ADAPT OR DIE.

Advancements to Accelerate Execution in Football's Modern Passing Game

Dub Maddox

FIRST EDITION

ISBN: 978-1-946466-37-2

Library of Congress Control Number: 2018937595

Designed by Wendy Trubia

Published by

3741 Linden Avenue SE | Grand Rapids, MI 49548

Printed in the United States of America

TABLE OF CONTENTS

PART ONE
The R4 Field Manual for Drops, Releases and Routes

PART TWO
The R4 Advancements

INTRODUCTION

The Evolution of Modern War and Football's Concept Passing Game

INTRODUCTION

Football is a game of two sides pitted against each other. It is rife with strategy and planning, and on the fly innovation. It is a model of war, and from studying war, we can gain a new perspective.

Fallujah, Iraq, in 2004, was the location of the heaviest urban combat the Marines have faced since 1968 in Hue, Vietnam. Operation Phantom Fury's goal was to take back the city of Fallujah that had been taken control of by an estimated 3,000 Al Qaeda (AQI) insurgents. 3,000 insurgents against the strongest military in the world didn't seem fair. The results, however, were surprising. AQI was winning, and they were doing it by fighting in unorthodox ways that the modern military could not match.

In Sun Tzu's Art of War, he writes:

The rule is, not to besiege walled cities if it can possibly be avoided.

Fallujah was a modern day walled city. The problem, however, is that it could not be avoided. The insurgency was growing and gaining recruiting momentum. Civilians and U.S. military were dying at a rapid rate.

The terrain in Fallujah was unlike any city that the Marines had trained for. It was random without boundary Zones for business, residential and industrial. The streets were narrow and lined with walls that easily pin soldiers in the line of fire. Houses connected with each other allowing insurgents to easily escape encounters. The houses were also made of thick brick that prevented fragmentation from grenades to penetrate through it. In other words, this city was a deathtrap for Marines.

The other factor in the insurgent's favor was that they knew the militaries rules of engagement and tactics. With the internet, the information of rules and strategies was more accessible to the enemy. The enemy would also observe how the military reacted to attacks and studied their tactics. The result was using the militaries rules and tactics to flip the strategy script in their favor.

Social media technology also played into the insurgent's hands. The used it to create propaganda to recruit more insurgents and fight for the cause. The insurgent's ability to blend in with the civilians prevented airstrikes. To get them out the U.S. military was going to have to go in and root them out room by room, building by building. This was a new kind of war that we were not fully prepared to fight.

These factors required military operations in urbanized terrain. This is known as (MOUT). Engaging with insurgents in these confined spaces is tactically known as close-quarters battle (CQB). CQB is not just reserved for the military. It is also used with S.W.A.T. and police forces in the world. CQB requires tactics executed by the operators to neutralize the opposing force (OPFOR) that is controlling the room. When the OPFOR is willing to die, the operator's tactics must be specialized.

Defenses Are Evolving Faster Than Before

The same challenges that the United States Military faced in 2004 and beyond are present in the game of modern football today. Since the existence of the game, the offensive side of football seemed to always be one innovative step ahead of the defense.

Defensive football up to the early 2000s consisted of more static coverages and fronts. You would see base Cover-2 or -3 the entire game with limited front movements. If the defense wanted to attack it was usually with an all-out feast or famine Blitz. These Cover-0 and -1 Blitzes required perfect execution or big plays and points resulted for the offense.

But around the same time as the U.S. military was engaging in a new war against an unconventional insurgency, so was offensive football seeing an unusual shift in defensive strategy on the playing field.

Defenses were morphing from static coverage schemes into shapeshifting split field, blended and post-snap pattern matching coverages. These coverages are now combined with multiple fronts, stunts with mixtures of Zone and double-A gap Blitzes.

These advancements in football are not just seen in college and professional football on Saturday and Sunday. They will also be seen in high school games on Friday nights. How? Technology... Information that was once available only to the inner circles at the highest levels of football is now easily accessed on the screen of a novice's own phone. Ideas once reserved for elite can now be shared through social media and websites that accelerate advancements in scheme like never before.

So, what does that mean for you as a coach? Like the Marines, being exploited by a ragtag insurgency in 2004, you must be willing to change.

The Way We Have Always Done It

This is what the Marines discovered when fighting a war on the enemy's turf with rules and tactics that were known by all. Before 9/11 United States CQB operator strategies of clearing a room controlled by an (OPFOR) were basic. One of the most common CQB strategies taught in the military as well as police forces were dynamic immediate entries that used surprise, speed, and force to defeat the OPFOR. (FIG. 1)

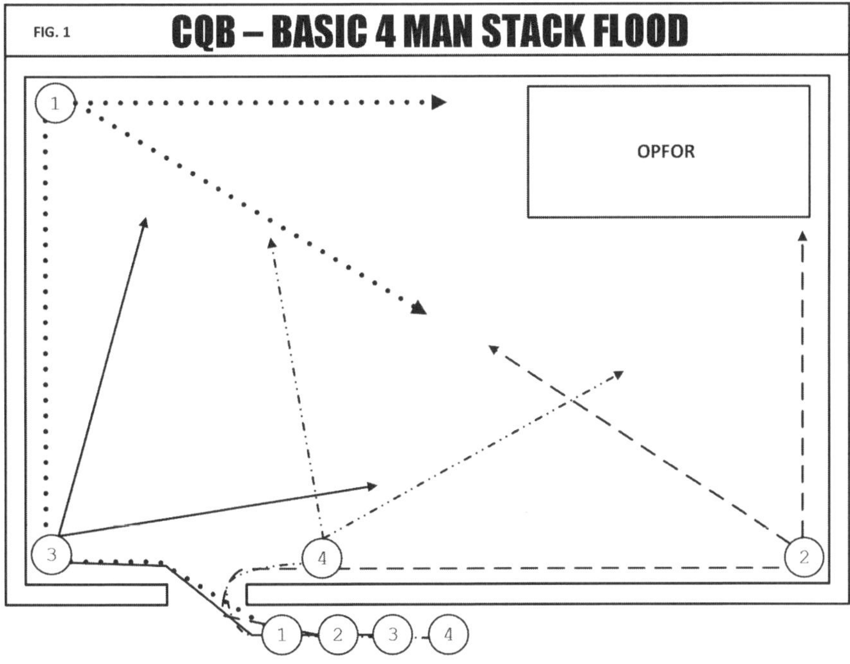

One of the most common tactics was a standard 4-man wall Flood. This tactic usually begins with stacking 4 operators along the wall ahead of the door. The #1 Man throws a flashbang into the room to disorient the opposing force. He then breaks the stack and runs into the room to occupy the hard-left corner. The #2 Man runs into the room to the right to occupy the hard-right corner. The #3 Man enters left to occupy the center and deep-left corner. The #4 Man enters right to occupy the center and deep-right corner.

These basic 4-man stacks with dynamic entry into a room worked in the environments for military and law enforcement at the time. However, in the Post 9/11 information age with an enemy that knew your strategy, these tactics were failing.

When Concept Passing Was King

A similar development was occurring in the offensive passing attacks of football. The West Coast offense of the 1980s and the Air Raid offense of the 90s and early 2000s ignited passing records across the country. These offenses attacked with a Rhythm, speed, and force like the Marines. The flashbang and 4-man Flood strategy of CQB was a mirror

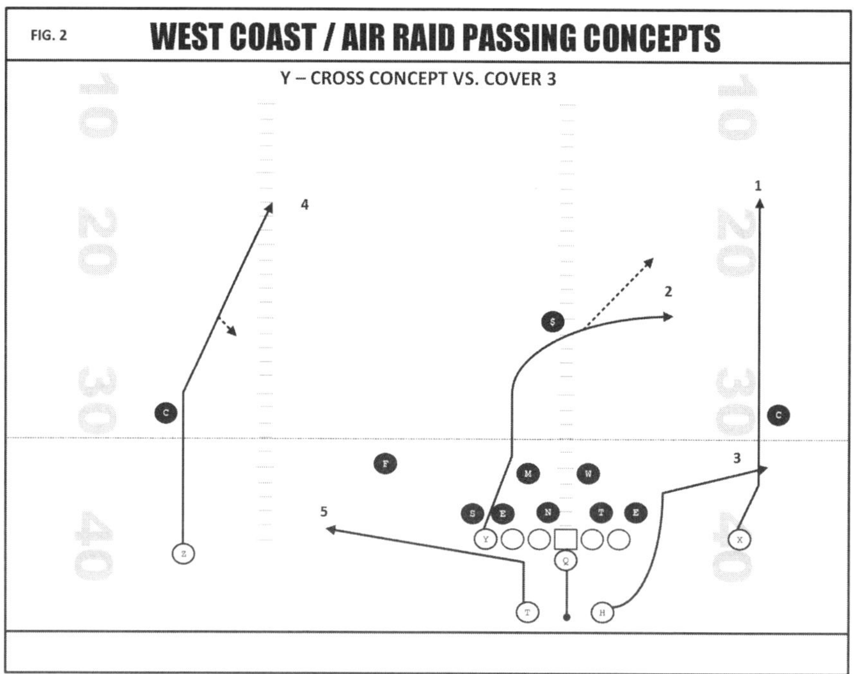

FIG. 2 WEST COAST / AIR RAID PASSING CONCEPTS

of the West Coast and Air Raid 4- and 5-man route progression tactics. These methods destroyed the static coverages defenses employed at the time. Defenses were disoriented by the full field attack and timing these offenses executed. Like the OPFORs in the pre 9/11 CQB age, the defense could not keep up. (FIG. 2)

Nothing Stays The Same

However, in 2004, the landscape on which the Marines and U.S. Military were fighting had changed.

1. The AQI insurgents were prepared for the Marine assault strategies like the 4-man wall Flood. This neutralized the element of surprise.

2. AQI was fighting using structures that allowed them to retreat, hide and slow the Marines down. This neutralized the Marines speed of attack.

3. AQI also had a different mindset. They were shooting to kill and not afraid to die in the process. This neutralized the Marine's ability to intimidate with force.

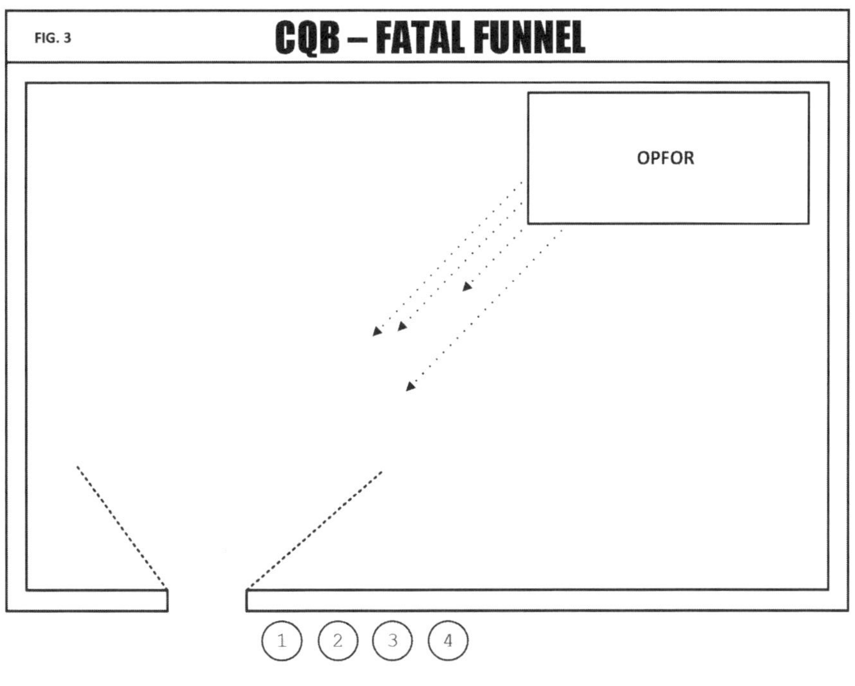

This evolution of the enemy. along with the environment the battle was fought in gave an outmanned insurgency the competitive advantage. (FIG. 3)

The problem with most of the CQB tactics taught in the U.S. prior to 9/11 was that it never dealt with immediate threats in the room. The operator in #1 man's job was to bypass an immediate threat in the room and cover the hard corner no matter what. The #2 Man was to do the same thing to the right. By that time, the #3 and #4 Man were dead men, walking through the fatal funnel of the door. These tactics did not mesh with the current environment and were getting soldiers killed.

Defenses in football made changes similar to the AQI insurgent's goal to defeat the air assault offensive tactics of the 80s and 90s.

Defenses were better informed on the alert and hot routes, as well as the quarterback progressions used in the pass-dominant offenses. This neutralized the element of surprise.

Defenses were using split-field coverage structures, post-snap movement, and pattern-matching to confuse and disrupt progression reads. This neutralized the speed of decision-making for the quarterback.

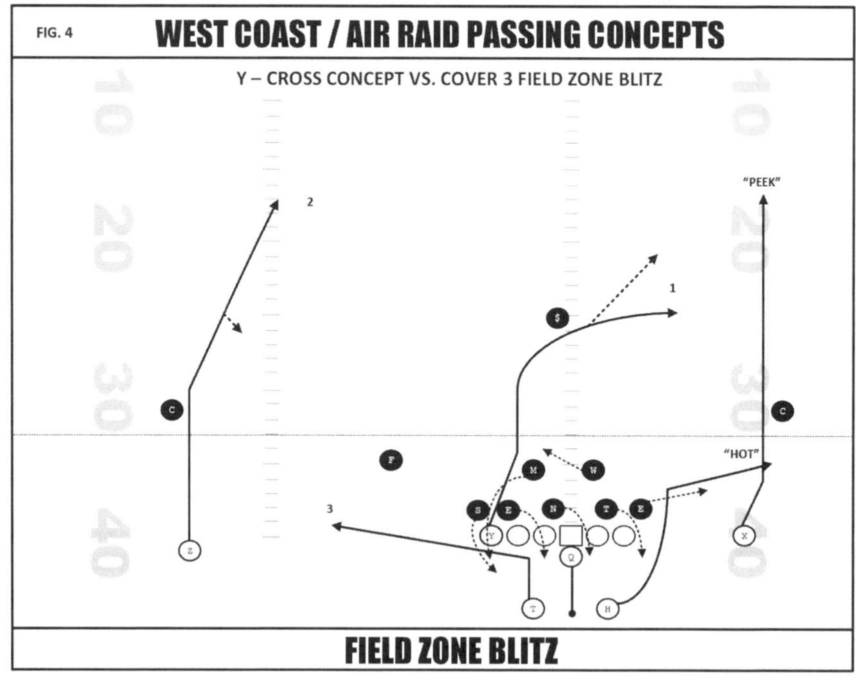

Defenses had a different mindset. They were using Zone Blitzes instead of Man Blitzes to create pressure. This neutralized the offense's threat of big-play potential that was likely against the Cover-0 and -1 all-out Blitzes.

These defensive evolutions reduced the time necessary for the QB to go through his pocket progressions, as well as disguising the space available to throw into. (FIG. 4)

The problem with most of the route progressions taught prior to these defensive changes was they never allowed the QB to read the Alert Route post-snap. QBs were taught to pre-snap the Alert Route in the West Coast offense or Peek Deep in the Air Raid. This worked, to an extent, with static coverage, but failed against pattern-matching and post-snap coverage movements. Without the ability for the QB to read vertical routes post-snap, explosive play opportunities decreased and incompletions and sacks increased. Zone Blitzes were used to bait a QB to throw the "hot" route only to find that the defense was one step ahead of them by Dropping a lineman into that area for an interception.

The Hurry Up No Huddle Solution

The offense's answer to combat these drastic defensive changes was to go faster. Speed, Surprise, and Force are three non-negotiables of CQB in modern war. The same is true in football. The hurry up, no-huddle strategy became the craze in football in the mid-2000s and is still present today. The strategy was to use speed to get the defense tired, out of position, and force them back into being static with their coverages. This caught many defenses off-guard, but like AQI observing the Marine's response to an attack so did defense's respond to operating at a no-huddle tempo.

To run an effective no-huddle today, against a defense that is prepared for it, requires an offense that has not only speed but superior firepower (force) over the opponent. In Iraq, this wasn't the case. AQI was prepared to die. This gave them one-up in the firepower (force) department. This motivated the Marines to look for different CQB strategies.

Thinking Outside The Box

Sometimes the first step to a better way is to admit that you don't know it all. This can be hard to do when you are the most dominant military in the world. However, there is always something to get better at. The nation of Israel has been at war for thousands of years. They live daily in the environment in which the Marines were at war. The result has fostered a different method of fighting called Israeli CQB tactical entry. (FIG. 5)

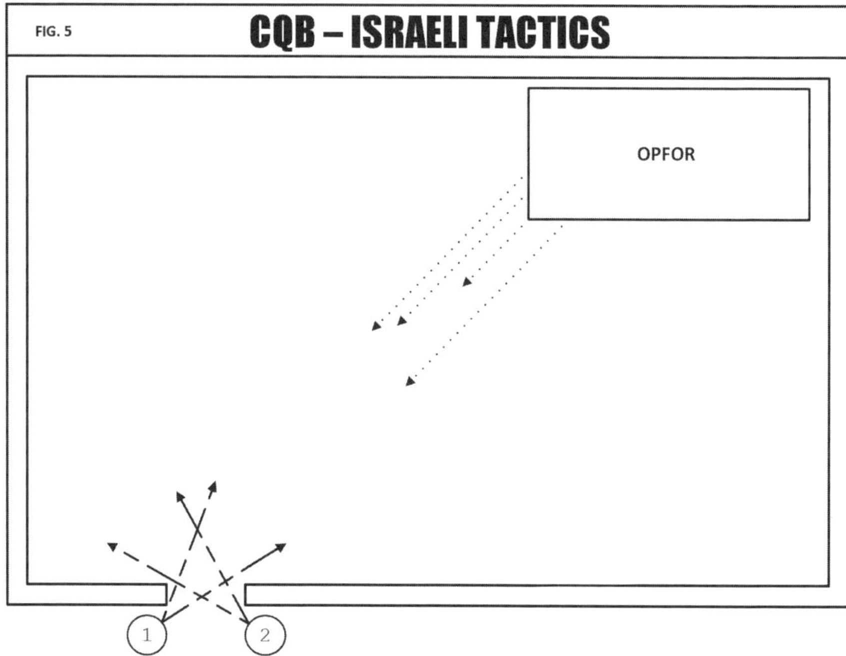

Israeli CQB was a counter-terrorism strategy developed in Israel to assault terrorists like the Marines were up against in Fallujah. Israeli CQB was different than U.S. strategy and designed on three principles:

1. First attack the immediate threats in the room.

2. Attack from the cover of exterior walls. There is no immediate entry. Limited entry occurs only when exposure-threat to OPFOR is at a minimum.

3. Increased accuracy is achieved through less movement.

Israeli CQB was centered around using the thick wall structures that is present in the Middle East buildings to provide better cover in fighting.

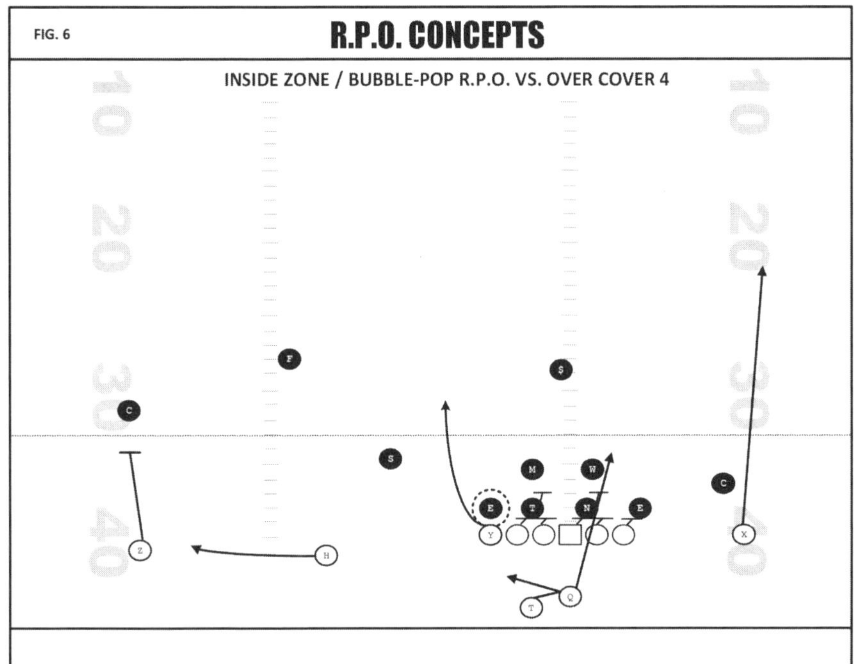

The Creation of RPOs

A similar evolution to the Israeli CQB tactic of room clearing was the RPO. RPO (Run-Pass Option) is a run play that is combined with a pass play. RPOs countered the defensive coverage and Zone Blitz adjustments that evolved to destroy the intermediate passing game. (FIG. 6)

They were built on three principles like Israeli CQB:

1. Isolate a single defender that has both run and route responsibilities and attack him immediately with a run and quick game route.
2. Attack with a pass under the guise of a run. Limited high percentage throws are only made when defenders ability to cover is at a minimum.
3. Increased passing accuracy because of less time in the pocket and quick game movement.

Just as Israeli CQB was centered to fight around the thick wall structure of the environment, so was the RPO concept developed around the thick run blocking structure of the play. These similar tactics have changed the CQB in counter-terrorism and offensive landscape of football today. But they are no silver bullet.

While Israeli CQB tactics provide better cover for the operator to fight from, the need to clear the room of the OPFOR is necessary. When the element of surprise, speed, and force is equal, then it's a 50/50 battle. These are not odds a soldier looks for.

Conversely, when a defense decides to remove the run/pass conflict of dual-read defenders with Man Coverage, the element of surprise, speed, and force is equally neutralized in the RPO scheme. This is the current state of many offensive teams that have sold out to RPOs in football today. Like the Marines found out in the bloodiest battle since Vietnam, being efficient at one method is no longer the best solution. Adaptability is more important than efficiency in modern warfare and football.

The Next Evolution In The Modern Passing Game

This was discovered during the inception of the R4 system and writing the first book *From Headset to Helmet.* R4 was created to accelerate decision-making under pressure for quarterbacks and coaches in the intermediate passing game. R4 brought the Alert Route online post-snap by providing the quarterback the non-negotiable tools to identify what "open" looks like. R4 linked routes together with meaning to create space and synchronization through a common language and sequential teaching process. The result was an increase in offensive efficiency of explosive plays and a decrease in turnovers. However, just as we learned through military history, defenses adapted.

Like the modern military learned, we had to create an environment in our offense that maximized adaptability and prioritized it over efficiency. We found that just as the Marines cannot enter a defended room the same way over and over, the quarterback and coach could not progress through a passing concept the same way over and over. We needed the ability to communicate and comprehend the intent of these adaptable defensive coverages, alignments, and post-snap personnel movements. Like the Marines discovered, if the enemy can adapt and change faster than you, they drastically increase their chances of winning, even if they are not the superior team.

The focus of this book is in two parts. Part One is Chapters 1-9. This section is a coach and player field manual that creates a common language and goes deep into the details of the toolbox families of quarterback drop footwork. This is critical to understand so the quarterback can operate and manipulate time. Next, we open the wide receiver toolbox of release strategies, so they can learn how to stay within the timeline constraints of a play. Finally, we go deeper into the details of the Rhythm, Read, Rush, and Release Route families. We unpack the receiver techniques and timing for every route that is needed to create "open" space for the quarterback. The result is building better fundamental weapons to use with progression advancements to create and attack space like never before.

Part Two is Chapters 10-12. This section covers the evolutions that we have created in the system to accelerate adaptability with simplicity in passing concepts. These advancements begin with a seamless process using the R4 language that allows you to pilot your quarterback through different progressions using the same pass concept. After that, you will be taught route rules to build and blend (quick-game and intermediate mixtures) passing concepts, followed by how to make them adaptable to defensive coverage and reactions. Finally, we will gain a grasp on how to maximize RPOs by building different route attachment answers for post-snap defensive reactions.

It is not required, but I highly recommended first reading *From Headset to Helmet* to better understand the R4 terms and definitions. This will also provide a starting point to see how the evolution of the modern passing game has developed.[1]

[1]Maddox, Dub. *From Headset to Helmet,* Reliance Media Inc., 2011

CHAPTER 1

The R4 Timeline

THE R4 TIMELINE

Space, time, and talent create the boundaries of the environment for football play. The mixture of these three elements creates a chaotic climate. This environment can make it difficult for players and coaches to perform well. Coaches and players who know where to go with the ball on a whiteboard is entirely different than knowing where to go on the field when the bullets are firing. Like the Marines in Fallujah, accelerating better decision-making under pressure requires understanding the limits of your environment, the weapons you have, and the weapons the enemy is using against you. The R4 System was created to accelerate performance through better decision-making within these pressured-packed limits.

> *A quarterback with awareness of the limits of time can learn strategies to manipulate and maximize the timeline boundaries.*

The first limit a quarterback must submit to is the element of *time.* The goal, however, is not submission; it is manipulation. A quarterback with awareness of the limit of time can learn strategies to manipulate and maximize the timeline boundaries. The amount of time available on any given down is never the same. Field position, pass concept, protection, and defensive strategy are just a few of the factors that dictate the amount of time that exists on a given play. However, it's the quarterback Drop footwork that drives the timeline.

The 5 Under-Center Drop Families

Knowing what drives the timeline allows a quarterback to adjust his Drops. These adjustments provide adaptability to different environmental factors that may show up on a play. The baseline Drops for a quarterback begin under-center. There are 5 base Under-Center Drop families.

They are the **1-step, 2-step, 3-step, 5-step, and 7-step Drops.** The Drop family the quarterback used is generally tied to the pass concept called. (FIG. 7)

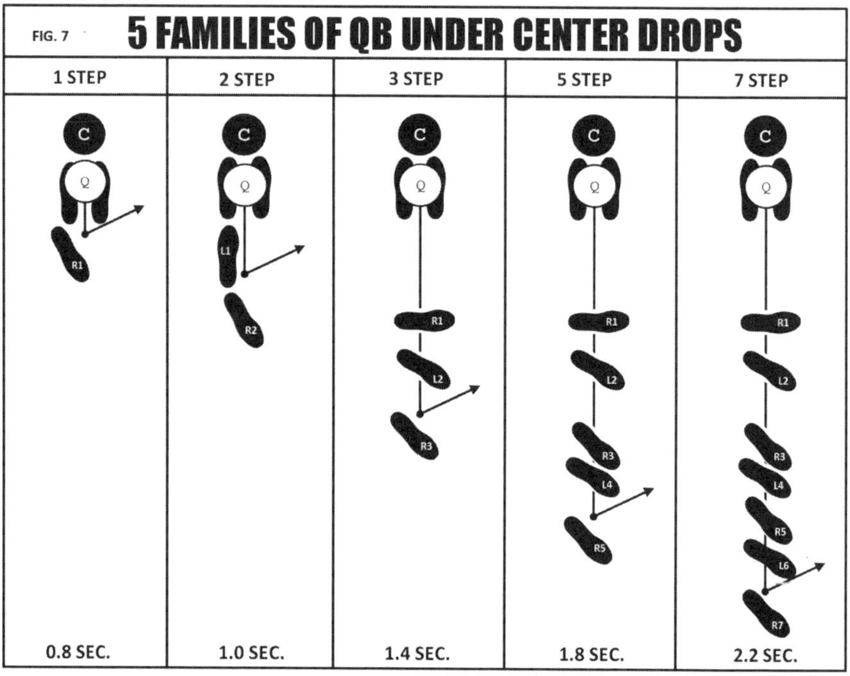

FIG. 7 **5 FAMILIES OF QB UNDER CENTER DROPS**

1 STEP	2 STEP	3 STEP	5 STEP	7 STEP
C, Q, R1	C, Q, L1, R2	C, Q, R1, L2, R3	C, Q, R1, L2, R3, L4, R5	C, Q, R1, L2, R3, L4, R5, L6, R7
0.8 SEC.	1.0 SEC.	1.4 SEC.	1.8 SEC.	2.2 SEC.

1-step – Under-Center Drop – 0.8 Sec.

Used with Now Screens, uncovered receivers, or when a receiver is UNCAPPED with a soft-zone defender.

2-step – Under-Center Drop – 1.0 Sec.

Used with Fade Routes when a receiver is UNCAPPED with a press-man defender, it is often selected for the Short Fade in the Red Zone. The second step allows a receiver more time to release against the jam technique of a defender.

3-step – Under-Center Drop – 1.4 Sec.

Used with quick-game routes like a Hitch, Slant, or Quick Out, it is also used with quick-game concepts like Double Slants, Fade-Out, or Stick.

5-step – Under-Center Drop – 1.8 Sec.

Used with Vertical Routes like the Corner and Post, it is also used with intermediate pass concepts, like Smash, Curl, and 4-Vertical plays.

7-step – Under-Center Drop – 2.2 Sec.

Used with deep-play-action concepts like Y-Cross, Drive, and Flood.

Manipulating the Timeline with Under-Center Drops

The differentiation between Drop families is identified by the time it takes for them to develop. This time stamp attaches to routes and concepts that contain breaks occurring at the same moment. A quarterback can use time-traits within each Drop family as a tool to manipulate the timeline. This is achieved by using a different Drop when elemental factors inhibit the Base-Drop attached to the play. (FIG. 8)

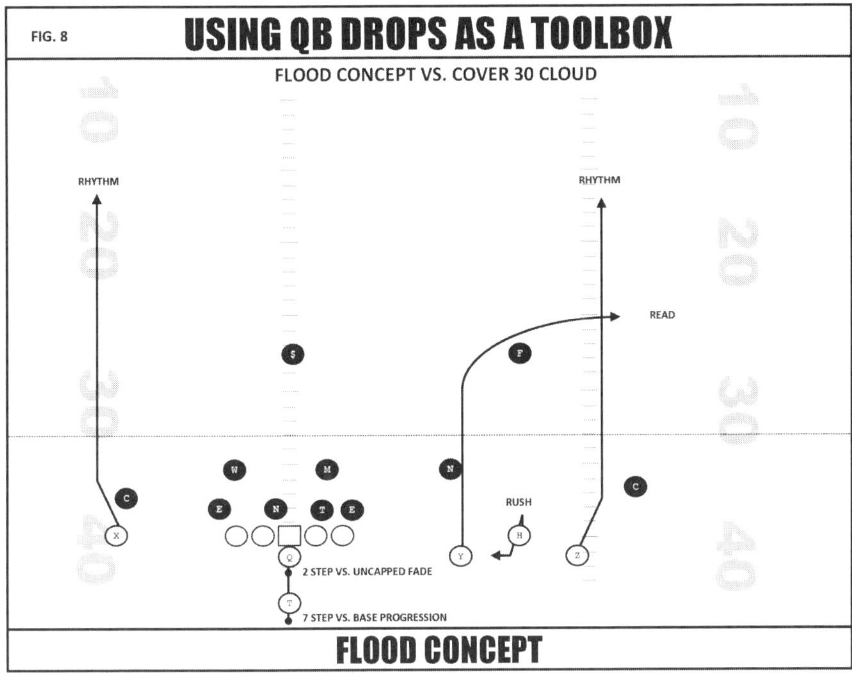

EXAMPLE: The play call is a 7-step play-action Flood concept taught to be run from under-center. The quarterback must take a 7-step Drop due to the time it takes for the play-fake and Vertical Stretch of the Flood to develop. However, Drop-timing disciplines can provide a framework for timeline manipulation when different environmental situations present themselves. One situation would be a boundary corner who is playing press-man against the backside X receiver. The quarterback could adjust his footwork to a 2-step Drop to get the ball out faster to the receiver before the defender can get his eyes around to make a play on the ball.

Adjusting the number of steps of the Drop is only one example of timeline manipulation. A seasoned quarterback knows how to adjust the speed of a specific Drop based on the environmental factors, as well. Zone Coverage creates an environment that provides 3 seconds of pocket-time, on average. Man Coverage creates 2 seconds of pocket-time, on average. (FIG. 9)

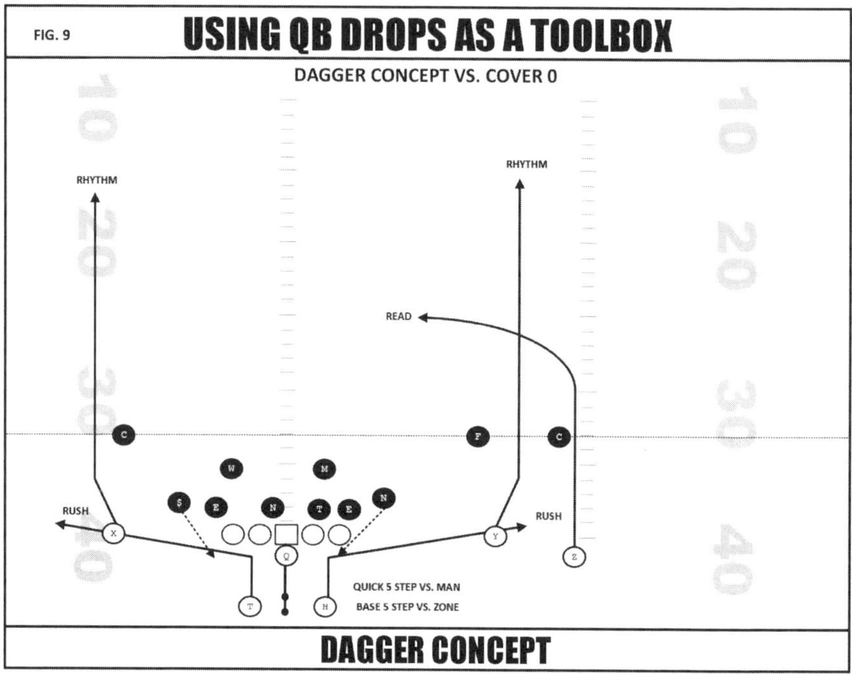

EXAMPLE: The play call is a Dagger concept run out of a pro-set from under-center with a 5-step Drop. A quarterback who is facing a Zone Coverage would incorporate a smooth 5-step Drop. However, against Man, he would need to manipulate the speed of the Drop into a quick 5-step. This would allow him to work within the reduced time available against a possible Blitz and get the ball out before the Man defenders can get back in phase to CAP the route.

The 5 Shotgun Drop Families

Shotgun Drops cut out the needed depth requirement, which can be achieved with Under-Center Drops. Since the quarterback has positioned himself with enough pre-snap depth, he can have manipulation freedom with the timeline and footwork used post-snap. There are 5 families of Shotgun Drops. They are the **1-step (Pop), 2-step, 3-step, Punch 3-step, and Punch 5-step Drop.** (FIG. 10)

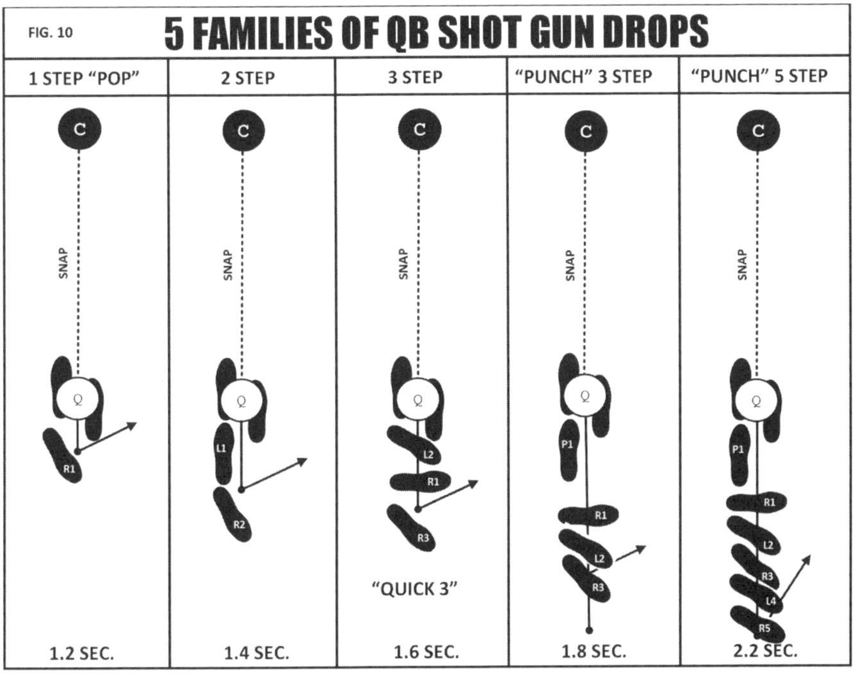

FIG. 10 **5 FAMILIES OF QB SHOT GUN DROPS**

1 STEP "POP"	2 STEP	3 STEP	"PUNCH" 3 STEP	"PUNCH" 5 STEP
C, SNAP, Q, R1	C, SNAP, Q, L1, R2	C, SNAP, Q, L2, R1, R3	C, SNAP, Q, P1, R1, L2, R3	C, SNAP, Q, P1, R1, L2, R3, L4, R5
		"QUICK 3"		
1.2 SEC.	1.4 SEC.	1.6 SEC.	1.8 SEC.	2.2 SEC.

1-step (Pop Drop) – Shotgun Drop – 1.2 Sec.

Used with Now Screens, uncovered receivers or when a receiver is UNCAPPED with a soft-zone defender, it is also used with RPO concepts. This Drop is referred to as a "Pop Drop." The name is derived from defining the movement that the hips and feet make to "Pop" in place after the snap or play-fake. In Shotgun, it is essentially a resetting of the hips and feet to a target.

2-step – Shotgun Drop – 1.4 Sec.

Used with quick-game-routes like a Hitch, Slant, or Quick Out, it is also used with quick-game concepts like Double Slants, Fade-Out, or Stick. A Shotgun 2-step Drop is equivalent to the same timing as a 3-step Under-Center Drop. The time it takes for the snap to get back to the Shotgun quarterback must be factored in.

3-step – Shotgun Drop – 1.6 Sec.

Used with Quick-Game Routes and concepts, it can also be used with Intermediate concepts with a route in the progression that breaks at 1.8 seconds or less. The base 3-step Shotgun Drop is achieved by catching the ball and driving off the front foot to create the first big step with the right foot. The next step is small by crossing over with the left foot. The final step is another small step by the right foot that sets the hallway with the route-space that is first in the progression.

However, the speed and technique of the 3-step Drop can be manipulated by the quarterback to better serve the route he intends to throw. The most commonly implement style of a 3-step Shotgun Drop is a hybrid "Quick 3" Step Drop in which the 2nd step of the Drop does not cross over the 1st step. The benefit of the "Quick 3" Step Drop is that it allows the quarterback more time to process a quick-game throw to a side than a 2-step Drop. It also makes it easier for the quarterback to reset his feet to another route in the progression.

Punch 3-step – Shotgun Drop – 1.8 Sec.

Used with vertical routes like the Corner and Post, it is also used with intermediate pass concepts like Smash, Curl, and 4-Vertical plays. A Punch 3-step Drop is used to give the quarterback more time to process route-side space development.

The quarterback will catch the snap, find the laces, and then take a 6-inch punch-step back. He will go into a standard 3-step Drop after the punch-step. A Punch 3-step Shotgun Drop is equivalent to a 5-step Under-Center Drop. This is due to the time it takes the quarterback to receive the Shotgun snap and find the laces.

Punch 5-step – Shotgun Drop – 2.2 Sec.

Used with deep Flood or play-action concepts, the Punch 5-step is closely related to the 7-step Under-Center Drop. This Drop elongates the timeline for deeper routes and stretches to develop. This Drop should be used in conjunction with concepts that have route breaks beyond 15-yards downfield.

The timeline of the Punch 5-step Drop begins at 2.2 seconds. This allows Read Routes to be treated as a Rhythm Route in the progression. It is important that coaches be strategic in how their concepts are structured to maximize the timeline benefit of the Punch 5-step Drop.

Manipulating the Timeline with Shotgun Drops

Shotgun Drops can be adjusted to manipulate the timeline in the same way as Under-Center Drops.

EXAMPLE: A quick-game spacing concept contains routes that require Drops to develop in 1.6 seconds or less. A quarterback who determines the Slant-Swing combo to the left is optimal could use a 2-step Drop to get the ball out to the Slant in 1.4 seconds. (FIG. 11)

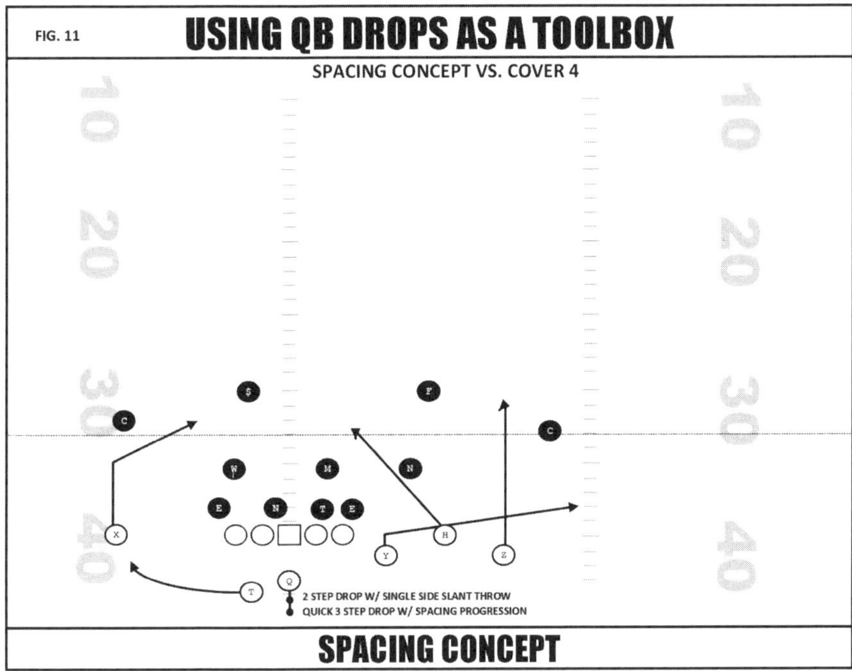

He could also use the same 2-step Drop for the Spacing concept to the right. However, the Spacing concept has 3 quick-routes that break open in 1.6 seconds or less. A spacing concept that creates a quick horizontal stretch could be better navigated by using a quick 3-step Shotgun Drop. The quick 3-step Drop still allows the Spot Route to be thrown in 1.6 seconds. It also allows for an easier reset of the feet to the remaining routes in the progression.

Another example of using the 5 families of Shotgun Drops to manipulate the timeline would be in the Snag concept. The Snag concept consists of a Rhythm Corner Route that breaks open in 1.8 seconds. A quarterback would match this Rhythm break by using a standard 3-step Shotgun Drop. A 3-step Shotgun Drop breaks open in 1.8 seconds. (FIG. 12)

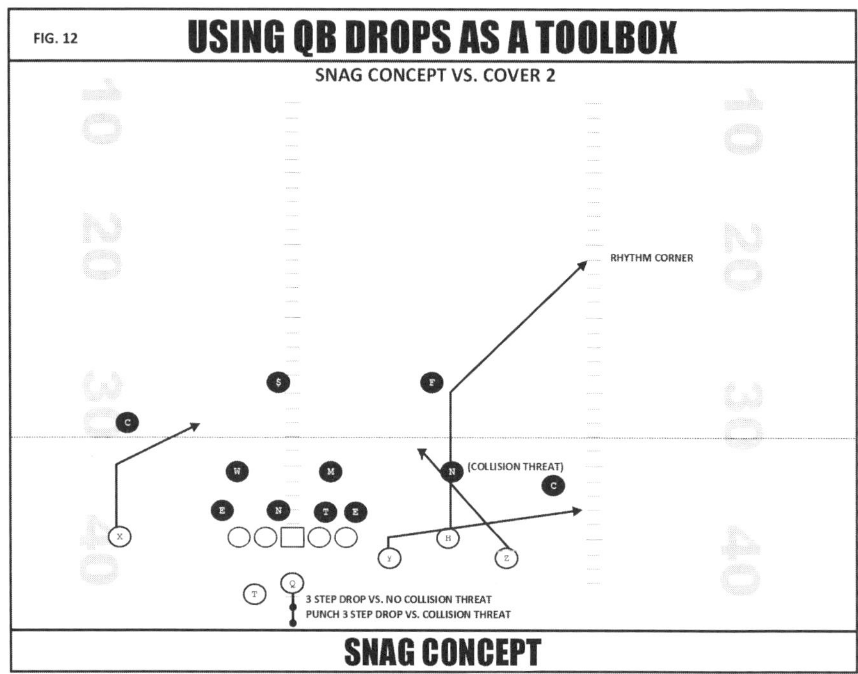

The primary weapon that a Rhythm Corner Route must defeat is collision by a defender. Collision can derail the route stem and timing of the throw. A quarterback can increase the release time a receiver needs to avoid collision by using a Punch 3-step Drop. The Punch 3-step Drop increases the timeline .2 tenths of a second. This allows the quarterback to stretch the Rhythm timeline and still reset to the remaining routes in the progression.

Teaching the timing and technique of quarterback Drops is mission-critical to any successful passing game. The main takeaway is to understand that Drops are a tool. There should never be an absolute when it comes to the Drops used within a concept. There should be a starting reference point with the time needed to navigate a concept, but fluidity of Drop adjustments is key. Different situations require a different tool to best handle that situation. The 5 families reveal the relationships between Drops and provide context to the coaching needed to teach what Drop may work best.

CHAPTER 2

The R4 Space Race

THE R4 SPACE RACE

Wide receivers use routes to create and control space on the football field. Defenders attempt to close and cover space that routes are designed to attack. These non-negotiables require the quarterback to maintain an ability to process the post-snap movements of receivers and defenders to determine what route space is "open."

The post-snap weapons the defense uses to close and cover space are Cushion, Collision, and C.A.P. Understanding the defensive weapons allows them to become mental decision-making accelerators for the quarterback. The pass accelerators provide a common language for the coach, quarterback, and receivers to clearly define what is "open" and how to get "open." (FIG. 13)

FIG. 13 **DEFENSIVE PASS ACCELERATORS**

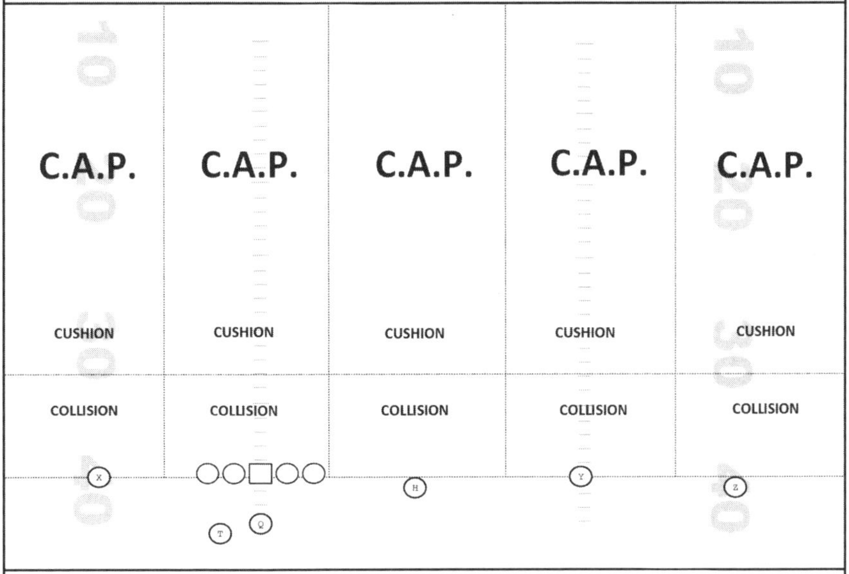

C.A.P.	C.A.P.	C.A.P.	C.A.P.	C.A.P.
CUSHION	CUSHION	CUSHION	CUSHION	CUSHION
COLLISION	COLLISION	COLLISION	COLLISION	COLLISION
X	T Q	H	Y	Z

DEFINING OPEN

Collision is the first weapon a receiver must defeat. *Collision* is the delay or disruption of the stem or release of a route. If a quarterback processes collision, he should immediately go to the next route in the progression, or release from the pocket. This is because collision destroys the Rhythm timing needed for a quarterback to make a throw before a receiver becomes open. It also inhibits the creation of space by route-stretches placed on defenders.

***Collision** is the delay or disruption of the stem or release of a route.*

Cushion** is the maintaining of a minimum **of 4-yards of vertical space over a receiver.

Cushion is the next weapon a receiver must defeat. *Cushion* is the maintaining of a minimum of 4-yards of vertical space over a receiver. The probability of beating a defender vertically is lowest when a defender can maintain a minimum of 4 yards or more of cushion over the receiver. If a quarterback processes a receiver within 4 yards of cushion on the Drop, he should stay on the route until the last step of the Drop. If a quarterback processes a cushion of 4 yards or more on the Drop, he should go to the next route in the progression.

CAP is the final weapon that a receiver must defeat. CAP is the action acronym of covered. The CAP confirms to a quarterback if a route is covered or open. The letters stand for:

CAP: *Coverage + Angle + Personnel*

Coverage: The dominant vertical and horizontal position of a defender at a fixed moment in time.

Angle: The position of the hips of a defender at a fixed moment in time.

Personnel: The closure ability of a defender at the break of a route or release of the ball.

Each layer of CAP reveals the reality of space that a defender can cover at a fixed moment in time. The CAP provides keyframes of reference through a common language that allows the coach, quarterback, and receivers to process space with the same mind's eye.

A CAPPED route is "not open." It means that the Coverage, Angle, and Personnel of that defender is in position to cover and close on the route-side space. An UNCAPPED route is "open." It means that the defender is not in position to cover and close on the route-side space. The defense is trying to C.A.P. the route-side space within a concept on a given play. The Cushion, Collision, and C.A.P. pass accelerators provide the mental weapons a quarterback will use to determine which route is "open" on a play.

Wide receivers must also understand how to read and process the defensive pass accelerator weapons of Cushion, Collision, and C.A.P. Defeating these weapons begins at the line of scrimmage by using the proper exit strategies to own or create route-side space. Exit strategies are not random. They must fit into the framework limits of the timeline to create space.

The WR Stance and Start

Every exit strategy that a receiver can use originates from the stance. The purpose of a good receiver stance is to eliminate false steps to waste no movement and provide maximum acceleration off the line of scrimmage. One of the most commonly misunderstood mechanics of the receiver stance is in the placement of the front foot. Some coaches prefer their receivers maintain an "inside" foot-up stance placement. Others prefer an "inside" foot-back stance placement. Some do not care and tell their receivers to do what they feel is best.

To understand what forward foot placement is best, we must determine the highest priority threats to the defense. Vertical value is one of the biggest threats to the defense. A receiver that can gain more vertical distance in a limited number of steps creates more route-space and strain on a defense.

7-steps is the distance that determines the vertical value of a receiver. This is because a 7-step Under-Center Drop is the biggest Rhythm Drop a quarterback can take and remain in the pocket. This is also why the hard-deck is placed at 7 yards. The hard-deck is a horizontal line that provides a frame of reference to define vertical space from flat space. The base hard-deck line is at 7 yards. This is because the vertical distance that a receiver will gain in 7 steps is equivalent to his level of speed. Therefore, at a minimum, an average receiver should be able to get 7 yards of depth in 7 steps.

One of the keys in generating explosive pass plays is the ability to get the ball out on Rhythm. In R4 terms throwing on Rhythm means getting the ball out on the last step of the Drop. It also means that the receiver must break the route or become open in 7 steps or less.

The placement of the front foot forward or back will determine how many inside and outside breaks can be made in 7 steps or less. The following picture helps determine the benefits of having the inside foot up versus back in a stance. (FIG. 14)

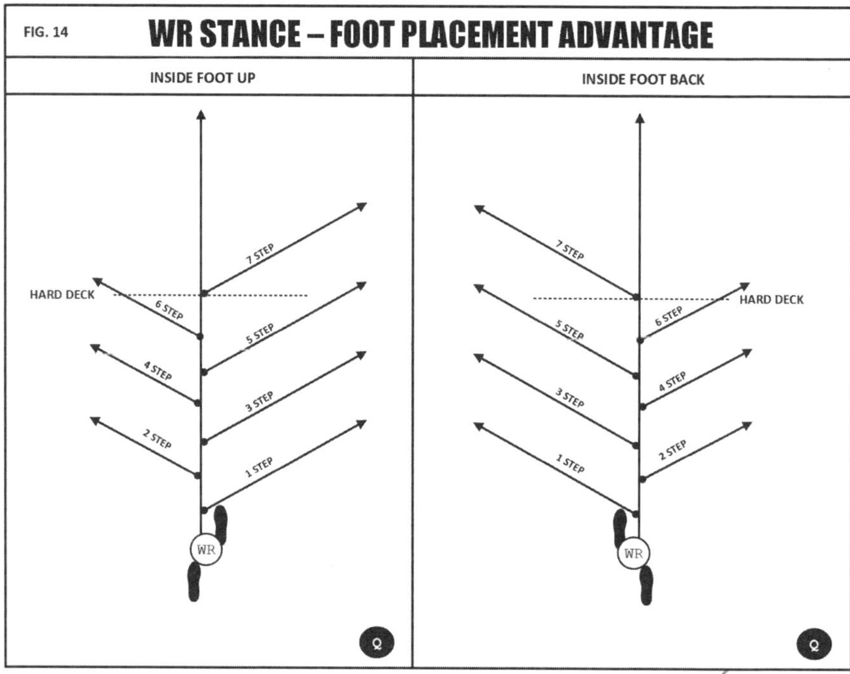

A receiver with the inside foot up can have four inside breaking routes thrown on Rhythm and only 3 outside breaking routes made on Rhythm.

A receiver with the inside foot back can have only 3 inside breaking routes thrown on Rhythm and 4 outside breaking routes made on Rhythm.

In-breaking routes are a higher priority threat to the defense because they are shorter, easier throws for the quarterback, and the attack interior pressures. This threat is why we teach receivers to maintain an inside foot up on their stance. It also keeps the timing for all route progressions consistent. However, in certain situations, we may coach a receiver to switch inside foot back to gain an exit strategy advantage on a defender.

The 5 WR Release Families

Exit strategies are called releases. Releases for receivers are identical to the Drops for the quarterback. Releases set up the receivers to avoid Collision, close Cushion, and UNCAP route-side space. There are 5 base release families for wide receivers. They are the Shave, Stutter, Seam, Slide, and Slice Release. (FIG. 15)

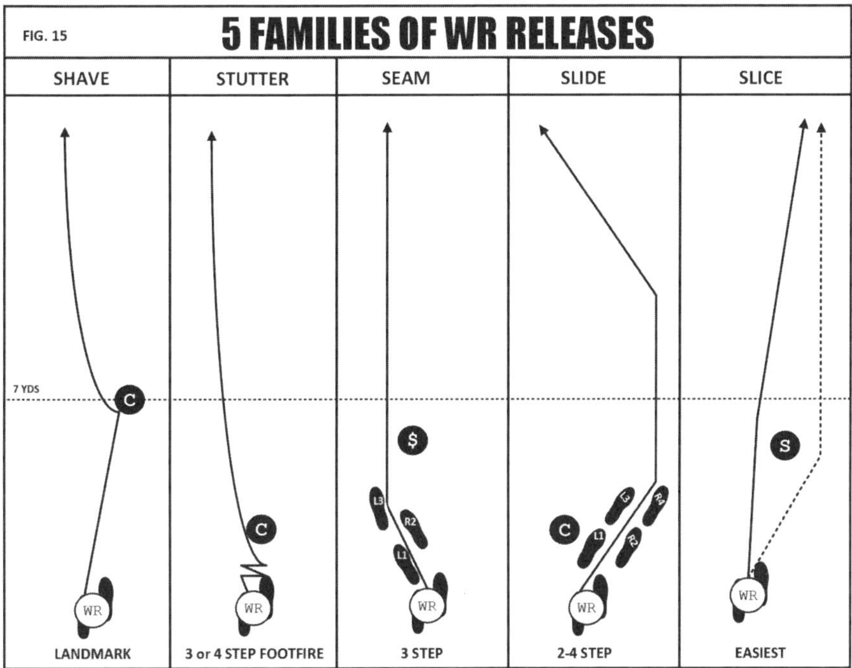

Shave Release: The Shave Release stems directly at the shoulder of a defender. The initial rule is to attack the route-side space shoulder of the immediate-threat defender.

EXAMPLE: On a Fade Route against an inside-leveraged Man defender, the receiver will Shave the outside shoulder of the defender. This release will help keep the defender in place with inside leverage, allowing the receiver to own outside vertical-route space. The key is the receiver must make the stick of his Fade route just before he gets into the personnel space of the defender.

There are times, however, when the defender may be playing with head-up leverage on the Fade. A Man defender is taught to not get beaten inside. In this situation, the receiver could Shave the inside shoulder to get the defender to aggressively CAP inside-space, then stick the inside foot crossing the face of the defender to return in the outside route-space of the Fade. When a receiver Shaves the opposite shoulder of the route-side space we call that a "return" move. This move should only be used when the receiver knows that the defender is going to aggressively close and CAP the initial move. (FIG. 16)

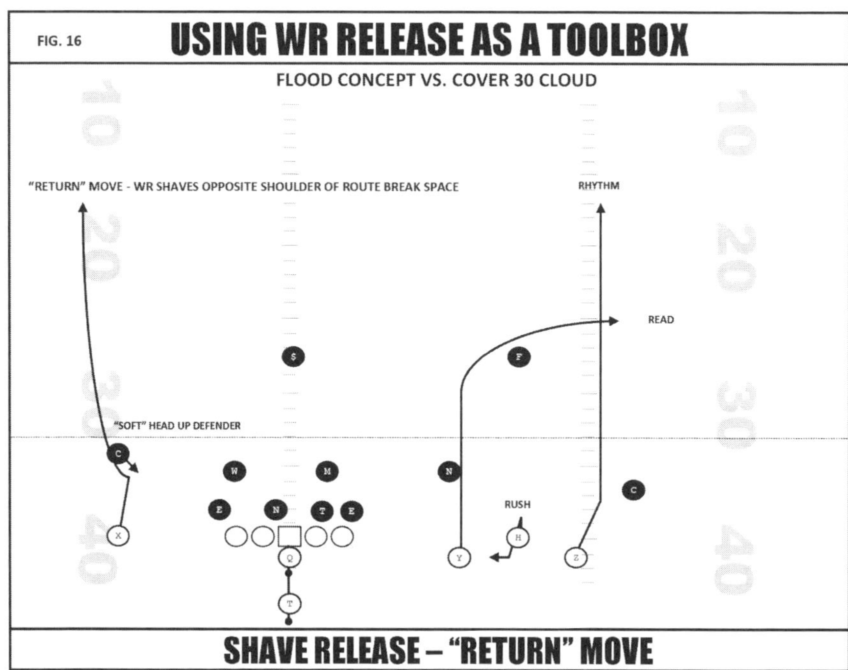

Stutter Release: A Stutter Release is a foot-fire stick-and-release to the route-side space. Outside breaking routes will use a 4-step foot-fire stick move. A receiver running a Rhythm Fade will start with the inside foot up in his stance at the line of scrimmage and fire his feet in a 4-step rapid Rhythm. The emphasis on the stick of the last step is to get the defender to shoot his hands into the chest of the receiver. At this point, the receiver will use a hand strike move that will relocate the defender's hands to avoid collision.

Inside-breaking routes will us a 3-step foot-fire stick move. The 3-step foot fire stick is effective to use against a press "jam" defender with head-up to inside leverage. The receiver will foot-fire his feet in a rapid 3-step Rhythm and stick on the 3rd step. The goal, again, is to get the defender to shoot his hands so the receiver can relocate and avoid collision at the line of scrimmage. (FIG. 17)

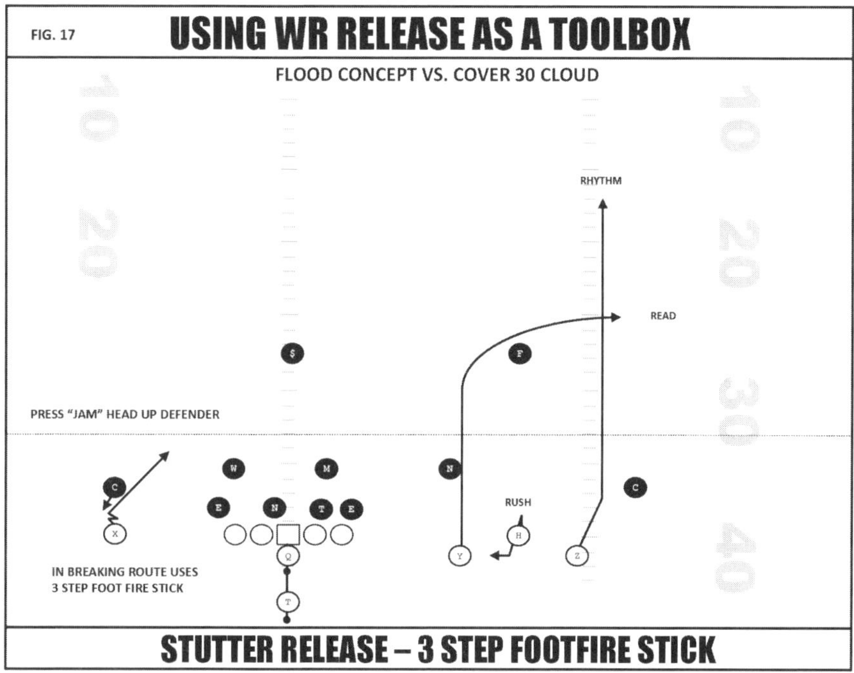

Seam Release: The Seam Release is a 3-step move off the line of scrimmage with an angle of departure aiming just outside the shoulder of the impeding defender. We call this outside-release move a Seam Release because it is most frequently used when running a Seam. On the 3rd step, the receiver will anticipate collision with an impeding defender. It is important to have a one-hand "hook" or "rip-hand" strike ready to defeat this oncoming contact. (FIG. 18)

The Seam Release must own the outside space by the 3rd step of the exit. If a collision defender is still over and outside the receiver on the 3rd step, then the receiver must get vertical and take the inside-space that is given to him. The 3rd step decision is required to maintain the route timing integrity with the quarterback's Drop. If this occurs, the receiver must attempt to win route-side space back at the top of the route or route-break.

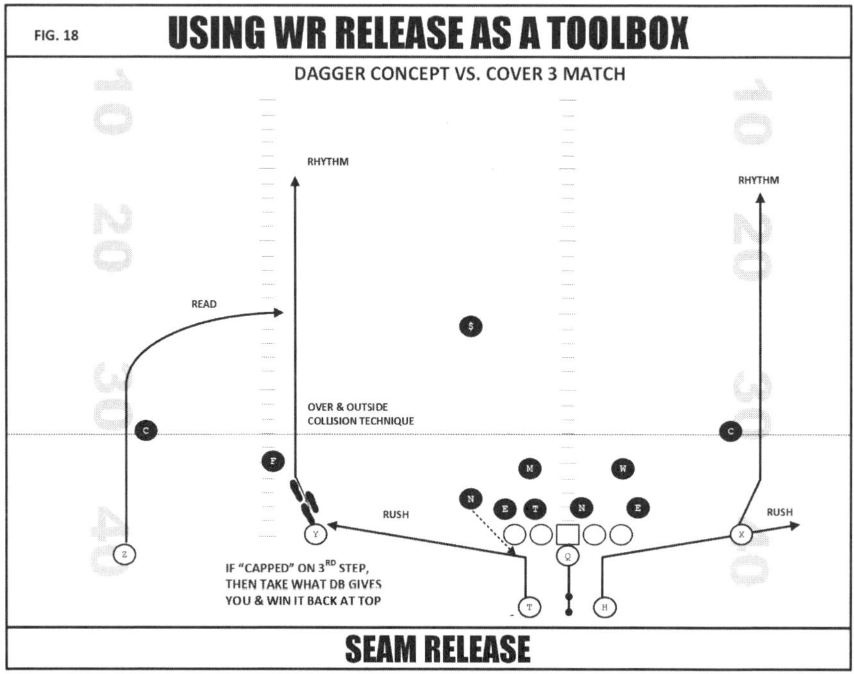

Slide Release: The Slide Release is a mandatory inside release on the collision or carry defender. The Slide Release is a minimum 2-step and maximum 4-step inside-release to avoid collision and create space for a route. A Slide corner is the most common route in which a Slide Release is used. It is effective against a hard Cover-2 collision cornerback or a 2-trapping corner that jumps the flats post-snap. (FIG. 19)

The Slide Release will take the sharpest inside angle of attack needed to avoid collision, and own inside-space off against a collision defender. If the receiver gets inside the defender on his 2nd step, he will get vertical immediately. Otherwise, he must get vertical at his 4th step of the Slide move. The receiver should be ready to use a "hook" or "rip" hand strike on the stick-step to get vertical; the hand strike used to avoid collision by a defender.

If the receiver cannot own inside-space by the 4th step of the Slide Release, then he will get vertical on the 4th step and take the outside space given to him by the defender. This would require the receiver to win the route-side space back at the top of the route.

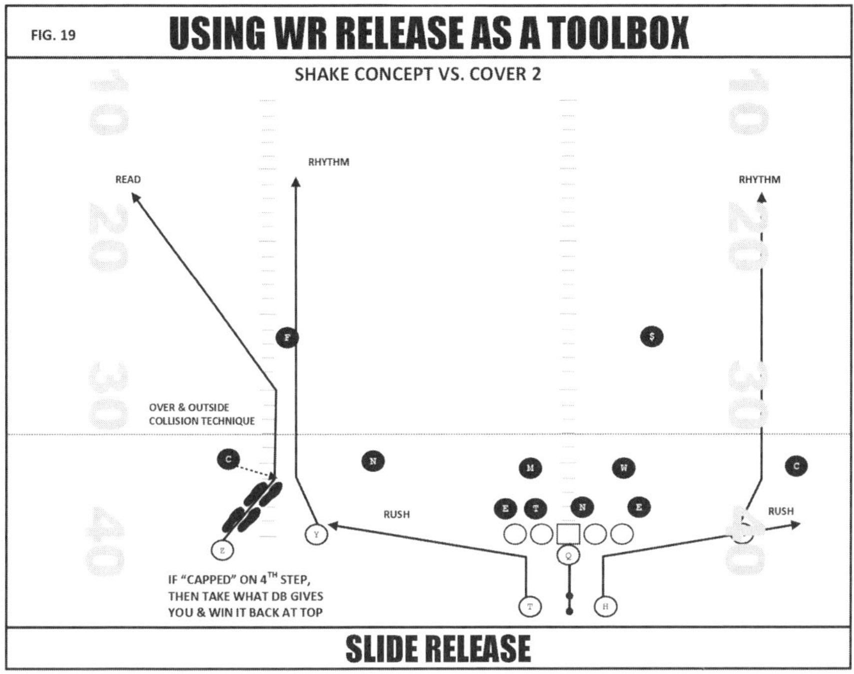

Slice Release: A Slice Release informs the receiver to take the easiest release based on the alignment and attack path of the collision defender. The Slice Release allows the receiver to determine the intent of the collision defender and provides freedom to inside- or outside-release. The Slice Release is a landmark release that does not require a step count. The highest priority is to avoid collision at all costs and get into the vertical tubes of space. (FIG. 20)

The Shake concept provides a good example of when a Slice Release is best used. The cross-route is the Rhythm Route in this concept. This route must avoid collision and attack the inside-space in the middle of the field. Defenses will adjust collision techniques to keep the cross-route from attacking the middle-of-field space. This could be a technique adjustment within the same coverage or a different coverage entirely. Either way, the receiver will determine the collision intent and take the space that is given to the defender.

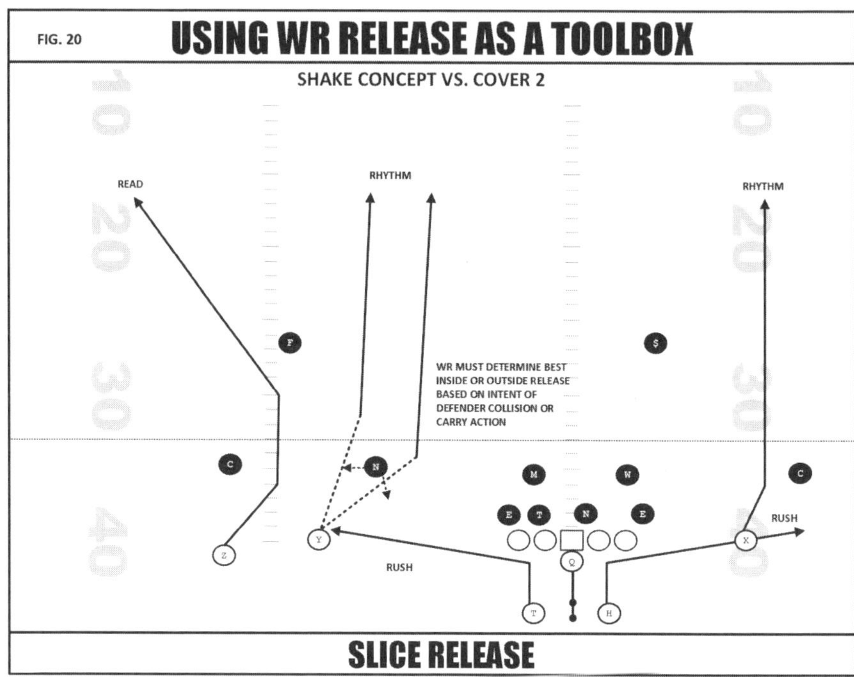

The 5 Release families make up a toolbox of exit strategies that can be attached to any route. The common language of the family names and traits provide a platform for accelerated adaptability and adjustments in a game. Comprehension of the properties of each release family informs the best exit strategy to employ against a myriad of defensive actions and alignments. Releases are a space weapon that must be developed to accelerate explosive play production for your offense.

CHAPTER 3

Understanding the 5 Base Rhythm Route Family

UNDERSTANDING THE 5 BASE RHYTHM ROUTE FAMILY

Routes are the offensive passing weapons that create and control space on the football field. Assembly of these weapons requires an understanding of the relationships between the moving parts. Routes are the means of transport to get receivers into a space at a specific moment in time. While all routes are not the same, they share key commonalities that confine them to the time and space limits of football. These commonalities generate a "genetic code" that places routes with similar "DNA" into like families.

The 4 families of routes are the **Rhythm, Read, Rush** and **Release** families. This family tree of routes provides the building blocks for most of the core passing concepts used in the game of football. (FIG.21)

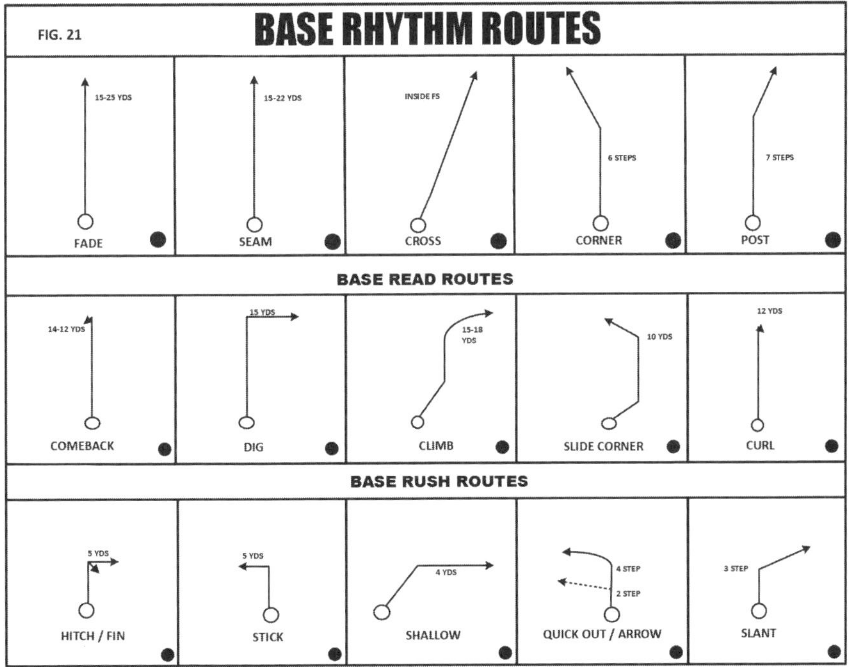

Placing the routes into families based on their DNA allows coaches and players to see the relationships in and between families. Understanding the properties that each route family contains provides a context for the quarterback on the space each route attacks and when on the timeline they fit within a progression.

The first family of routes is the Rhythm family. Rhythm Routes are designed to attack vertical space and must break in 1.8 seconds or less. 1.8 seconds is the equivalent time it takes a quarterback to hit the last step of a 5-step Drop from under-center or a 3-step Drop in Shotgun. Throwing a Rhythm Route on the last step of the Drop is one of the most challenging fundamentals that a quarterback must master, because Rhythm throws require the quarterback to decide to throw before the receiver breaks open. The R4 language provides a deeper understanding of route design and defensive intent that accelerate decision-making under pressure. There are 5 base Rhythm Routes in football. They are the Fade, Seam, Cross, Corner, and Post.

Rhythm Fade: The Rhythm Fade route is best used to attack Man Coverage vertically. This route is a landmark route that is run off yardage. (FIG. 22)

The ideal landing space for the Rhythm Fade ball is between 18 to 25 yards outside the bottom of the numbers. This is a difficult throw for most quarterbacks because it requires the ability of the quarterback to drain power from his throw. To do this the quarterback must shorten his Drop by taking a 2 step or quick 3 step Drop in Shotgun or under center with no stride on the throw. The quarterback can bleed power out of the throw by elevating quickly and using the extension of his arm and turn of the body to get the nose to quickly turn over and Drop in the route-side space landmark. By getting the ball to land under 22 yards places the defensive back in a visual disadvantage to track the ball as he attempts to get in phase to CAP the route side space of the vertical route.

A Man defender is trying to get his hips and hands in front of the receiver quickly to CAP and carry the vertical route space. If executed correctly the vertical space is CAPPED. A defender however cannot simultaneously CAP both vertical and horizontal route space. In this case, a quarterback and receiver can attack horizontal space underneath

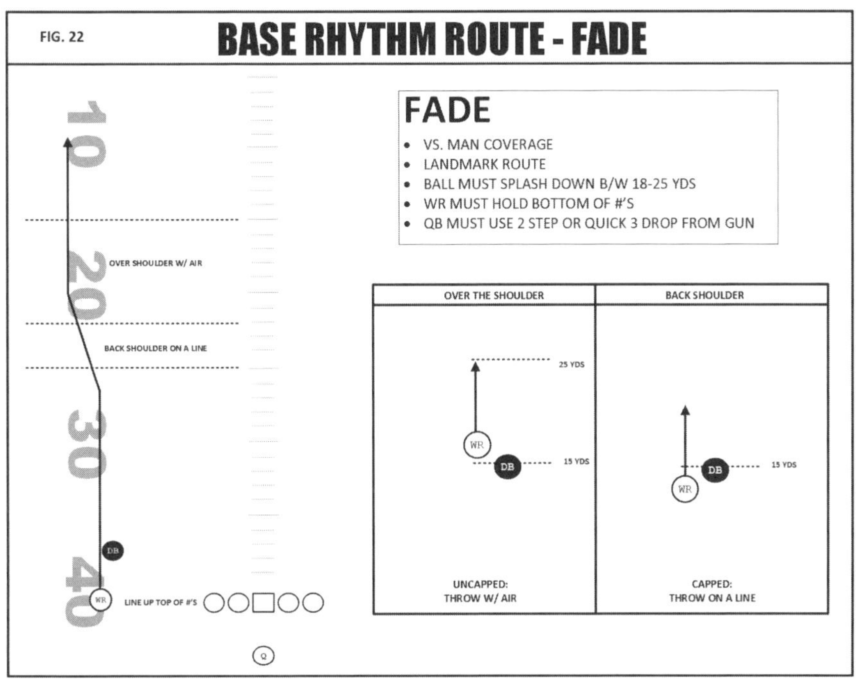
FIG. 22
BASE RHYTHM ROUTE - FADE
FADE
VS. MAN COVERAGE
LANDMARK ROUTE
BALL MUST SPLASH DOWN B/W 18-25 YDS
WR MUST HOLD BOTTOM OF #'S
QB MUST USE 2 STEP OR QUICK 3 DROP FROM GUN
OVER SHOULDER W/ AIR
BACK SHOULDER ON A LINE
LINE UP TOP OF #'S
OVER THE SHOULDER
BACK SHOULDER
25 YDS
15 YDS
15 YDS
UNCAPPED:
THROW W/ AIR
CAPPED:
THROW ON A LINE

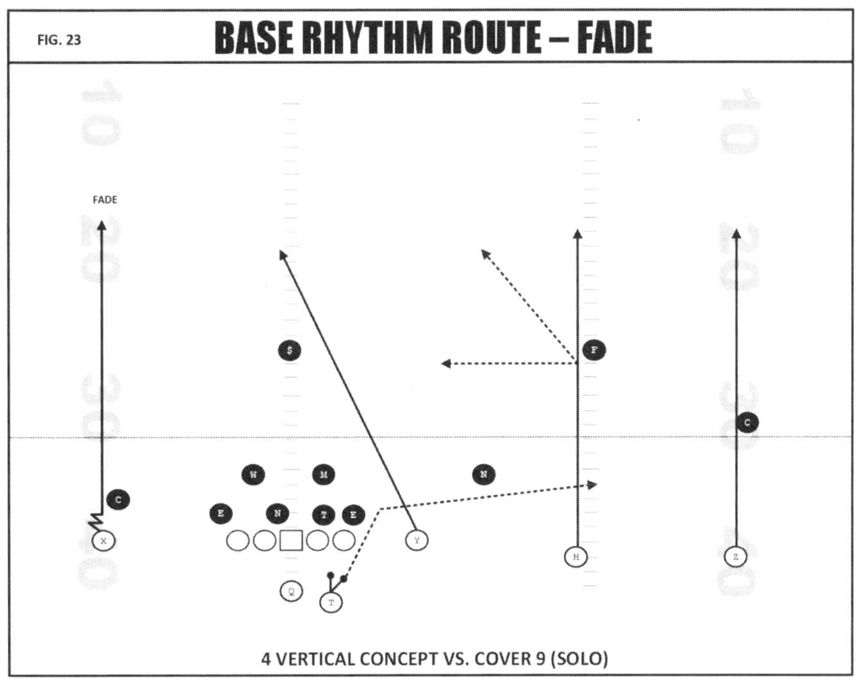
FIG. 23
BASE RHYTHM ROUTE – FADE
FADE
4 VERTICAL CONCEPT VS. COVER 9 (SOLO)

the defender by throwing the Fade on the back shoulder of the receiver. To do this the quarterback must throw the ball on a line at 15 yards or less before the defender can recover.

The Rhythm Fade route is most often thrown out of 3 x 1 formations. 3 x 1 formations can cause defensive coverage to push to the trips-receiver side and force a 1-on-1 isolation with a single defender. A 4-vertical concept is a common play used to throw a Rhythm Fade. (FIG. 23)

The receiver must determine what type of Man technique the defender is playing before he exits the line of scrimmage. There are two main types of press-man technique, press-jam and press-bail. (FIG. 24)

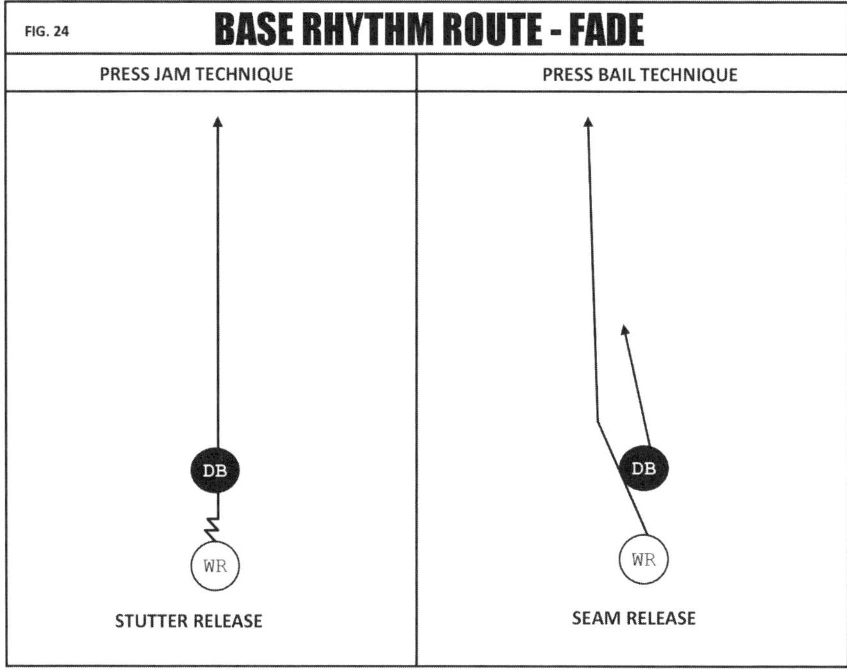

Against press-jam, the defender is trying to collision and carry the receiver. In this situation, the receiver will need to incorporate a Stutter Release.

Against press-bail technique, the defender is using the sideline for help by forcing the receiver out-of-bounds. This closes the route-side space of the Fade and CAPS the route. The receiver must use a Seam Release with no false steps to clear the hips of the press-bail defender.

The goal for the receiver on the Fade route is to get his hips and inside hand ahead of the defender to UNCAP the vertical space of the Fade. It is also important that the receiver does not widen and create too much space upon the release against the defender. The receiver needs to attack the outside shoulder as the press-bail defender opens the door by turning his hips to bail. The defender will attempt to place his inside arm on the near hip or on top of the near hand of the receiver to CAP the vertical space. The receiver should use a hook move with his inside hand to combat the defender's hand and UNCAP the vertical space. The receiver should not look for the ball until this occurs.

If the quarterback does not see the hips and hands of the receiver even or in front of the defender by the last step of his Drop, he should throw the back-shoulder Fade on a line, or go to the next route in the progression. This is not an absolute rule, however. When the personnel ability of a receiver is better than the defender, a quarterback can throw the ball off a reset step in the Drop.

The Rhythm Fade is also designed to attack soft-Man Coverage as well. Soft-Man Coverage is generally played anywhere from 5-7 yards from

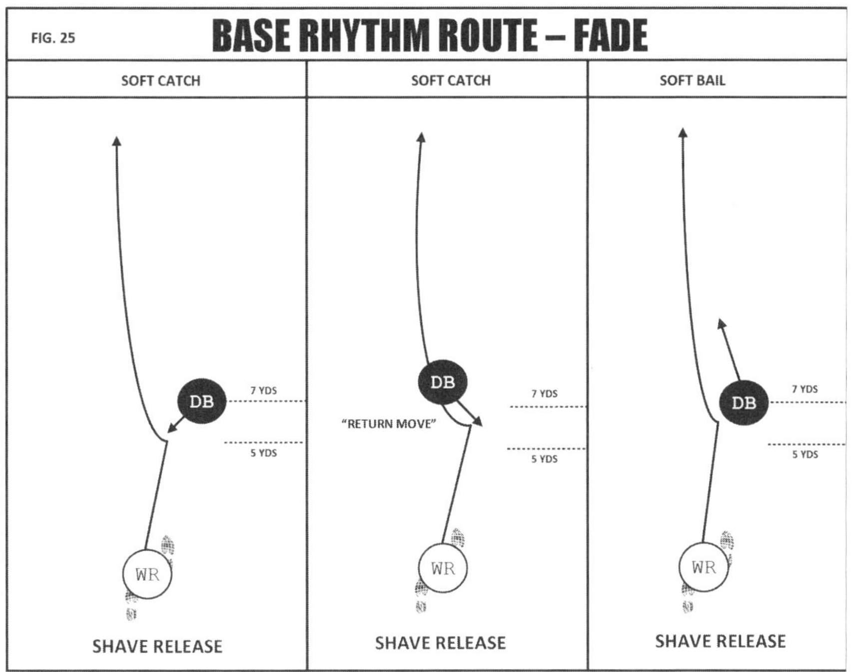

the line of scrimmage, and 1 yard to inside eye alignment on the receiver. There are two main types of soft-Man Coverage techniques. Soft-catch and soft-bail. The purpose of soft-catch technique is it allows the defender space to jump any quick-game route along with the ability to catch and absorb the receiver with collision if he runs a vertical Fade route. The soft-bail technique allows a defender who may be outmatched physically more cushion to bail and CAP the Fade route.

Receivers should use a Shave release against soft-catch or soft-bail Man defenders. Against a soft-catch Man technique, the receiver will need to be ready to use a release-hand strike move. Against soft-bail, it is more about closing the cushion.

The standard Shave release rule is to attack the route's side-space shoulder of the Man defender. When the receiver gets into the personal space of the defender, he will stick and explode, fading to the ball that is being thrown. (FIG. 25)

If the defender is over-aggressive with the catch-man technique, then the receiver can use a return move on the Shave release. The return

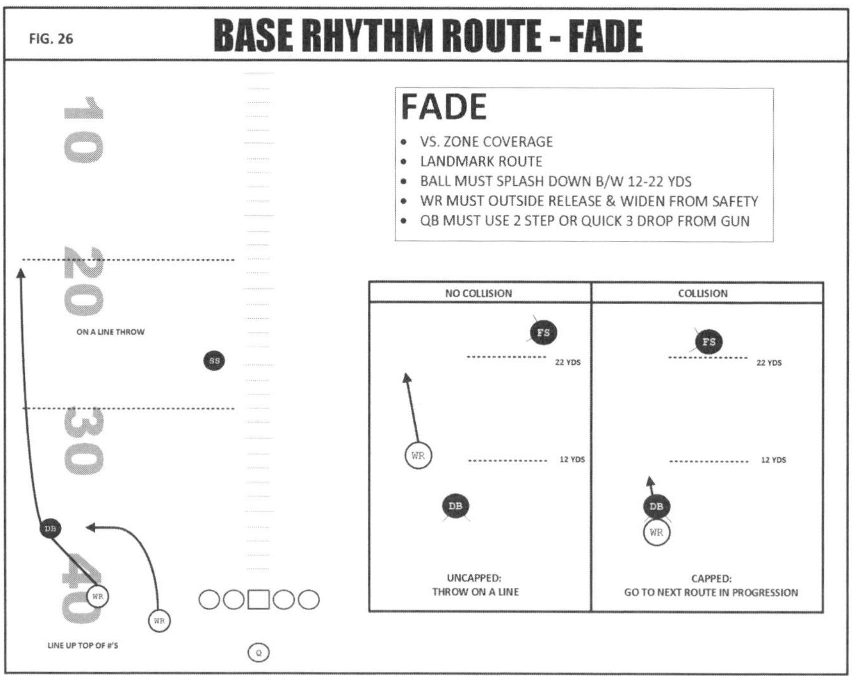

FIG. 26 BASE RHYTHM ROUTE - FADE

move is used to attack the opposite side of the route-side space to get the defender to CAP it. Then the receiver will stick and use a hand-release to win back the original route-side space. The key to using the return move is that the receiver must know the defender is going to CAP the initial setup move before he decides to use it.

Fade routes thrown into Zone Coverage require more time to close the cushion of a defender. This makes it more difficult to throw Fades on Rhythm into Zone Coverage. Proper complementary routes must be used alongside the Fade route to protect vertical route-space and also increase the timeline to throw the Fade off a reset step by the quarterback.

The best Zone Coverage that can be attacked by a Rhythm Fade is Cover-2. (FIG. 26)

The UNCAPPED space in Cover-2 is between 12-22 yards from the line of scrimmage. We refer to this space as the hole in Cover-2. Throwing the Fade in the hole requires the receiver to use a Seam Release to get the outside cornerback defending the flat space. There are different techniques that cornerbacks will use while playing Cover-2. Some will use a heavy-collision technique and others will play soft and carry the vertical release until they see another route threaten the flat space.

This requires the quarterback to read collision on the Drop. If there is no collision then the quarterback will throw the Fade in the hole with low trajectory and maximum velocity. If there is collision, then he will reset to the next route in the progression.

Rhythm Seam: The Rhythm Seam is a landmark route used to attack Man and Zone Coverage. In Zone Coverage, the Seam is designed to attack the vertical space between 15 and 22 yards. In Man Coverage, the route must be hit on Rhythm under 25 yards.

The Rhythm Seam Route is best used to attack 3-deep-zone Coverage. Throwing the Rhythm Seam Route into a 3-deep-zone requires low trajectory and maximum velocity. Zone Coverage places the eyes of defenders on the quarterback, allowing them to see when the ball is being thrown. This also allows defenders to break faster on the ball.

If the ball is thrown off Rhythm or with too much air, interception and incompletion probability increases. (FIG. 27)

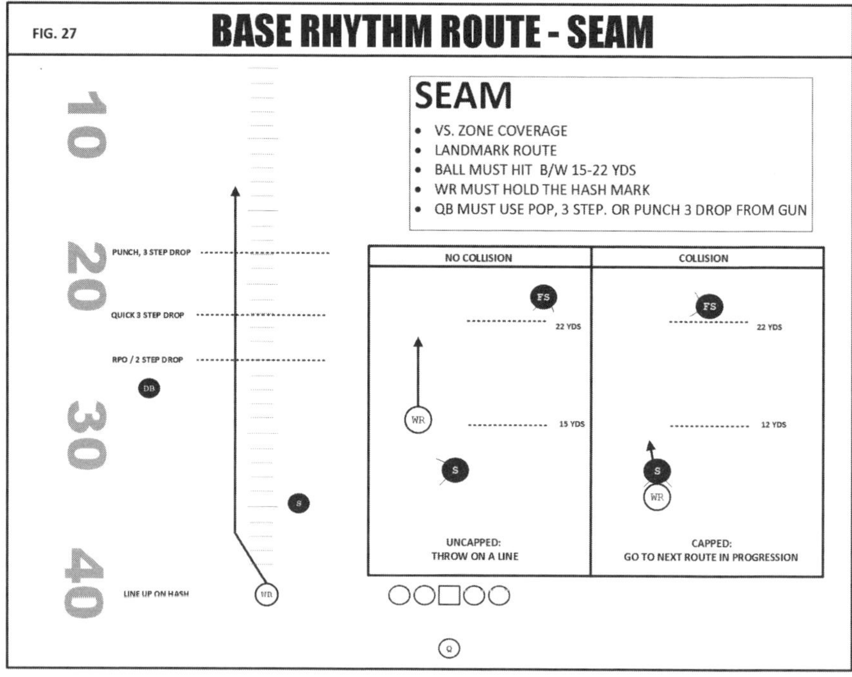

In 3-deep-zone, the middle of the field safety and cornerback are the potential CAP threats to the Seam Route. The curl/flat defender is a collision threat to the Seam. Therefore, timing the throw of the Rhythm Seam is critical. Timing can be manipulated by the type of Drop the quarterback uses post-snap. The quicker the Drop, the shorter the throw. The floor of the Seam Route is at 15 yards. This is the minimum distance needed to clear the curl/flat defender. The key for a quarterback is to learn how to manipulate the curl/flat defender who is trying to collision or carry the Seam post-snap.

One of the best ways is by using an RPO (Run/Pass Option) scheme that neutralizes the collision of the defender because he must honor the run-action between the quarterback and running back. (FIG. 28)

If there is no collision and the Seam is UNCAPPED, then the quarterback will pull the ball, pop his hips and set his hallway in line with the Seam Route-space. We refer to the mechanics of this style of Drop used with

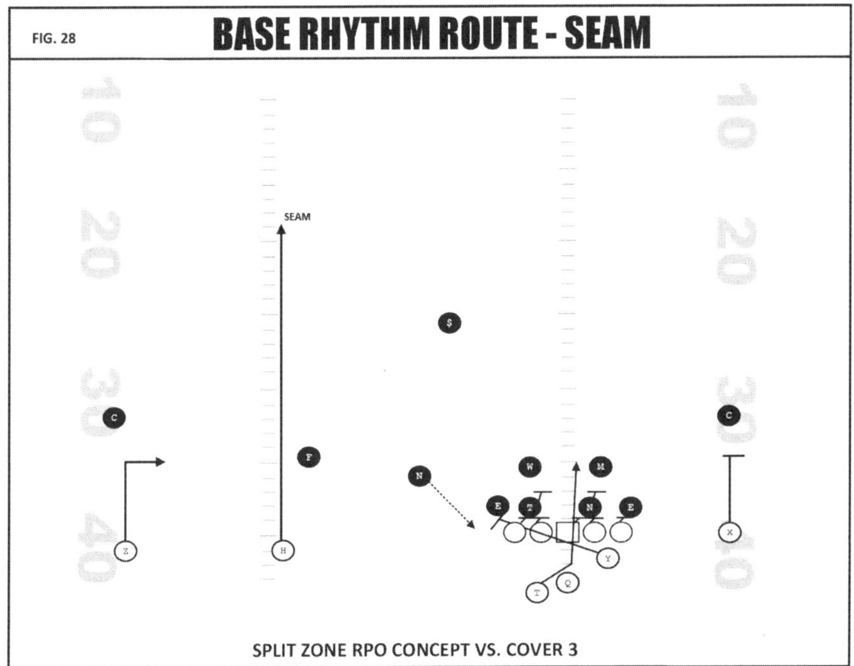

RPOs as a Pop Drop. A Pop Drop is a no-step Drop that resets the hips and feet in place, allowing the quarterback to hit the Seam at 15 yards from the line of scrimmage.

If play-action is not used when throwing the Seam Route, then the quarterback will have to rely more on using the R4 accelerators to process if it will be open. R4 accelerators allow quarterbacks to anticipate the opening of the Seam Route as it occurs between 15 and 22 yards. Accelerators are the primary defensive actions that defenders use to delay and disrupt route timing and mental decision-making by the quarterback.

> ***Accelerators** are the primary defensive actions that defenders use to delay and disrupt route timing and mental decision-making by the quarterback.*

Collision is the primary accelerator that defenders use to neutralize routes run by inside receivers. A quarterback can provide himself more time to process collision with different Drop footwork.

The baseline Drop in Shotgun is using a 3-step Drop. This Drop allows for a throw to be on Rhythm and places it in a landing Zone of 18-22 yards. However, if a quarterback needs more time to process the Rhythm Seam he can take a punch 3-step Drop.

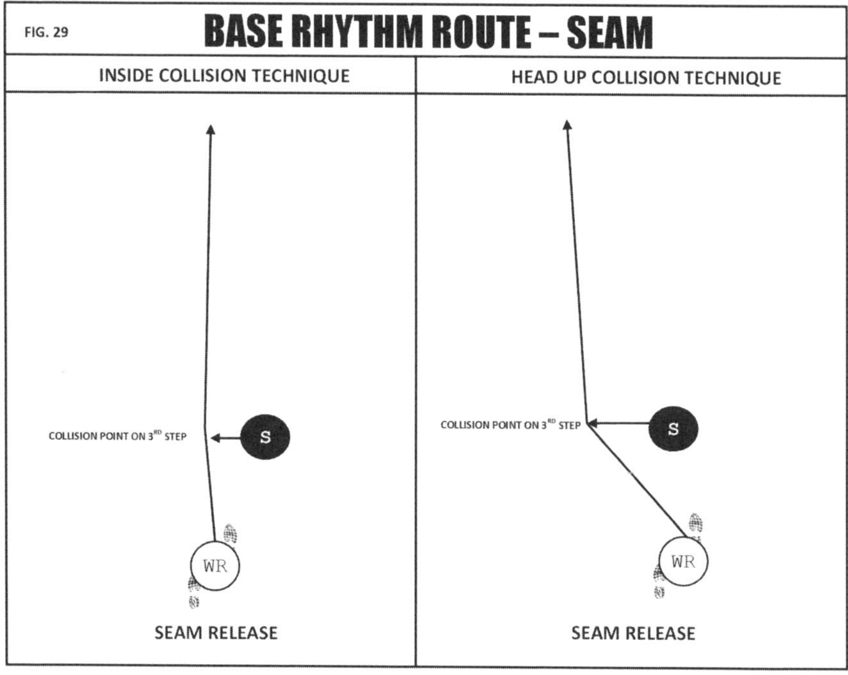

Collision must be avoided by the receiver, as well. To attack this defensive weapon, the receiver running a Seam Route must use a Seam Release. Like we discussed on the Fade route, the Seam Release is a 3-step outside release that is used to attack a defender who is trying to delay or disrupt a vertical route. The angle of departure on the release is relative to the alignment of the curl/flat defender. (FIG. 29)

There are two main alignments for defenders using collision. They are *inside* or *head-up* alignment over the receiver. A receiver who has a defender aligned inside will not have to take an aggressive Seam Release angle off the line. He will still use the first 3 steps off the line, however, to position his body and hand-strike for contact with the defender. The 3rd step places the outside foot in the ground at the collision point between receiver and defender. This allows the receiver to lean back into the contact while incorporating a one-hand strike move with the inside arm. A receiver will use either a *hook* move or a *rip* move at this moment in time.

A *hook* move is a violent one-hand circular over-the-top strike that is aimed at the arm-bar of the oncoming collision of the defender. A *rip* move is an aggressive turn of the shoulders away from contact, along with a down-to-up ripping action of the inside arm through arm-bar of the oncoming collision of the defender.

The quarterback and receiver must understand that there is a difference between *contact* and *collision. Contact* is inevitable between and receiver and defender and necessary to create space and separation with a route. The difference is that contact does not delay or disrupt the receivers route-stem or break. Collision does.

If the curl/flat defender is not attempting to collision the Seam Route, then he may be using a *carry* technique. A carry technique is also referred to as a wall technique by some coaches. There are two main types of carry technique. They are an *inside-* or *outside-leveraged* technique. (FIG. 30)

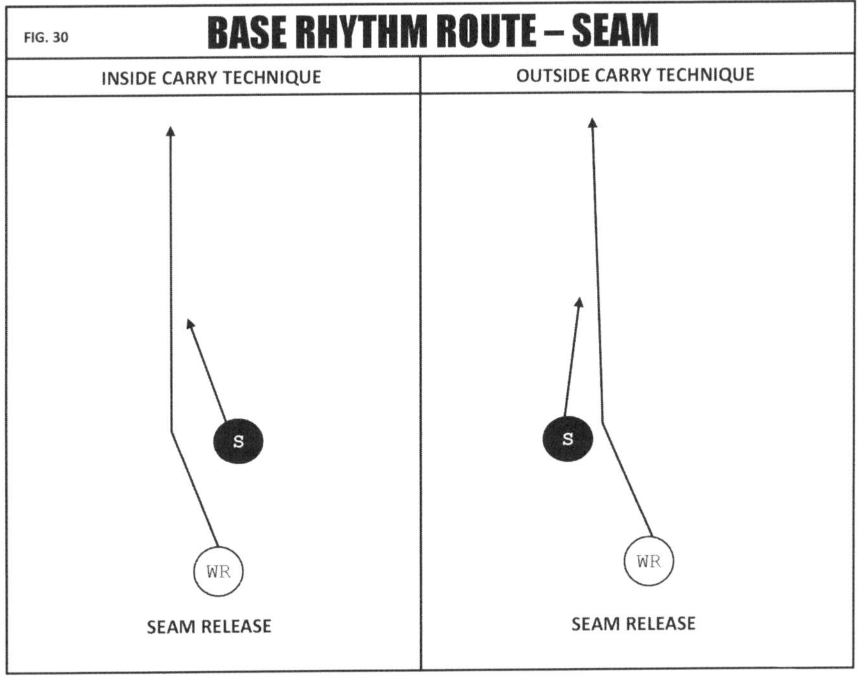

The inside carry technique is used to CAP the vertical stem of the receiver to the hard-deck line at 7-10 yards and pass the route off to a secondary defender. After the route is passed, the defender will Drop down and look to CAP any receiver in the flat route-space. The benefit of this technique is that it delays the decision-making for the quarterback on the vertical route, and entices the quarterback to throw the flat route. The carry defender can rally to tackle the flat route, prevent the explosive play on the Seam, and force the offense to execute with shorter throws in the passing game.

The receiver uses a Seam Release to attack an inside carry technique. The receiver must explode out of his stance with no false steps, and clear the hips and hands of the defender. The benefit of the inside carry technique is that the eyes of the defender are away from the quarterback. This prevents him from seeing the ball being thrown and hinders his ability to make a play on the ball. A quarterback must be aggressive and throw on-Rhythm against the inside carry technique.

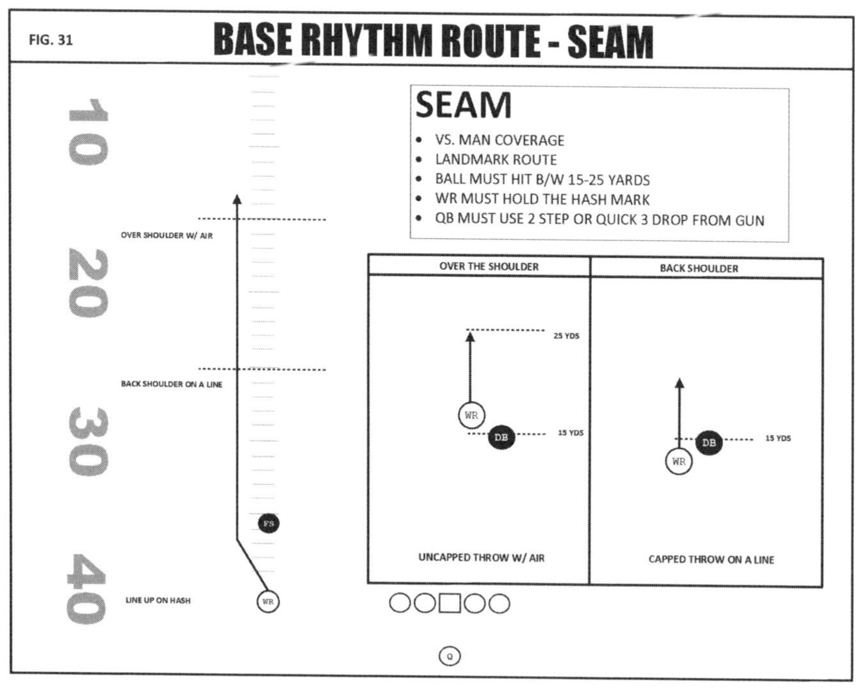

The outside carry technique has evolved over the years in pattern-matching variations of Cover-3. One of the most popular is Nick Saban's Rip/Liz pattern matching Cover-3. In this coverage, the outside carry technique places the defender over and outside of the slot receiver in a pre-snap CAPPING position on the Seam Route. This allows the defender to maintain a CAPPED position on the Drop and squeezes the vertical Seam to the middle of the field safety.

The receiver will use a Seam Release to attack an outside carry technique. The receiver must take an aggressive attack angle at the outside shoulder of the defender. If the receiver cannot own outside space by his 3rd step of the Seam Release, then he will have to take the inside space that the defender is giving him and win outside route-space at the top of the route. This technique puts the quarterback in a high-risk throwing position. The defender had the advantage by CAPPING the outside space of the Seam while being able to keep his eyes on the quarterback to see the throw. It is recommended that this throw is only made against a clear personnel mismatch in the offense's favor.

The Rhythm Seam Route is also an effective route against Man Coverage. Specifically, Cover-0 with no safety help deep. (FIG. 31)

The issue with Cover-0 is that the defense is usually bringing 1 more defender than the offense can block, so throwing on-Rhythm is a must. The biggest challenge with throwing the Rhythm Seam against Cover-0 is that most quarterbacks overthrow the route. The main factors that contribute to this are being too amped up because of the Blitz threat and not understanding how to bleed power out of the throw. Throwing the Seam Route against Cover-0 requires minimal power. The key is getting the nose of the ball to turn over and land under 25 yards. 25 yards in the ceiling for even the fastest receiver to get to when the quarterback throws off a quick 2- or 3-step Drop from gun.

Another benefit of getting the nose of the ball to turn over and land before 25 yards is that it is challenging for a defender to get in position to CAP the Seam and get his eyes around to locate the ball in that short amount of time. The quarterback must process either pre-snap or on the Drop depending on the receiver's ability to get his hips and hands in front of the Man defender on him. Like the Fade, the quarterback

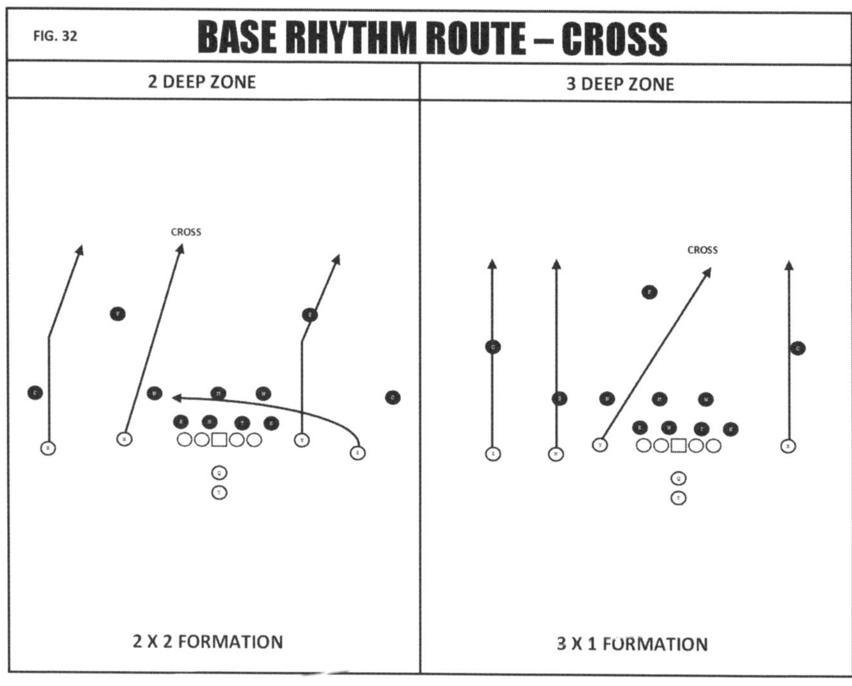
FIG. 32
BASE RHYTHM ROUTE – CROSS
2 DEEP ZONE
3 DEEP ZONE
CROSS
CROSS
2 X 2 FORMATION
3 X 1 FORMATION

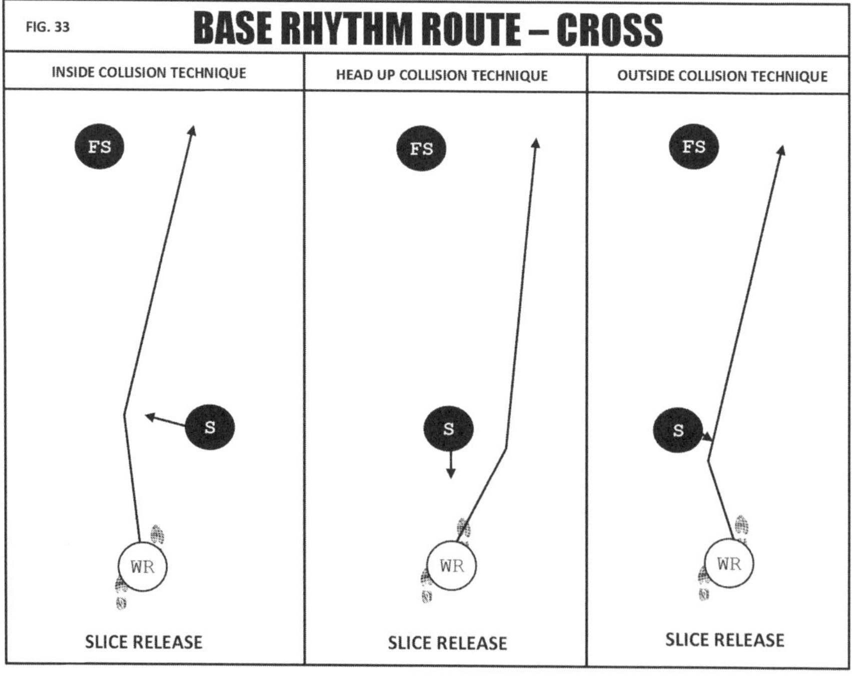
FIG. 33
BASE RHYTHM ROUTE – CROSS
INSIDE COLLISION TECHNIQUE
HEAD UP COLLISION TECHNIQUE
OUTSIDE COLLISION TECHNIQUE
FS
S
WR
SLICE RELEASE
FS
S
WR
SLICE RELEASE
FS
S
WR
SLICE RELEASE

can also throw a back-shoulder Seam if the defender is quickly in a position to CAP the vertical routes space.

Rhythm Cross: The Rhythm Cross Route is another landmark route designed to attack Zone Coverage between 15 and 25 yards. The best coverages that are vulnerable to the Cross Route are 2-deep or 3-deep-zones. Against a 2-deep-zone Coverage, the Cross Route should be run by a slot receiver out of a 2 x 2 formation. Against a 3-deep-zone Coverage, the Cross Route should be run by a #3 receiver out of a 3 x 1 formation. (FIG. 32)

A slot receiver running a Cross Route must focus on avoiding collision and securing space for the quarterback to throw the ball into. A Slice Release is the best release that defeats collision when running a Cross Route. (FIG. 33)

Once collision is avoided, the function of the Slice Release taken on the Cross Route is to cut into the UNCAPPED space of the zone. To do this, the receiver must understand which defender to attack so he can maximize route-side space for the quarterback to throw into.

Against a 2-deep-zone Coverage, the receiver needs to Slice just inside the near safety. If you take the space between the near field safety and

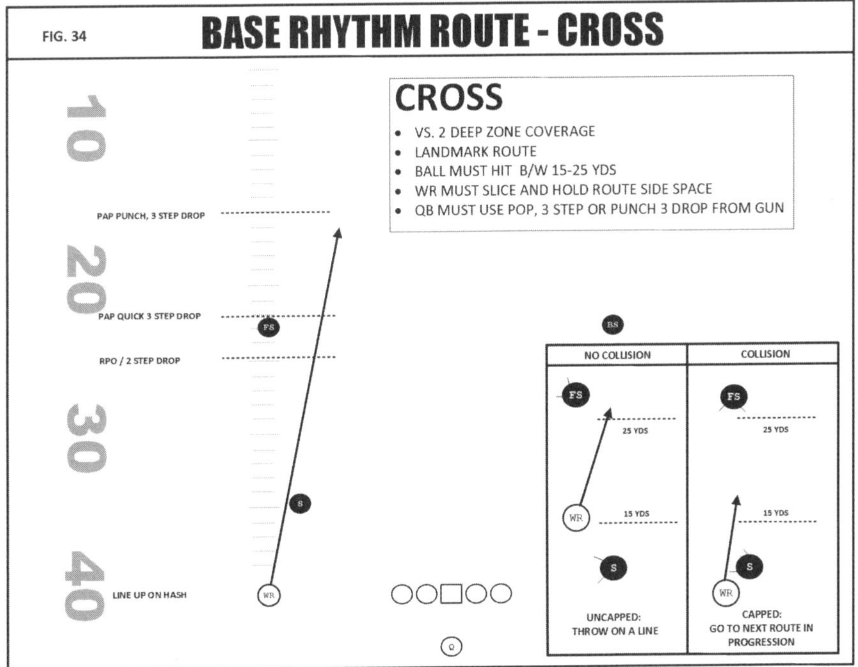

boundary safety as 100%, then the receiver would need to attack the inside 5% of that space and keep the rest of the 95% open for the quarterback. A big mistake that some receivers will make is attacking the space right down the middle of the safeties leaving only 50% of UNCAPPED space for the quarterback to throw into. (FIG. 34)

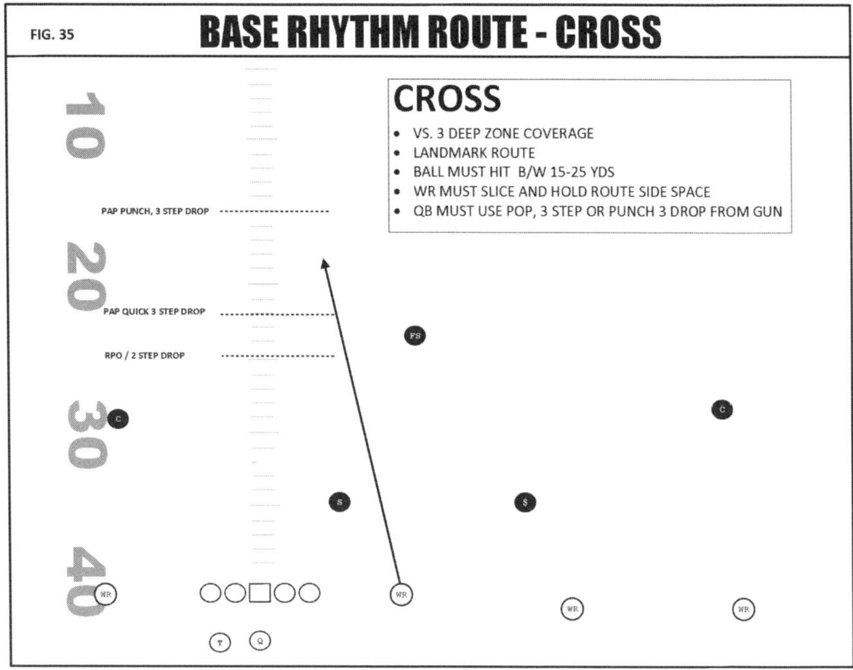

A quarterback throwing the Rhythm Cross Route must determine the best Drop to associate with the concept being called. A play-action fake is highly recommended when throwing the Cross Route. This places dual threat collision/run defenders in a bind, and allows the slot receiver to stretch and secure the UNCAPPED Zone space faster. Some example of play-action gun Drop footwork here could be an RPO pop, play-action quick 3-step or play-action punch 3-step Drop.

On a play-action fake, the quarterback will determine if there is collision. If there is no collision, he will read the route-side space of the Cross Route. If the space is UNCAPPED by the safety, he will throw the ball on-Rhythm with low trajectory and maximum velocity.

If there is collision or the safety is CAPPING the route-side space of the cross, the quarterback will go to the next route in the progression.

Against 3-deep-zone Coverage, the Cross Route is best used by a #3 receiver in a 3 x 1 formation. (FIG. 35)

This route is commonly used in a 4-Vertical concept. The mechanics of the Cross Route against a 3-deep-zone are almost the same. The only change is that the receiver must understand the UNCAPPED space is now between the high safety and cornerback. Therefore, after collision is defeated, the receiver needs to attack inside the 5% of space inside the high safety to hold 95% of UNCAPPED space for the quarterback to throw into on-Rhythm.

Rhythm Corner: The Rhythm Corner Route is designed to attack both Man and Zone Coverage. (FIG. 36)

The Rhythm Corner must be run off steps instead of yards. This differs from the previous Rhythm Routes discussed. The reason is that the corner route has a distinct break angle. This requires the throw to be made just as the break occurs. The angle of attack out of the break is based on the type of coverage it is going against. Against Man Coverage,

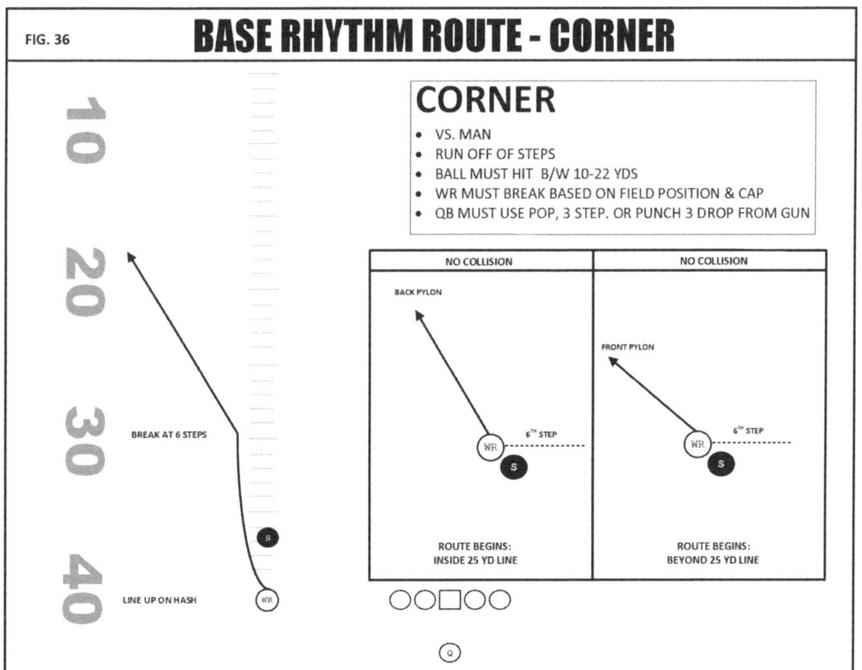

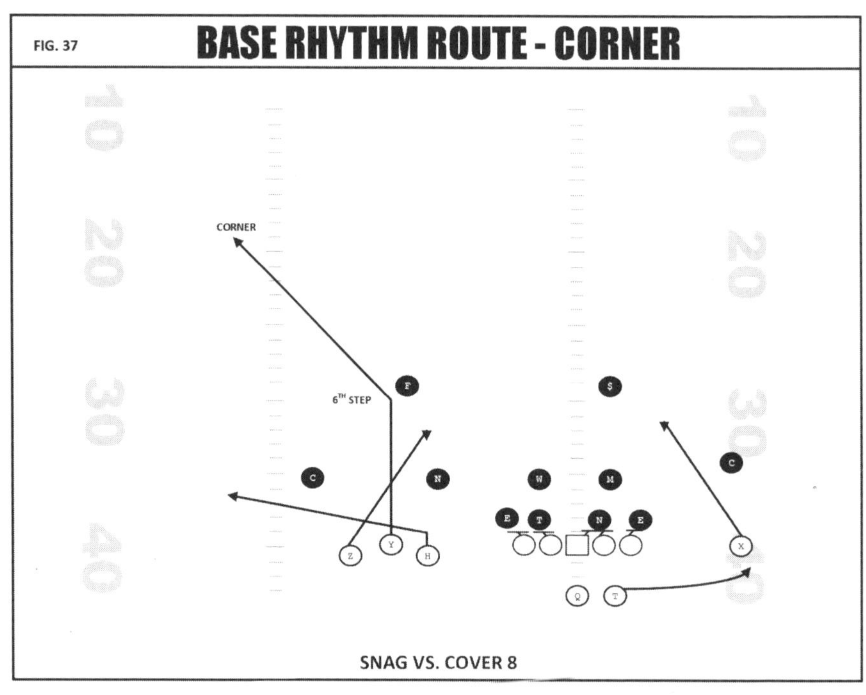
FIG. 37
BASE RHYTHM ROUTE - CORNER
CORNER
6TH STEP
F
$
C
N
W
M
C
E
T
N
E
Z
Y
H
X
Q
T
10
20
30
40
SNAG VS. COVER 8

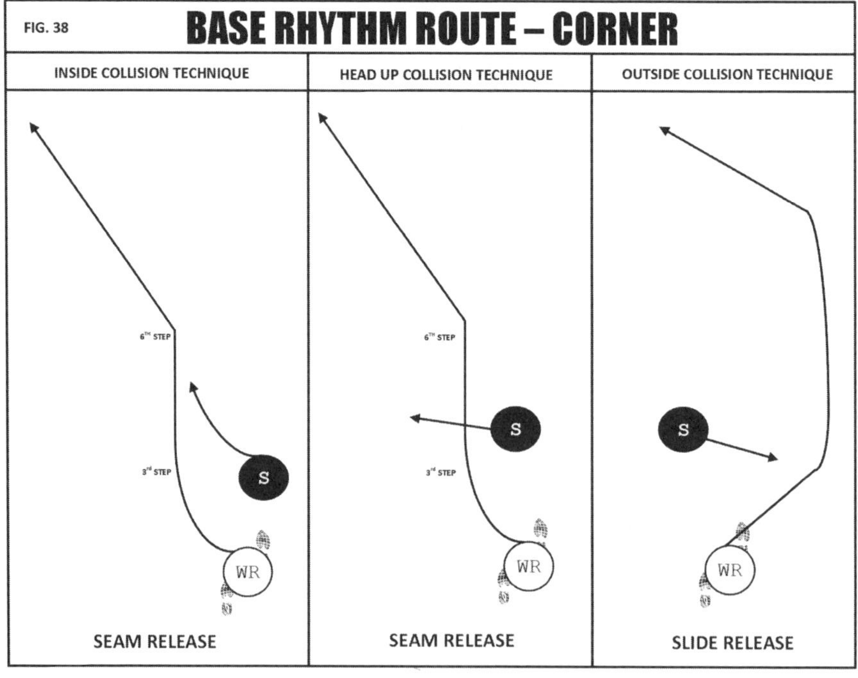
FIG. 38
BASE RHYTHM ROUTE – CORNER
INSIDE COLLISION TECHNIQUE
HEAD UP COLLISION TECHNIQUE
OUTSIDE COLLISION TECHNIQUE
6TH STEP
3rd STEP
S
WR
SEAM RELEASE
6TH STEP
3rd STEP
S
WR
SEAM RELEASE
S
WR
SLIDE RELEASE

the angle of attack out of the break is based on field position. If the route begins inside the red Zone (25 yards to goal line) then the route break is aiming at the back pylon of the end zone.

The Rhythm Corner is the vertical threat route for the Snag concept. (FIG. 37)

The Corner provides the spacing needed for the horizontal stretch to develop between the Pivot and Flat Route. The key to generating an explosive play is created by the receiver's ability to release off the line of scrimmage without collision. It is also critical that the receiver stems to own the route-side space and break at the proper angle on the corner to maximize route-space for the quarterback.

The route break of the corner will adjust base on the field zone it is being run in, as well as the CAP position of the defender. If the route begins beyond the red zone, then aim the route break at the front pylon of the end zone. These rules are used to provide a frame of reference that maximizes route-space.

Receivers running Rhythm Corner Routes against Man Coverage must use the best release to avoid collision. (FIG. 38)

The best release to use against head-up or inside-aligned defender is a Seam Release. The Rhythm Corner must break on time at 6 steps. So the receiver must, at all cost, get vertical after the 3rd step of the Seam Release. If the defender still owns outside space on the 3rd step of the Seam Release, then the receiver must take the inside-space given and win back the outside-space at the top of the corner route break.

If the defender is playing Man with an outside alignment or preventing a Seam Release, then the receiver will have to use a Slide Release. A Slide Release is used by a receiver who is trying to avoid a hard-outside collision defender. A Slide Release is a 2-step inside release. If the receiver has not gained inside leverage by the 2nd step, then he can continue to 4 steps but no further. It begins with a receiver in a stance with his outside foot back. The key is that the receiver must get vertical as soon as he gains inside leverage on the collision defender.

A receiver who is using a Slide Release on a Rhythm Corner against press-man will not have a distinct break at the top of the route. The receiver will still break on the 6th step, but the route will be more rounded because of the sharp angle of the Slide Release. We call this route a banana route because of the shape it makes when it is being run.

Against Zone Coverage, the angle of attack out of the break is based on the defender's position. If there is no defender in a position to CAP route-side space out of the break, then the corner route will break at the highest angle, using the pylon positioning rules in Man Coverage. If there is a defender in position to CAP route-side space, then the route will snap the break flat to attack the horizontal UNCAPPED space underneath the CAPPING defender. (FIG. 39)

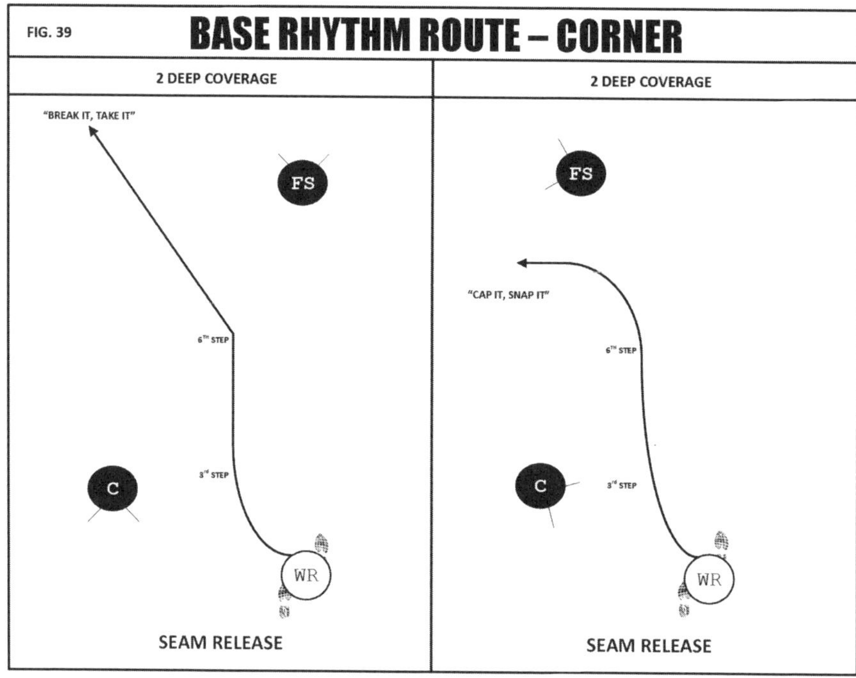

We use the phrase, "If we break it, we take it." Meaning if we can break the CAP and no defender is in position to CAP the vertical space, then we take that space out of the break. We use the phrase, "If they CAP it, we snap it." Meaning if the defender is positioned to CAP the route-side space, then we must snap the break flat to win back horizontal space.

A quarterback can maximize his processing time for the Rhythm Corner by manipulating his Drop footwork based on the defensive coverage.

Against Man Coverage, there is less time needed because of the 1-on-1 match-up between receiver and defender. The quarterback will generally use a base 3-step Drop in gun, or a quick 5-step Drop from under-center. However, when the Rhythm Corner route is being run in the tight red Zone (10-yard line – goal line) the route steps and Drop footwork must shorten. (FIG. 40)

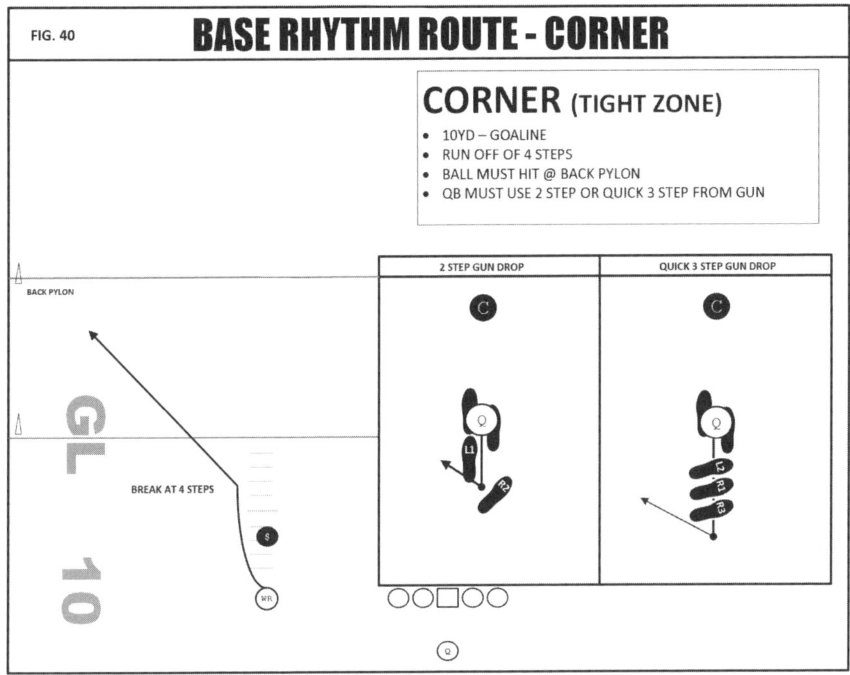

This is because of the reduced amount of route-space availability and defensive pressure increasing in the tight Zone area. In the tight Zone, the receiver will run a 4-step Rhythm Corner and break at the back pylon of the end zone. The quarterback will adjust his footwork to get the ball out faster. From under-center, the quarterback will use a basic 3-step Drop. In Shotgun he has two options:

1. Use a Quick 2-step Drop from gun.
2. Use a Quick 3-step Drop from gun.

The Quick 3-step Drop differs from a basic 3-step Drop in that the 2nd step of the Drop does not cross over the 1st step. The 2nd step resets 6 inches from where it starts in the stance. and stops just in front of the

1st step in the Drop. The benefit of the quick 3-step Drop allows for an easier reset of the hips and feet to the backside of the play if the Rhythm Corner is CAPPED. It's more difficult to reset to the backside off a 2-step gun Drop. The quarterback should use the 2-step or quick 3-step based on his determination of staying frontside with the ball or having a possible backside option if the corner is CAPPED.

Against Zone Coverage. there may be more time needed because of the post-snap movements of multiple defenders in the Rhythm-corner route-space. A basic 5-step under center or 3-step gun Drop is generally used in these situations. A quarterback can create more time in gun by using a punch 3-step Drop. (FIG. 41)

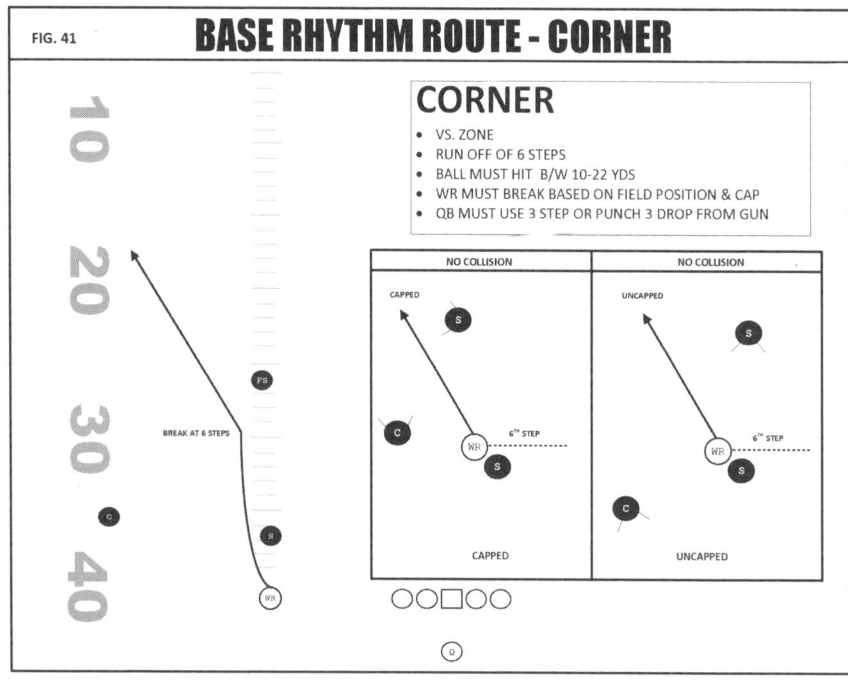

Processing the Rhythm Corner on the Drop requires the quarterback to first read collision. If the route gets collision on the release, then the quarterback should go to the next route in the progression. If there is no collision, then the quarterback's eyes must maintain soft focus on the route-side space of the corner route. The quarterback must be able to process the dominant position and hip angles of any defenders in the area who can CAP the route. Cover-2 and pattern-matching coverages, like 2 read, can present a challenge to a quarterback who doesn't know what to look for.

A soft focus allows the quarterback to maintain a wider field of view. The result is being able to process multiple defenders' positions at a moment in time and determining their ability to close on route-side space by the last step of the Drop.

EXAMPLE: If the cornerback is over and outside the receiver, with a full turn of the hips, can CAP the route-space of the corner. Furthermore, if a free safety is over and outside the receiver, with a man turn of the hips, CAPs the route as well.

Conversely, if the cornerback is under and outside the receiver, with a square hip turn the route-side space of the corner is UNCAPPED. If the free safety is over and inside with square hip angle, then the route is UNCAPPED, as well.

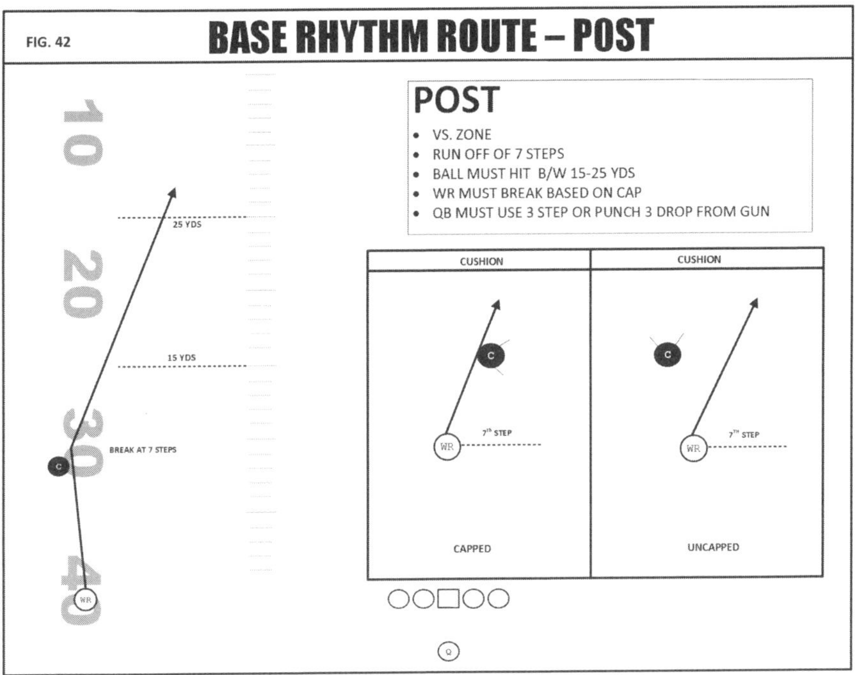

The final factor that must be considered when determining if the route is CAPPED or UNCAPPED is the personnel of the receiver against the defenders threatening route-side space. Personnel trumps dominant positions of defenders. A defender may be in position to CAP route-side space, but if the personnel ability of the receiver is better, then the space can still be considered UNCAPPED.

It also works the other way. A receiver may have UNCAPPED space, but if the defensive personnel is better than the receiver, he can make up for his bad position and close and CAP the space on the throw. This is where film breakdown and game-planning are critical to determine defender's personnel ability and then communicate those abilities properly to your quarterback so he can add that to his pre-snap decision-making on the called concept.

Rhythm Post: The Rhythm Post Route is primarily designed to attack Zone Coverage, particularly 3-deep-zone Coverage. (FIG. 42)

The Rhythm Post is a 7-step route starting with the outside foot back in a receiver stance. The Shallow concept is a play that features the Rhythm Post. The Rhythm Post provides the vertical threat for the concept. This threat protects the horizontal stretch created by the dig and shallow route. (FIG.43)

When the Rhythm Post is run from an outside receiver position, the ball must be thrown on a line. The ball should land from 15 to 25 yards and in between the numbers and hash mark. Running the route-break between the numbers and the hash mark gives the Post a "skinny" look, and is why many refer to the Rhythm Post as a "skinny" post.
Timing and trajectory are critical for the Rhythm Post. If it is thrown off a reset step at the end of the Drop at 25 yards, then the cornerback can make a play on the ball by undercutting the route. The safety can also recover to CAP the route over the top. To prevent this, the quarterback must make sure that he throws the route off the last step of the Drop and process the route-side space correctly to anticipate if the route will be UNCAPPED.

To do this, the quarterback must view the vector of the route break. Viewing the vector is maintaining a soft focus on the route-side break space to determine the CAP intent. If the cornerback is over and inside with a zone hip angle, then the quarterback would confirm that the Post

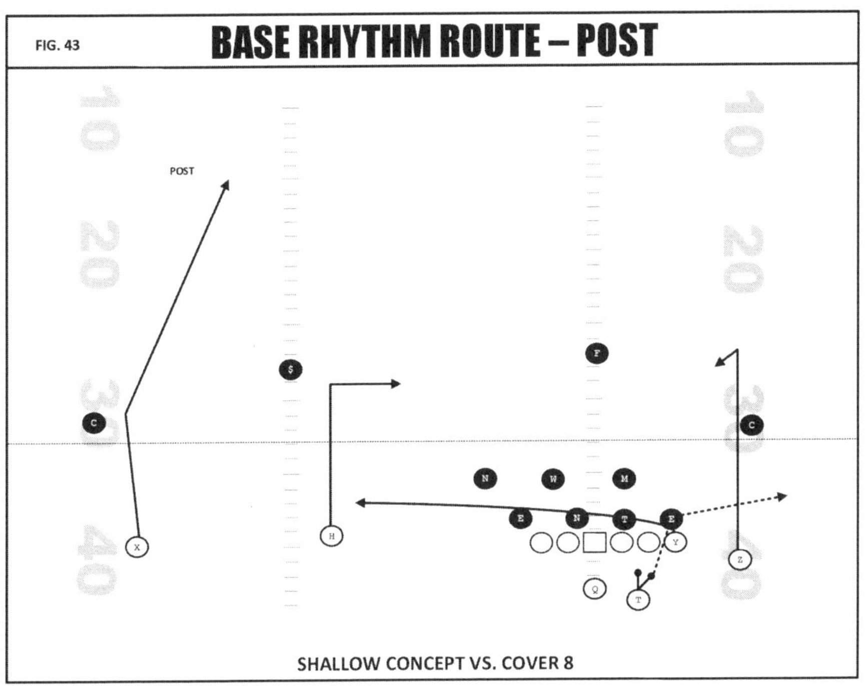
FIG. 43
BASE RHYTHM ROUTE – POST
POST
10
20
30
40
SHALLOW CONCEPT VS. COVER 8

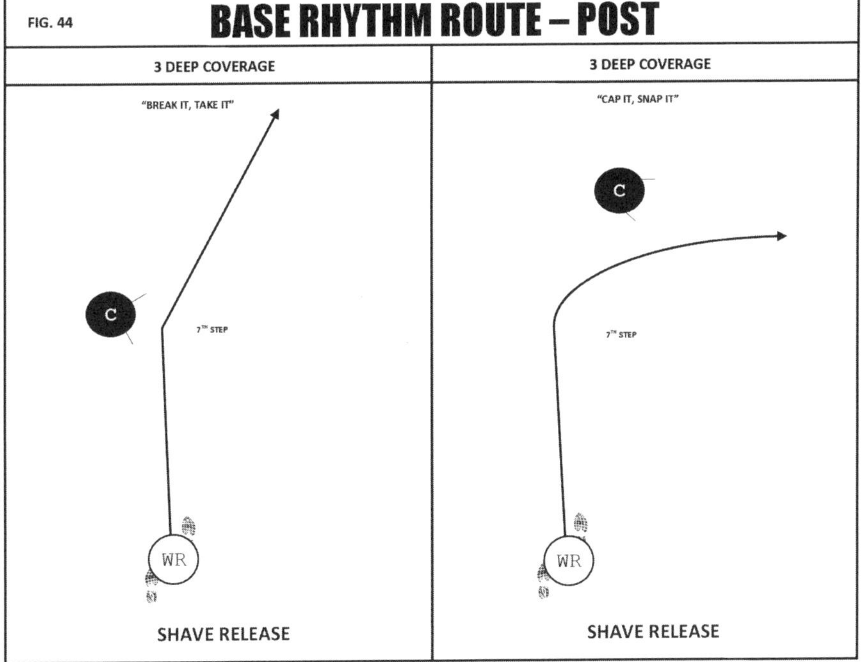
FIG. 44
BASE RHYTHM ROUTE – POST
3 DEEP COVERAGE
"BREAK IT, TAKE IT"
7TH STEP
C
WR
SHAVE RELEASE
3 DEEP COVERAGE
"CAP IT, SNAP IT"
C
7TH STEP
WR
SHAVE RELEASE

FIG. 45 **BASE RHYTHM ROUTE – POST**

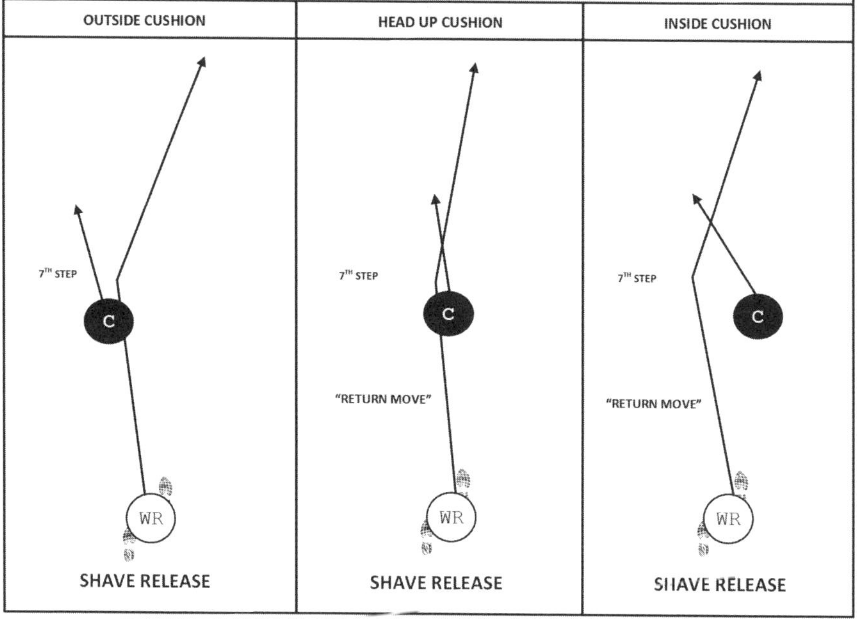

OUTSIDE CUSHION	HEAD UP CUSHION	INSIDE CUSHION
7TH STEP C WR SHAVE RELEASE	7TH STEP C "RETURN MOVE" WR SHAVE RELEASE	7TH STEP C "RETURN MOVE" WR SHAVE RELEASE

is CAPPED and go to the next route in the progression. If the cornerback was over and outside with a full turn hip angle. then the quarterback would confirm it as UNCAPPED and throw the ball on-Rhythm. (FIG. 44)

The Post Route can adjust the attack angle out of the break to win back route-side space if it is CAPPED. EXAMPLE: If the receiver can UNCAP the route-side space of the post, then the quarterback will take it. "Break it, take it"

However, if the route-side space of the Post is CAPPED vertically on the 7th step, then the receiver can win back the horizontal space by snapping the route break off flat. "CAP it, snap it"

Giving your receivers the freedom to win back space with route-break adjustments requires practice but can pay big dividends once mastered. It is easier for quarterbacks and receivers to adjust route-breaks that break to the same side of space.

Receivers can create more route space with proper releases from the line of scrimmage. The Shave release is the most common release used on the Post against Zone Coverage. (FIG. 45)

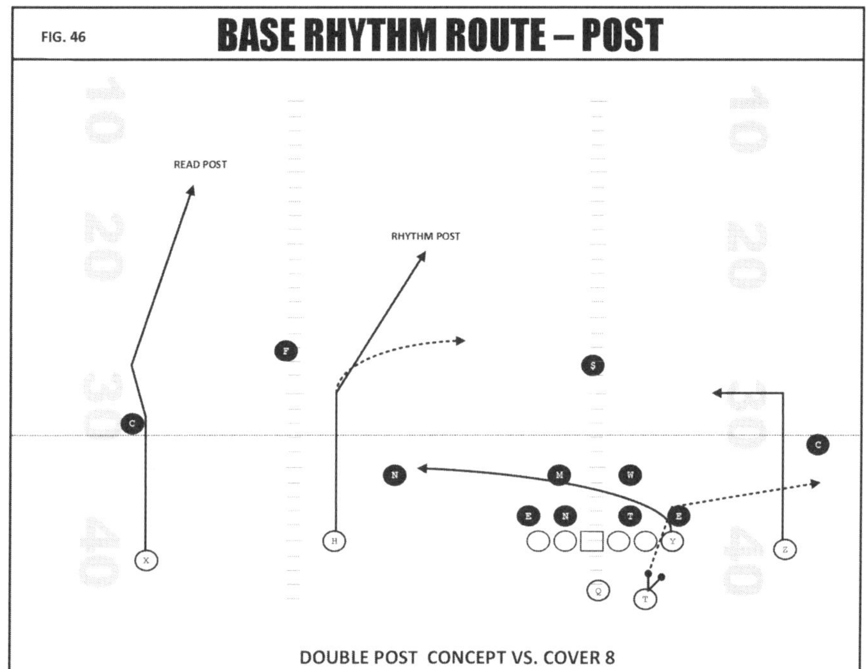

FIG. 46 **BASE RHYTHM ROUTE – POST**

DOUBLE POST CONCEPT VS. COVER 8

Against an outside-leveraged cushion defender, the receiver will Shave the inside shoulder of the defender and break on the post. Defenders who want to protect the UNCAPPED Seam space in a 3-deep-zone Coverage may play with more of a head-up or inside-leveraged cushion. This would place them in a better pre-snap position to CAP the inside space of the post. To attack this alignment, the receiver can Shave the outside shoulder opposite of the route break. This a "return move" previously discussed on the Fade route.

The key is to attack the opposite shoulder to make the defender think you are running an outside vertical, or breaking route and get the defender to widen to CAP that space. As the defender widens, the receiver will stick the route on his 7th step and cross the face of the defender to attack the UNCAPPED space with the post. The quarterback can use a punch 3-step Drop in gun to furnish more time for the receiver to set up the defender on the return move.

Against 2-deep or 4-deep coverages, the Rhythm Post is best used from an inside receiver position. This can best be illustrated with the Double Post concept out of a 2 x 2 formation. (FIG. 46)

FIG. 47

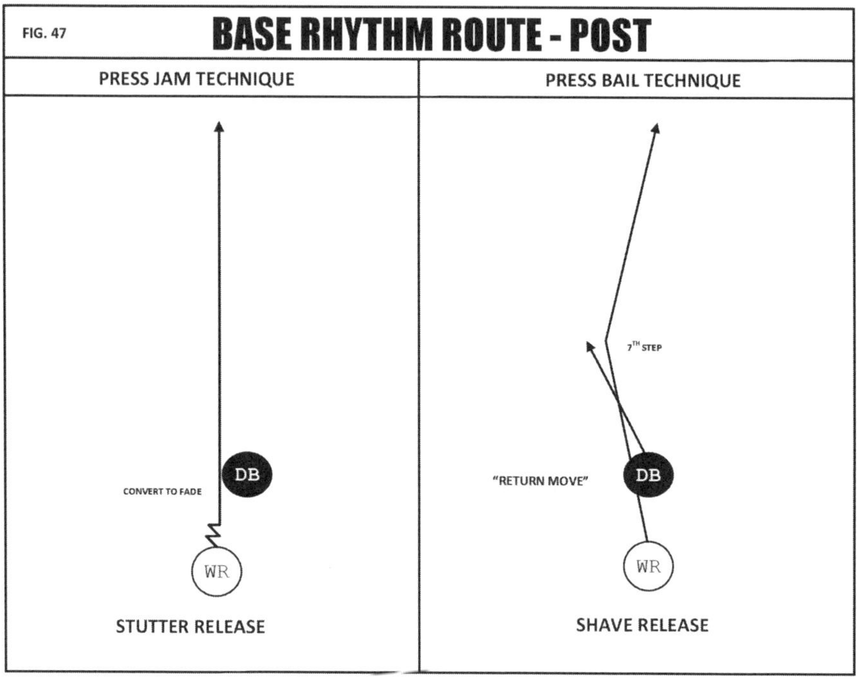

BASE RHYTHM ROUTE - POST

PRESS JAM TECHNIQUE	PRESS BAIL TECHNIQUE
CONVERT TO FADE DB WR	7TH STEP "RETURN MOVE" DB WR
STUTTER RELEASE	SHAVE RELEASE

There are more accelerators to process when running the Post from an inside receiver position. The collision accelerator is the highest threat to the Rhythm Post. A play-action fake is best used to neutralize collision on an inside receiver running a post. Once neutralized, the quarterback must view the vector of the route-side space of the Post Break. The dominant position of the near safety will determine the route break of the post. If the safety is over and outside the route-side space, then the Post will break skinny down the middle of the field. If the safety is over and inside, then the Post will break flat to attack the horizontal space in the middle of the field.

The quarterback must process the hip angle and closure ability of the defenders to confirm if the route is CAPPED or UNCAPPED. This confirmation will tell him to throw or go to the next route in the progression.

There are times when a Post route concept is called to attack Zone Coverage and the defense may come out in Man Coverage. (FIG. 47)

If this occurs against a press-man coverage with a defender trying to jam at the line of scrimmage, then it is best to convert the Post to a Fade

Route. There is no sense in banging your head into a brick wall trying to attack a space that has a defender in optimal position and technique to take the space away. However, if the defender is playing a press-bail Man technique or a Soft-Man technique, a Shave Release attacking the outside shoulder with a return move can UNCAP the route-side space of the Post and win space back at the top of the route. These are some adjustments to consider against Man Coverage.

CHAPTER 4

Understanding the 5 Snap Rhythm Routes

UNDERSTANDING THE 5 SNAP RHYTHM ROUTES

Every base family of routes contains a sub-group that maintains the same timing traits of the routes but differs in the space the routes attack. The sub-group for the base Rhythm-route family is the snap-Rhythms. Snap-Rhythms are routes that break at 1.8-seconds on the timeline and must be thrown off the last step of the quarterback's Drop. The difference is they do not attack vertically; each route in this group snaps at the break and attacks horizontal intermediate space instead of vertical deep space.

Snap-Rhythms provide the adjustments needed to counter defender actions that are CAPPING vertical space. A defender cannot simultaneously defend both vertical and horizontal space at the same moment in time. If a defender is CAPPING a base-Rhythm Route, then a snap-Rhythm is the complement solution. Base- and snap-Rhythm Route adjustments are not always made on the run. Most adjustments are made off anticipated pre-snap defensive intent.

Snap-Rhythms also serves coaches by providing better Rhythm-route options in tight Zone (10-yard to goalline) situations where vertical space is reduced, and Blitz pressure is increased. They also create an edge against personnel match-ups where defenders are set on CAPPING vertical space.

Fall-Out Route: The Fall-Out Route is the snap adjustment to the Rhythm Fade Route. (FIG. 48)

The Fall-Out Route attacks horizontal intermediate route space. The Fall-Out Route is a landmark route that breaks at 9-yards. This route is best used against a defender who is good at CAPPING the Rhythm Fade Route. If a defender is consistently over and inside, with his hips and hands CAPPING the vertical Fade Route, then the Fall-Out is the route to counter and win the UNCAPPED horizontal space.

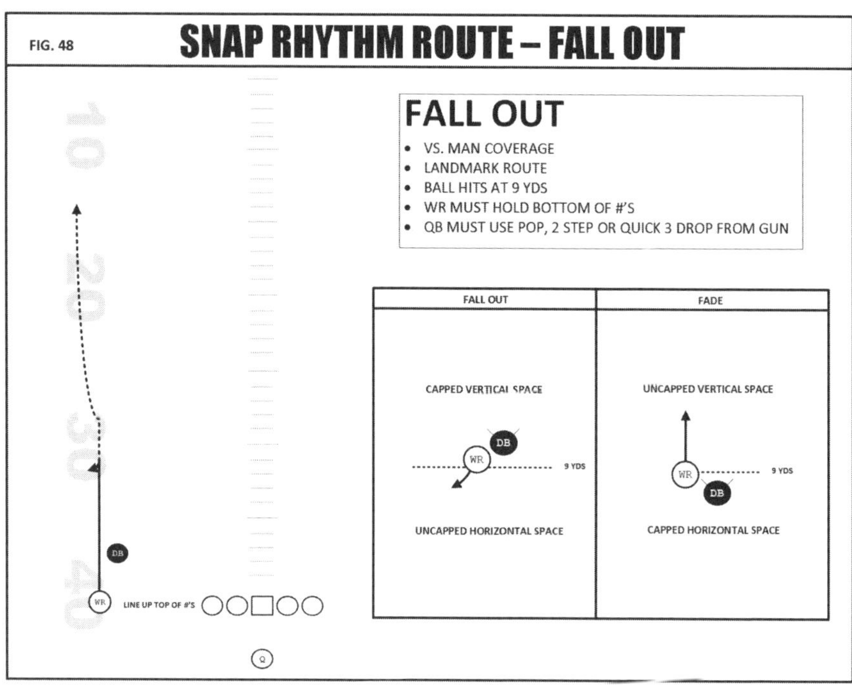

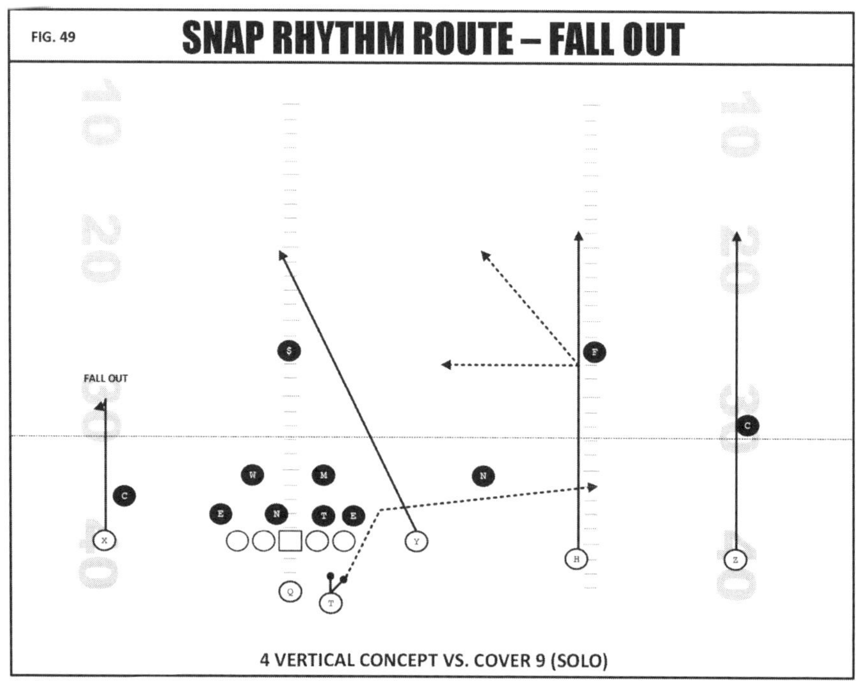

4 VERTICAL CONCEPT VS. COVER 9 (SOLO)

The Fall-Out Route is best used to the single-side receiver in a 3 x 1 formation. (FIG. 49)

These formations tend to generate Man Coverage against the single receiver. The defense will usually place its best cornerback to this side and rely on his athletic ability to CAP any vertical shot attempt against man-to-man. If the offense does not have a receiver who can UNCAP vertical space against this single-side man-to-man coverage, then the Fall-Out Route is a good route substitute to attempt. The Fall-Out is also a favorable route to use in the tight zone (10-yard to goalline), where vertical space is limited and Man Coverage increases. This Fall-Out can be signaled as an adjustment pre-snap at the line of scrimmage or tagged on an existing play-call.

Sit-Route: The Sit-Route is the snap adjustment to the Rhythm-Seam Route. (FIG. 50)

If the vertical space the Seam attacks is CAPPED by a safety, then the horizontal space can be attacked with the Sit-Route. The Sit-Route is a landmark route that breaks at 8-yards.

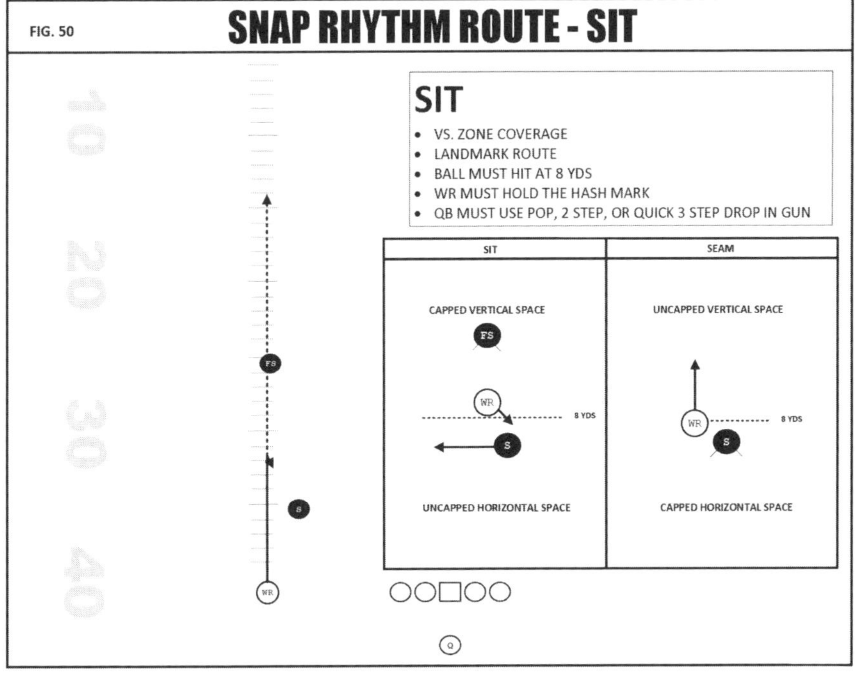

The Sit-Route works best from an inside-receiver position against a quarter's coverage with a flat defender who buzzes the flat space quickly, and the Sit-Route works best from an outside-receiver position against a 3-deep-zone Coverage with a flat defender who quickly buzzes the flat space.

The Sit-Route is best used in compressed or bunch formations. (FIG. 51)

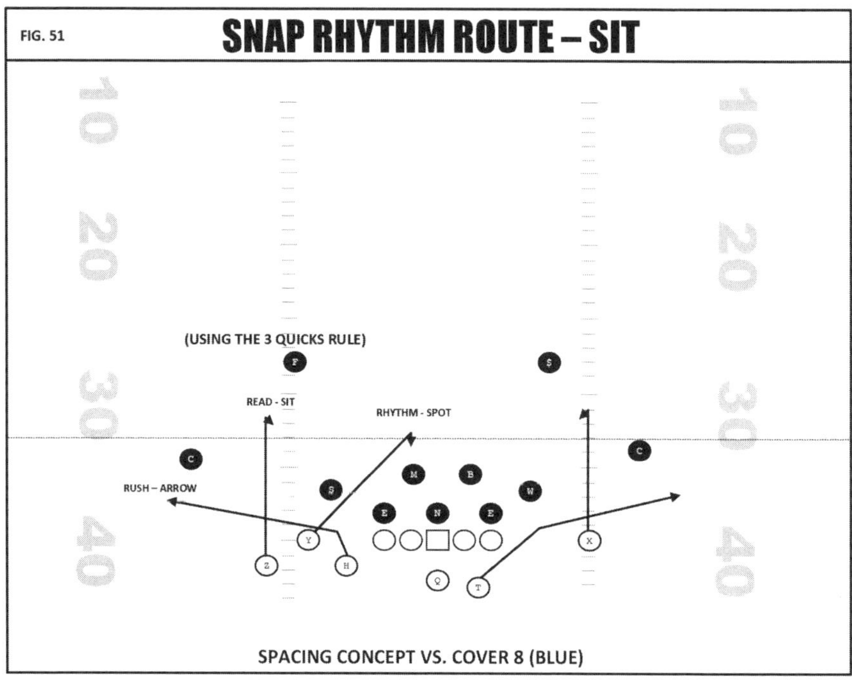

FIG. 51 **SNAP RHYTHM ROUTE – SIT**

SPACING CONCEPT VS. COVER 8 (BLUE)

Spacing concepts best suit the Sit-Route. These formations increase flat-space and force the flat-defender to quickly react post-snap. In the spacing concept, the Rhythm-sit can be treated as a read-route by using the 3-Quicks Rule or the two-Rhythms-make-a-Read rule. These rules would make the progression: Rhythm – Spot, Read – Sit, Rush – Arrow.

Using condensed splits helps inhibit collision and delays in reading the route-side space of the sit.

The Sit-Route is also a valuable route to attack a zone cornerback to the single-side of a 3 x 1 formation. (FIG. 52)

A hitch route is a popular route to throw against a Zone cornerback to the single-side. The vertical threat of a 5yd hitch rarely forces the defender to open his hips and bail. This can result in an interception. The Sit-Route that breaks at 8yards increases the vertical threat, forcing the

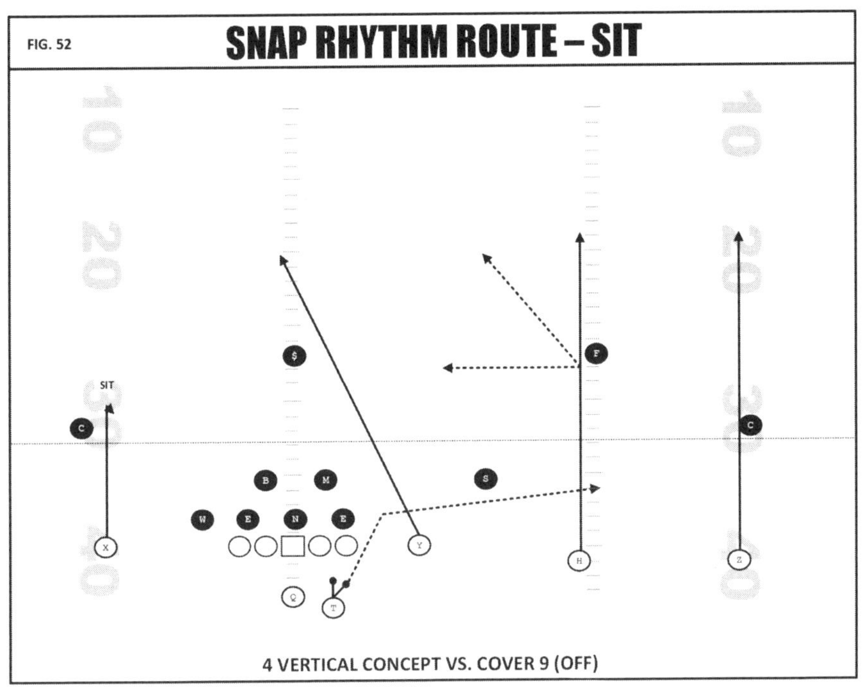
FIG. 52
SNAP RHYTHM ROUTE – SIT
SIT
C
$
F
C
B
M
S
W
E
N
E
X
Y
H
Z
Q
T
4 VERTICAL CONCEPT VS. COVER 9 (OFF)

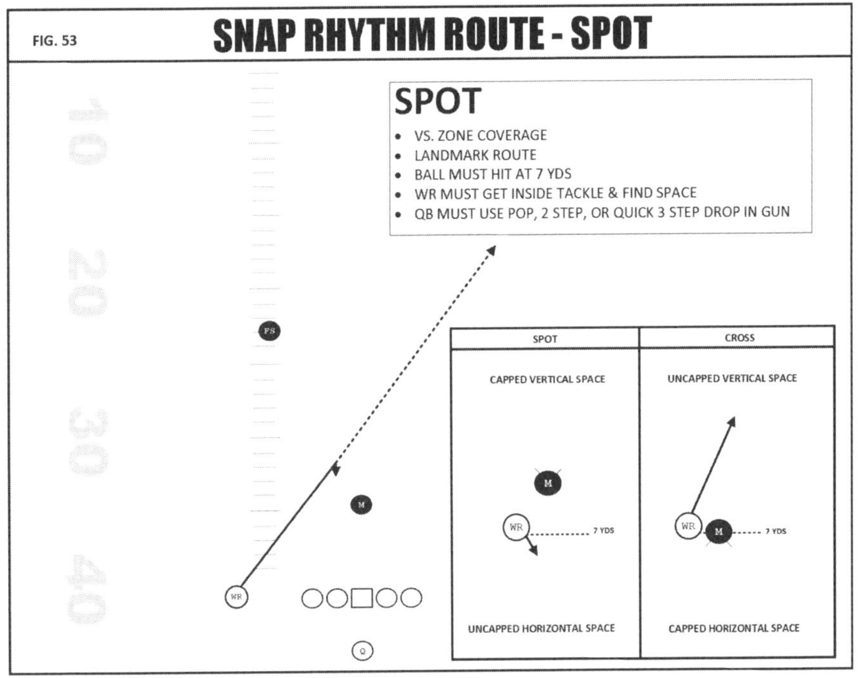
FIG. 53
SNAP RHYTHM ROUTE - SPOT
SPOT
VS. ZONE COVERAGE
LANDMARK ROUTE
BALL MUST HIT AT 7 YDS
WR MUST GET INSIDE TACKLE & FIND SPACE
QB MUST USE POP, 2 STEP, OR QUICK 3 STEP DROP IN GUN
FS
M
WR
Q
SPOT
CROSS
CAPPED VERTICAL SPACE
UNCAPPED VERTICAL SPACE
M
WR
7 YDS
WR
M
7 YDS
UNCAPPED HORIZONTAL SPACE
CAPPED HORIZONTAL SPACE

defender to back-pedal and open his hips. This can create more space and result in a safer throw against Zone Coverage.

Spot Route: The Spot Route is the snap adjustment to the Rhythm-Cross Route. (FIG. 53)

If the vertical space is CAPPED by a free safety or middle linebacker, then the intermediate space can be attacked by the Spot Route. The Spot Route is a landmark route that breaks at 7 yards. The Spot Route is a strong dual-threat route that attacks fast Zone-Dropping middle linebackers, as well as aggressive inside linebacker Blitzes.

Like the Sit-Route, the Spot Route is best used in compressed and bunch formations. (FIG. 54)

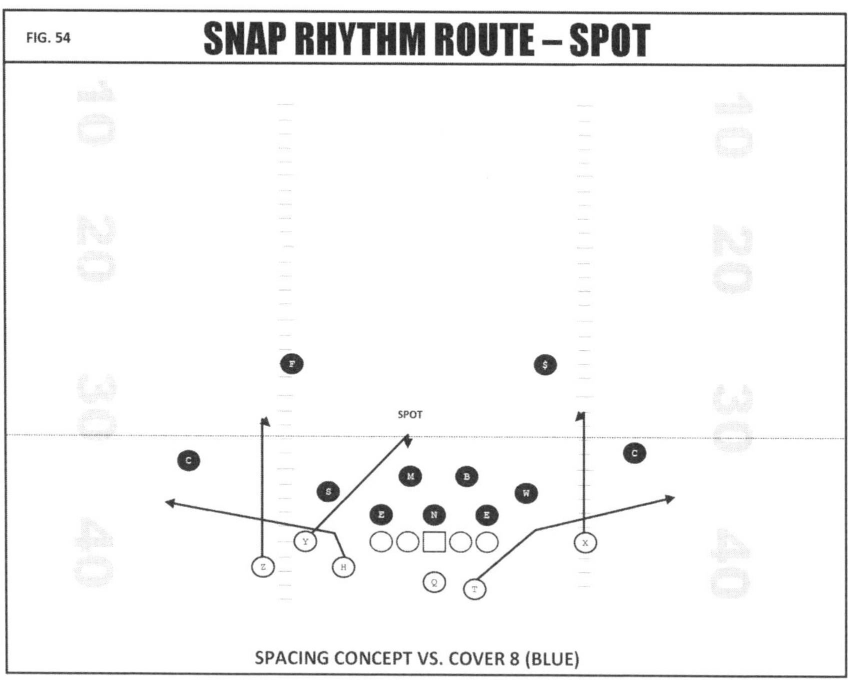

The Spot Route is best suited in spacing and curl-flat concepts. Spot Routes are generally run by inside receivers and tight-ends. Spot Routes increase value to a concept even if they are not open. When a quarter-back's eyes are on the Spot Route down the middle of the field, the mere existence of the route can be used to hold defenders in place on-Rhythm. This keeps defenders from breaking on other routes that become open later in the progression.

Out Route: The Out Route is a snap adjustment to the Rhythm-Corner Route. (FIG. 55)

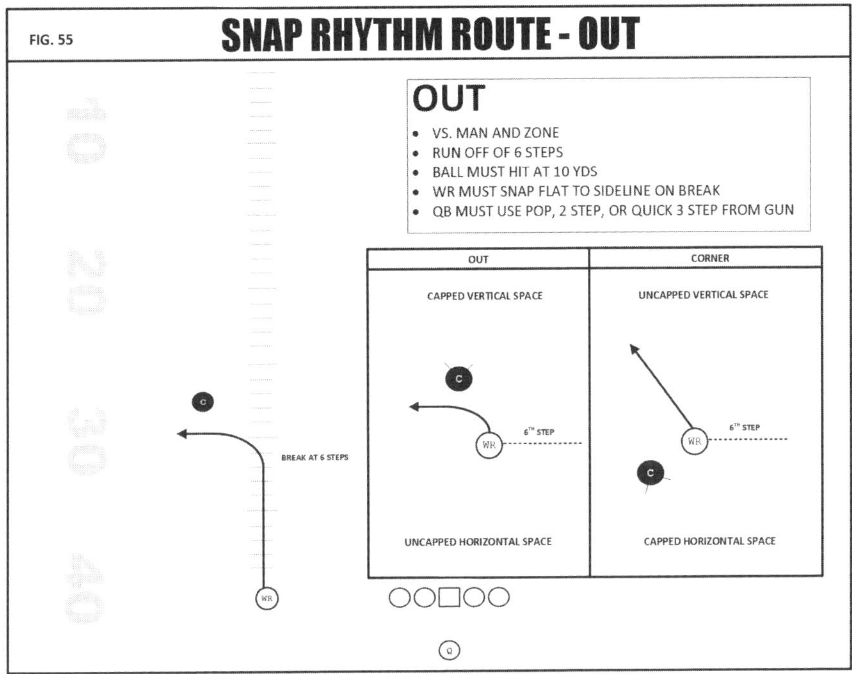

If the vertical space of the corner is CAPPED by a corner or safety, then the intermediate space can be attacked by the Out Route. The Out Route is a timing route run off 6 steps. It is a dual-threat route that is great at attacking both Man and Zone Coverage. The 6-step Out Route requires maximum power and accuracy by the quarterback. They ball must hit 18-inches outside the receiver at 10 yards from the line of scrimmage. The throw must by on-Rhythm with maximum velocity and straight line trajectory.

We have discussed how the Rhythm Corner can convert to a snap Rhythm out when it is CAPPED. This occurs when a Rhythm Corner is run by an inside receiver. Another way that the Rhythm out can be successful is when it is run by an outside receiver to the field. (FIG. 56)

A great way to do this is by putting formations into the boundary and singling up your best receiver to the field with the field cornerback. This creates maximum space for the Rhythm-Out to be thrown and puts an extreme amount of pressure on the field defender.

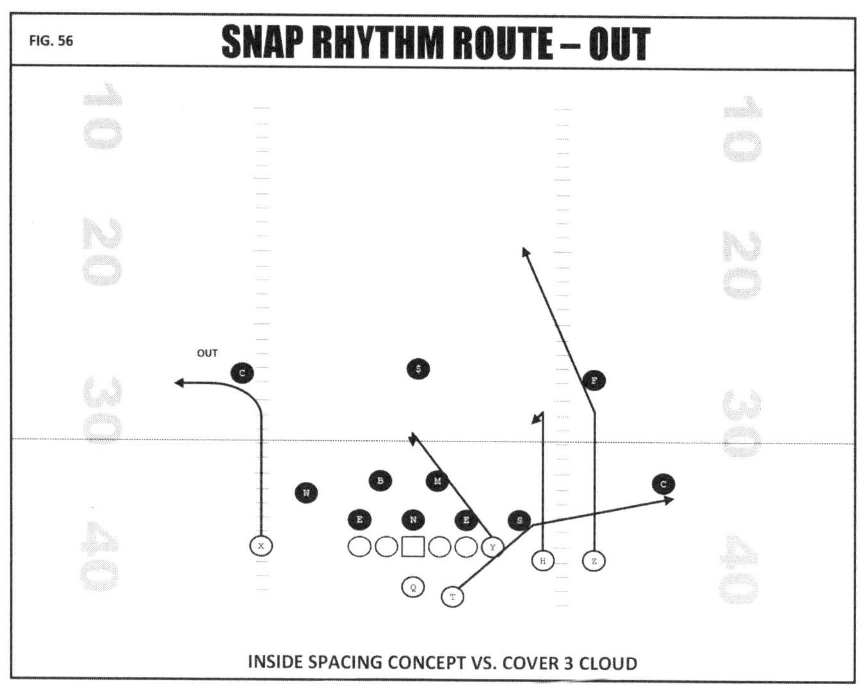
FIG. 56
SNAP RHYTHM ROUTE – OUT
OUT
INSIDE SPACING CONCEPT VS. COVER 3 CLOUD

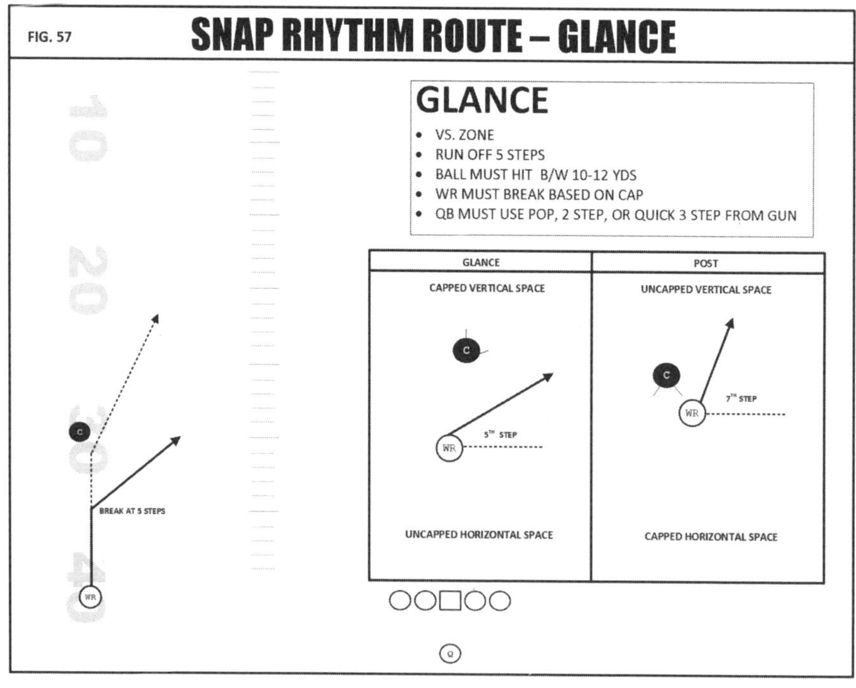
FIG. 57
SNAP RHYTHM ROUTE – GLANCE
GLANCE
VS. ZONE
RUN OFF 5 STEPS
BALL MUST HIT B/W 10-12 YDS
WR MUST BREAK BASED ON CAP
QB MUST USE POP, 2 STEP, OR QUICK 3 STEP FROM GUN
GLANCE
CAPPED VERTICAL SPACE
UNCAPPED HORIZONTAL SPACE
POST
UNCAPPED VERTICAL SPACE
CAPPED HORIZONTAL SPACE
BREAK AT 5 STEPS

Glance Route: The Glance Route is a snap adjustment to the Rhythm-Post Route. (FIG. 57)

If the vertical space of the Post is CAPPED with excessive cushion by the corner or safety, then the intermediate space can be attacked by the Glance Route. The Glance Route is a timing route run off 5 steps. Some instances where this common action occurs is against a fast-Dropping 3-deep or quarters coverage. If the receiver cannot get within 4 yards of the defender on his 5th step, then he can snap the route immediately to the UNCAPPED space underneath.

The Glance Route is also a beneficial tag on a 3rd level RPO concept. (FIG. 58)

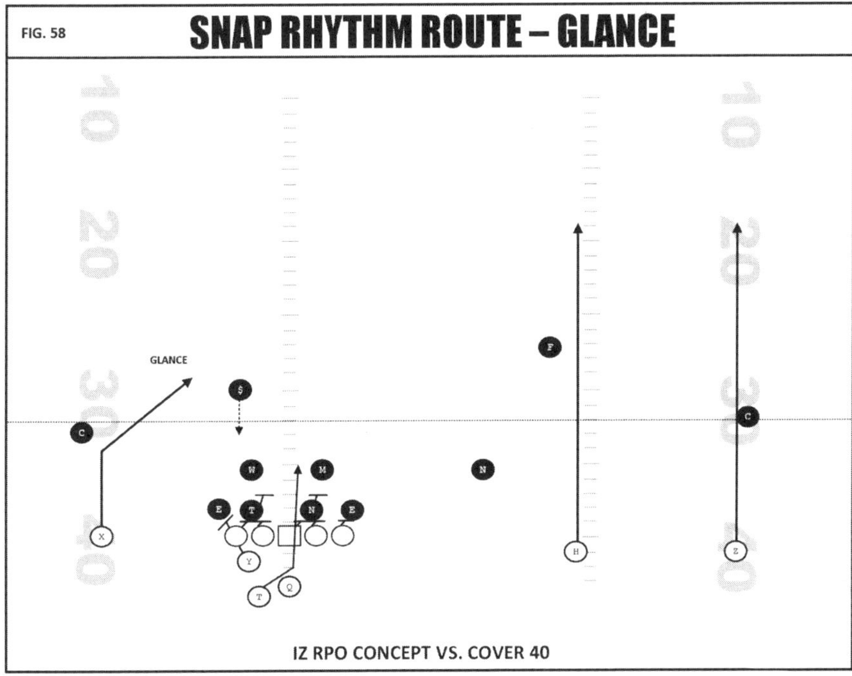

EXAMPLE: When paired with an inside zone run, the 5-step Glance Route provides the perfect route timing to allow the safety to declare his CAP intent on the run or pass. If a 7-step Post was used, the offensive linemen would be too far downfield. If a 3-step Slant was used, the safety at the 3rd level would still be able to recover and CAP the Slant Route.

CHAPTER 5

Understanding the 5 Base Read Routes

UNDERSTANDING THE 5 BASE READ ROUTES

The second Base Family of R4 routes are the Read Route family. Read Routes are double-move or decelerating routes that, by design, take longer to develop. Therefore, they are the second option in a passing progression. Read Routes break open between 2.2 and 2.6 seconds on the Drop timeline and attack horizontal, intermediate space. This requires the routes to be thrown off 1 or 2 reset moves after the Drop in the pocket. There are 5 Base routes in the Read Family. They are the Comeback, Dig, Climb, Slide Corner, and Curl.

Read Routes are fundamentally designed to attack Zone Coverage. Since Read Routes attack intermediate space, they have more than 1 potential defender who can CAP the route-side space. This results in proper pairing with Rhythm or Rush Routes to isolate defenders and create space. This is the genesis of progression passing. Progressions require precision with the eyes and feet. Quarterbacks who throw Read Routes must avoid staring down the route space before the break point. Receivers must remember that they are the second option in the progression, and that they have time to set up the route and get to the proper break depth.

Because of their delayed break time, Read Routes are rarely used as a standalone route. This also makes them less suitable to attack Man Coverage, but with the proper personnel and timing, Read Routes can be used to attack man.

The Read Route throw must be in sync with the route break-point by using 1 or 2 reset steps in the pocket. The route depth and number of breaks in the route stem determine if the Read Route is a 1- or 2-reset step throw. The speed of the receivers will also play a factor in this timing. It is important that the quarterback establishes the reset steps for each Read Route with his receivers before the season.

Comeback Route: The Comeback is a Read Route used to attack outside intermediate space between a deep-zone and flat defender. (FIG. 59)

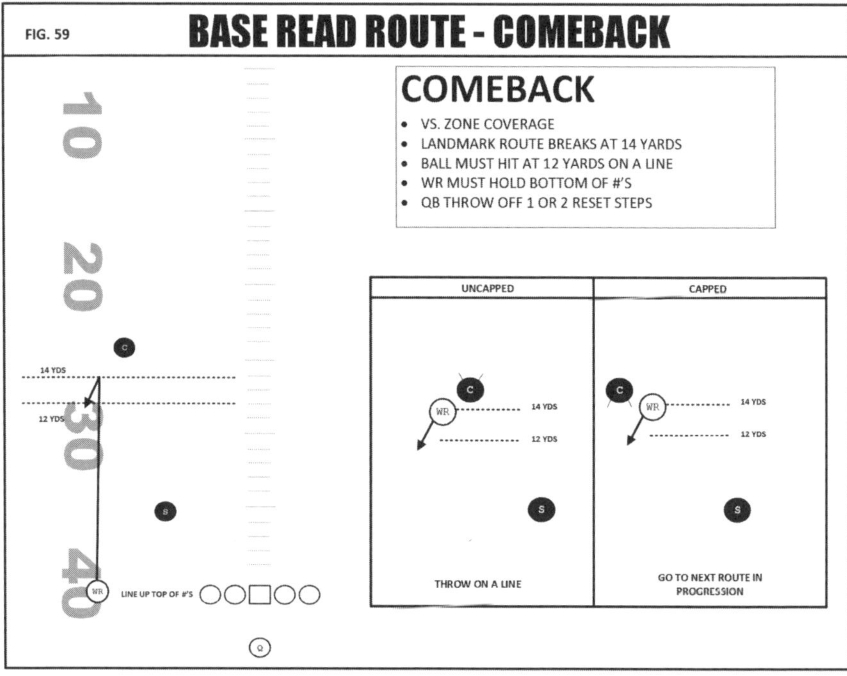

This is a landmark route run at 14 yards and breaks back to 12 yards. The premise of the route is to threaten the defender vertically, making him feel like it's a Rhythm Fade Route. The objective is to get the defender to open his hips and CAP vertical space, which in return UNCAPs horizontal space for the Comeback break. The quarterback will throw off 1- or 2-reset steps, depending on the speed of the receiver. The mark is to release the ball when the receiver is firing his feet to decelerate and break.

Before the ball is released, the quarterback must confirm the route-side space is UNCAPPED. Against Zone Coverage, the quarterback is looking for the defender to be in a dominant position over the receiver with a full-turned hip angle. This is a premium UNCAPPED look for the Comeback Route. A CAPPED route has a defender over the receiver with square-hip angle in line to break on the attack angle of the Comeback. The flat Zone defender would be controlled by a Rush Route.

The Comeback is a feature route adjustment used in the 4-Vertical concept. (FIG. 60)

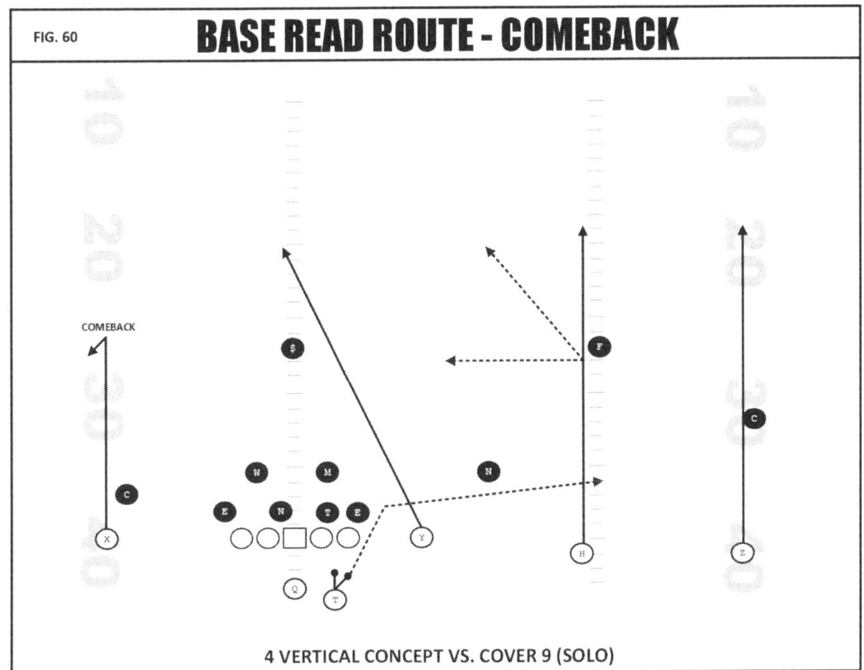

FIG. 60 **BASE READ ROUTE - COMEBACK**

4 VERTICAL CONCEPT VS. COVER 9 (SOLO)

The Comeback is an effective Read Route that counters defensive backs who are CAPPING the vertical Fade Route.

When facing Zone Coverage, the receiver must first determine the proper release. (FIG. 61)

The objective is to own outside-space for the Comeback Route. Quarters coverage, 3-Deep and 2-Read Coverage, will generally align the cornerback with an outside 7 x 1 alignment (7 yards off the receiver and 1 yard outside). A receiver uses a Shave Release against this technique. The Shave Release will attack the outside shoulder of the cornerback as he explodes off the line to his break-depth of 14 yards. The function of this release is to win back the outside route-space on the stem, while getting the cornerback to bail and CAP vertical space.

Not all Zone Coverages are played with the same technique. For example, some coaches prefer to play quarters and 3-Deep-zone Coverages with an inside 7 x 1 alignment. The mindset for this technique is to position defenders to cover space closer to the quarterback and force him to make longer, more difficult, throws. A receiver still uses a Shave Release against this technique. The Shave Release will attack the outside

FIG. 61 **BASE READ ROUTE – COMEBACK**

OUTSIDE ZONE TECHNIQUE	INSIDE ZONE TECHNIQUE
14 YDS 12 YDS C WR SHAVE RELEASE	14 YDS 12 YDS C WR SHAVE RELEASE

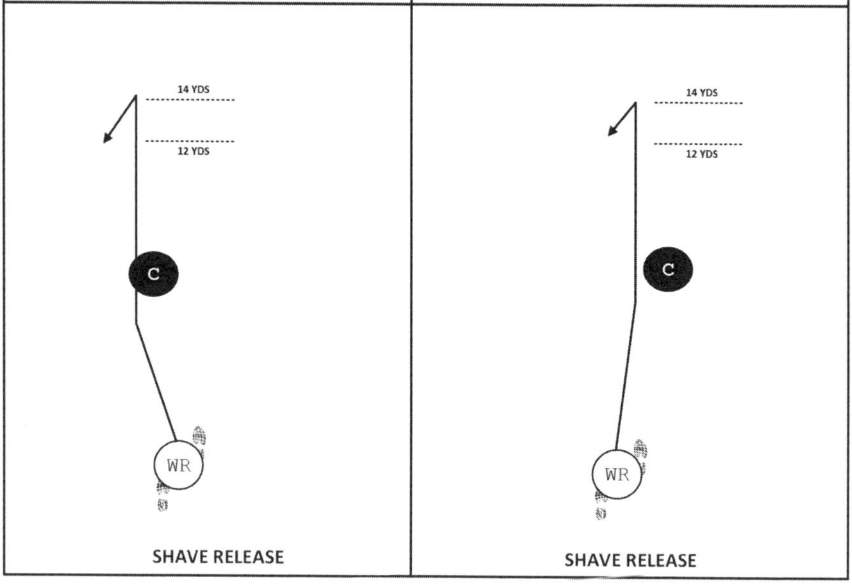

shoulder of the cornerback to maintain the outside leverage that is already in favor of the receiver pre-snap.

The Comeback Route can also attack a Man defender. However, Man Coverage places a defender in a more suitable position to CAP the route-side space of the Comeback. An athletic defender who is trailing a receiver with inside leverage can read the break of the route and undercut the Comeback for an interception. It is important that if you run a Comeback against Man that you make sure the defender is in a dominant position over the receiver CAPPING vertical route-space.

A receiver must explode off the line to force the defender to CAP vertical space. Against press-man, he will use a Stutter Release. Against press-bail, he will use a Seam Release. (FIG. 62)

Many coaches teach defenders who are beat vertically off the line of scrimmage to trail and recover by playing the eyes and hands of the receiver. The defenders are taught to not look back or make a play on the ball until the receiver looks up and extends his hands. A receiver can use this technique to his advantage when running a Comeback against Man Coverage.

FIG. 62

BASE READ ROUTE – COMEBACK

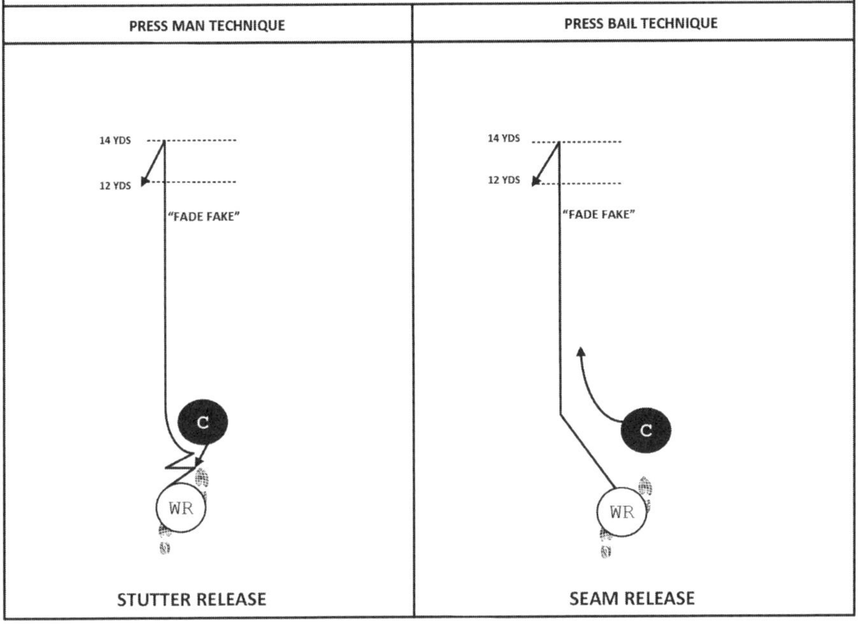

PRESS MAN TECHNIQUE	PRESS BAIL TECHNIQUE
14 YDS 12 YDS "FADE FAKE" C WR	14 YDS 12 YDS "FADE FAKE" C WR
STUTTER RELEASE	SEAM RELEASE

As the receiver runs through 10 yards, he should look up in the air and extend his outside arm as if he is catching a Fade Route. We call this a Fade Fake. A Fade Fake will trigger the defender to look up or make a play on the ball instead of looking at the quarterback's hips for the Route Break. As this occurs, the receiver should sink his hips and fire his feet to decelerate for the Comeback Break. This will help separation against Man technique.

Dig Route: The Dig is a Read Route used to attack intermediate-middle of the field-space between 2 deep-zone and hook Zone defenders. (FIG. 63)

This is a landmark route run at 15 yards and settles into UNCAPPED space. The premise of the route is to threaten the defenders vertically and make them feel like they are defending a Rhythm Seam. The vertical threat creates UNCAPPED intermediate-space underneath that must be CAPPED by linebackers.

The quarterback must confirm that the route-side space of the Dig is UNCAPPED. This is done by viewing the vector of the Dig Break and reading the dominant position and hip angle of the linebackers. Against 2-deep coverage there are 2 areas of space that the Dig can be thrown

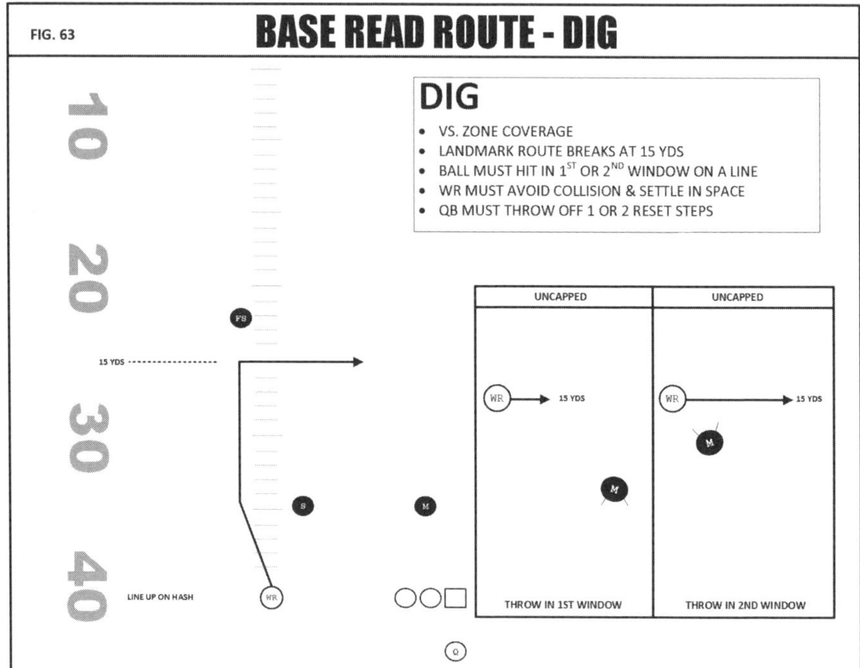

into. The 1st window is just out of the break of the route. This would be thrown off 1 reset step by the quarterback. The 2nd window is just on the other side of the middle linebacker. This would be thrown off 2 reset steps by the quarterback.

The Read Dig is enhanced in the Shallow Wheel concept. The Post and Wheel Route establish 2 immediate vertical threats that help create horizontal space availability for the Dig Route. (FIG. 64)

A receiver running a dig against Zone Coverage requires a Seam Release to avoid collision by an inside defender. There are two objectives to remember when running a Read Dig. The first is that receivers must not break the route early. The Dig Route must break at 15 yards. Many receivers get impatient and forget that they are the second route in the progression. The result is breaking the route at 10 to 12 yards. This reduces the stretch of intermediate route-space and takes the defenders into the space before the throw can get there. (FIG. 65)

The next factor that must be executed is the type of break to take at the top of the route. Linebackers who use a standard carry technique and pass over the receiver to the safety at 10 yards, allows for a

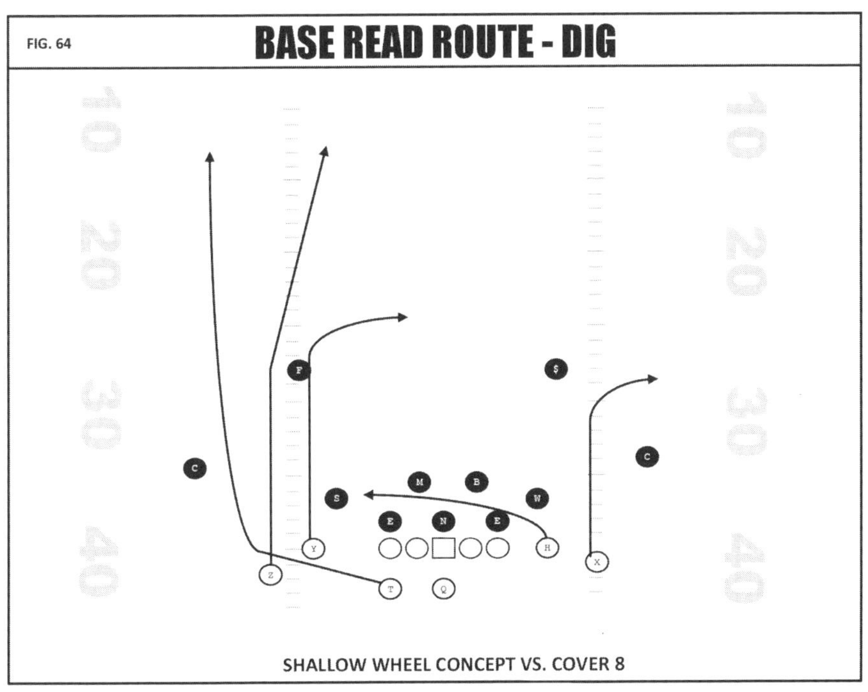

SHALLOW WHEEL CONCEPT VS. COVER 8

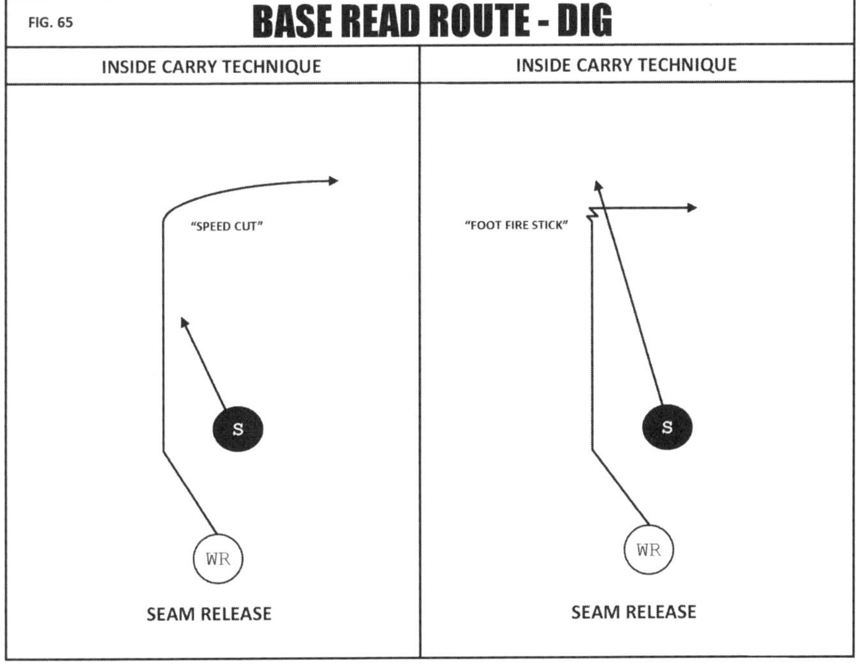

speed-cut at the top of the Dig Break. Linebackers who use an aggressive Spot Drop or Carry Technique may require the receiver to foot-fire and stick the route at 15 yards. On the Stick, the receiver will have to use a 2-move hand strike and throw the defender during the Route Break.

The Dig Route is not a good design against Man Coverage. However, the receiver still needs to learn release and break methods to overcome Man technique. The priority of a receiver is to determine if there is enough access to win inside dig-space at the line of scrimmage. A Slide Release is used to accomplish this. After the Slide Release, the receiver will get vertical to 15 yards with a foot-fire stick to create separation on the break. (FIG. 66)

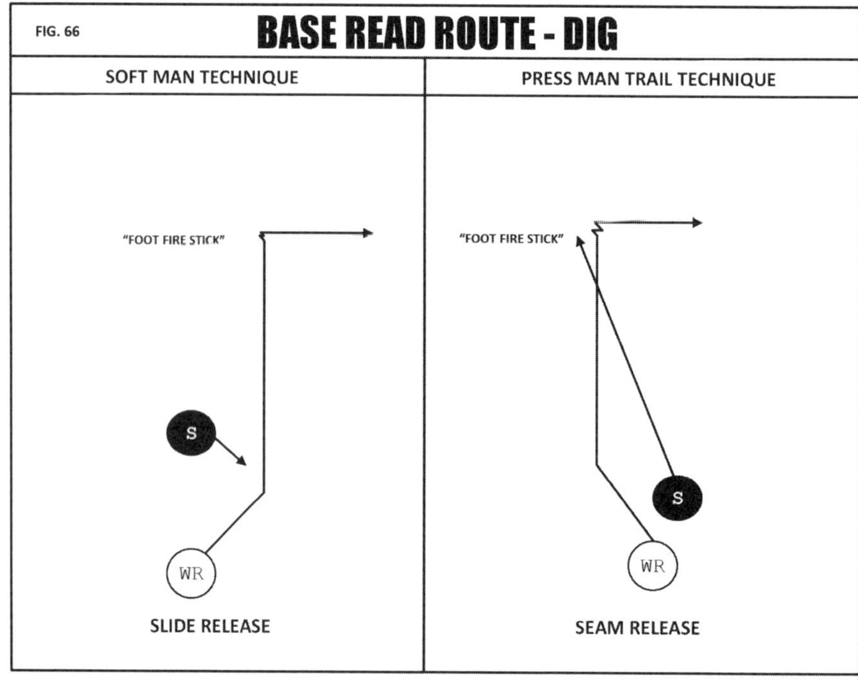

If the Man defender is playing press and not giving inside access, then the receiver will use a Seam Release and sell an out-breaking route at the top of the break. This can be done with an aggressive stick, like the receiver is running a Corner Route or a foot-fire stick as if he is running an out-route. After the stick, the receiver will accelerate to the dig space looking for the ball.

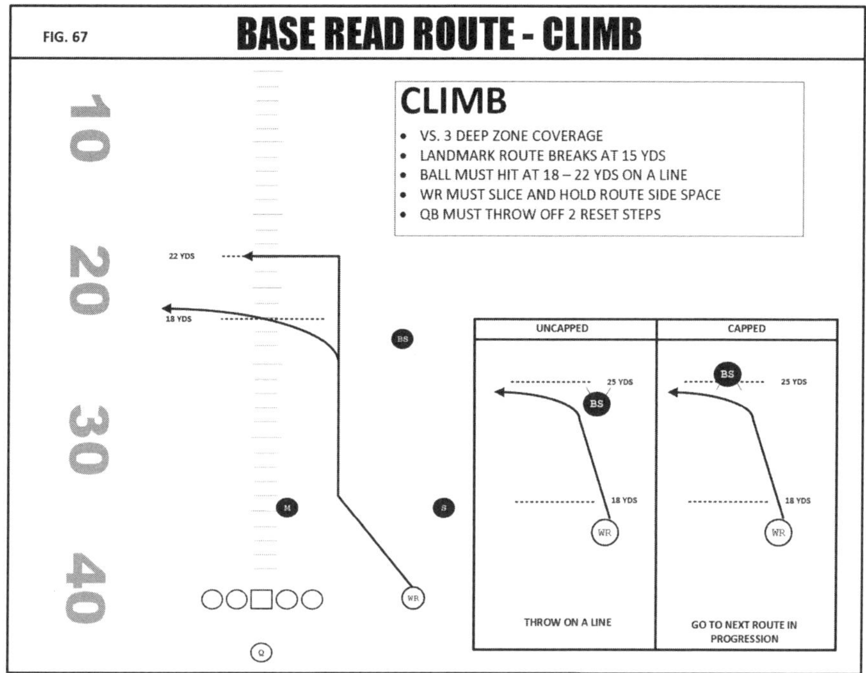

Climb Route: The Climb Route is a Read Route used to attack intermediate Seam underneath deep-zone defenders. This is a landmark route run at 18 to 22 yards. The depth of the Climb Route is deeper than the Dig Route, and best used off play-action to avoid collision by linebackers. (FIG. 67)

***Cross-key** is a term used for a boundary safety who is keying the #3 receiver in a Trips Formation who is attacking vertically across the centerline.*

The Climb Route is generally run by an inside receiver out of 3 x 1 formations. It is used to attack the weak-side boundary-Seam space. The Climb Route derives its name from the extended vertical climb of the route stem past 15 yards before it breaks. (FIG. 68)

The quarterback must buy time with a good play-action fake and work up into the pocket to create time and space for the climb to develop. This route is best used to attack a 3-deep-zone or cross-keying Zone Coverages out of 3 x 1. Cross-key is a term used for a boundary safety who is keying the #3 receiver in a Trips Formation who is attacking vertically across the centerline. The quarterback must locate

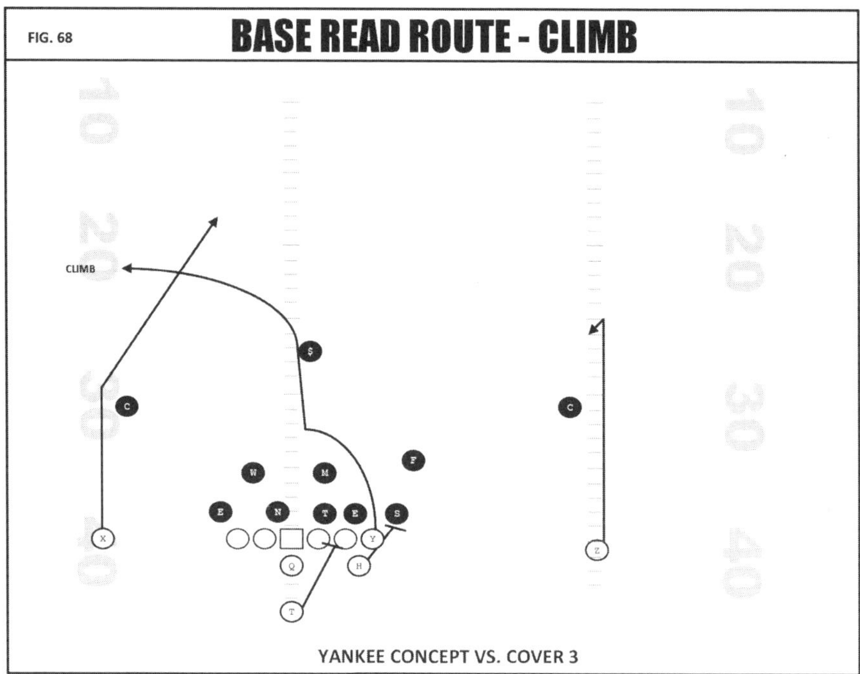

FIG. 68 **BASE READ ROUTE - CLIMB**

YANKEE CONCEPT VS. COVER 3

the route-side space of the climb on the reset and determine if the high safety is in position to CAP the route-side space.

The receiver running the Climb Route must use a Slice Release to avoid collision. (FIG. 69)

The Slice Release begins by taking the easiest access to avoid collision. The preferred release is to get inside the strong-side linebacker, then climb to 15 yards forcing the boundary safety's hips to turn and bail. The receiver will use a speed-cut at 15 yards to break over the top of the middle linebacker. This will allow him to own the route-side space on the other side.

A strong side linebacker with inside leverage using a hard carry or Man technique makes it difficult to Slice inside on the release. In this case, the receiver will have to Slice outside and climb between 18 and 22 yards to get the safety to bail. The extra climb depth is needed between the Release and Route Break, so the receiver can create a "stair step" action that forces separation away from the carrying or Man covering linebacker. A "stair step" move is accomplished by taking a sharp 90-degree cut after the release, climbing vertical, then making another

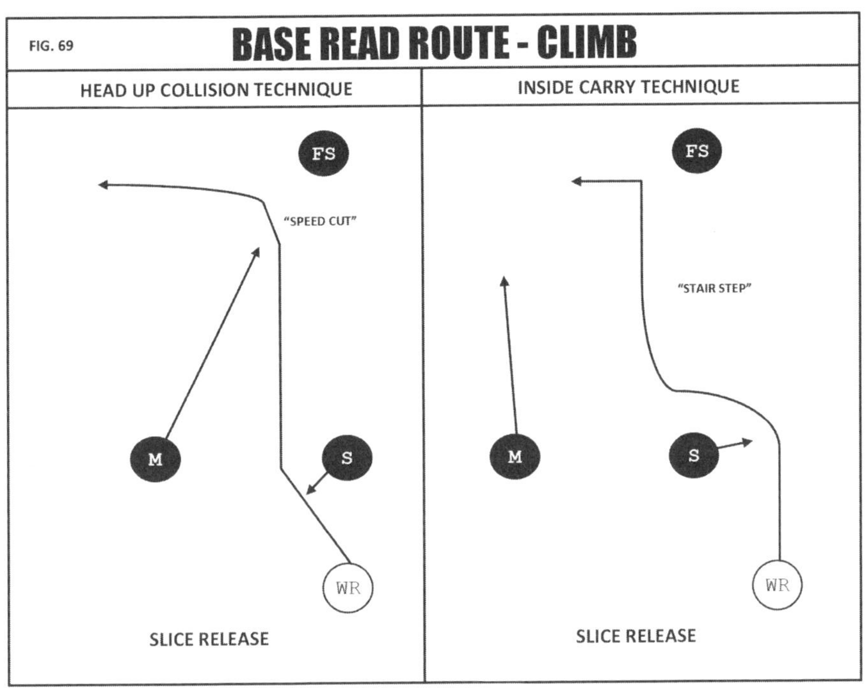
FIG. 69
BASE READ ROUTE - CLIMB
HEAD UP COLLISION TECHNIQUE
INSIDE CARRY TECHNIQUE
FS
"SPEED CUT"
M
S
WR
SLICE RELEASE
FS
"STAIR STEP"
M
S
WR
SLICE RELEASE

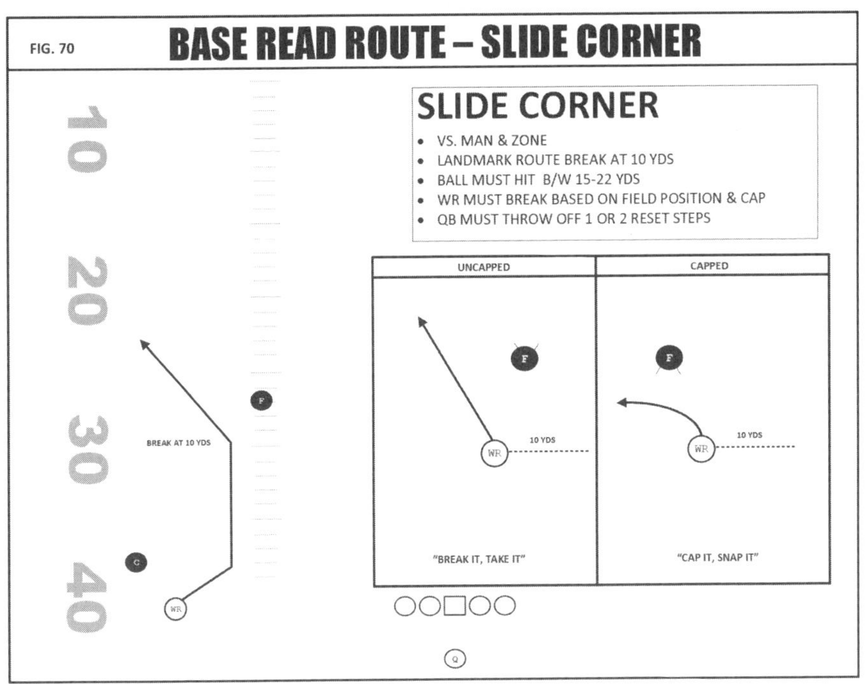
FIG. 70
BASE READ ROUTE – SLIDE CORNER
10
20
30
40
BREAK AT 10 YDS
F
C
WR
SLIDE CORNER
VS. MAN & ZONE
LANDMARK ROUTE BREAK AT 10 YDS
BALL MUST HIT B/W 15-22 YDS
WR MUST BREAK BASED ON FIELD POSITION & CAP
QB MUST THROW OFF 1 OR 2 RESET STEPS
UNCAPPED
CAPPED
F
10 YDS
WR
"BREAK IT, TAKE IT"
F
10 YDS
WR
"CAP IT, SNAP IT"
Q

sharp 90-degree cut at the top of the route break. The "stair step" move is very effective for creating space against a tight-covering defender.

Slide Corner Route: The Slide Corner Route is a Read Route that can be used to attack both deep and intermediate outside space. (FIG. 70)

The Slide Corner is a variation of the Rhythm Corner Route. The difference in the routes is that the Slide corner is a double-move route that breaks in 2.2 seconds. The Slide Corner is used to attack hard-outside leveraged flat defenders who are attempting to collision or carry receivers at the line of scrimmage. The Slide Corner is a landmark route that breaks at 10 yards.

The quarterback looks at the route-side space of the corner on the reset step in the pocket. As he views the vector of the break, he determines if a defender is CAPPING the route-side space. The Slide Corner Route can adjust the break based on the CAP of the defender. If it is UNCAPPED, the route will be hit at 22 yards. If it is CAPPED, the route will snap flat and be hit at 15 yards. The quarterback must throw the ball on a line in Zone Coverage, and with more air in Man Coverage.

The Slide Smash concept features the Slide Corner Route. (FIG. 71)

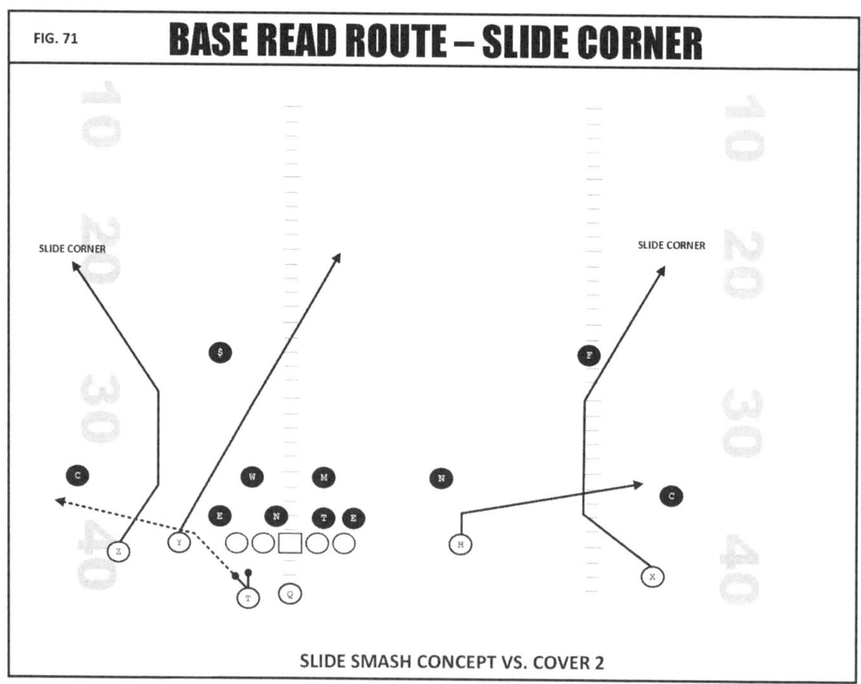

This concept uses a Rhythm Cross Route to isolate the play-side safety and force him to choose to CAP the Rhythm Cross Route or the Read Slide Corner Route. The Slide Corner is generally run by an outside receiver. It is a go-to route against coverages that are defeating inside corner routes with collision and free safeties who are successfully CAPPING the slot receiver vertically. It is also a great route concept to use against pattern-matching defenders who are keying the #2 receiver on a flat-route break under 7 yards.

The receiver running the Slide Corner will use a Slide Release off the line of scrimmage. (FIG. 72)

The receiver gets vertical as soon as he gets inside position and breaks the route at 10 yards. At 10 yards the receiver adjusts his break based on the CAP.

"If we break it, we take it" to 22 yards. "If they CAP it, we snap it" to 15 yards. Against Man Coverage with a carrying defender, the receiver gets inside on the Slide Release then break at 10 yards. The route will not have a distinct break at 10 because of the aggressive carry from the Man defender.

Curl Route: The Curl is a Read Route used to attack intermediate-Seam space between a deep-zone and flat-zone defender. (FIG. 73)

This is a landmark route run at 12 yards and breaking back to 10 yards. The premise of the route is to threaten the defender vertically and make him feel like he is defending a Post Route. The Curl Route is thrown off 1 reset step in the pocket. The Curl Route is often used in conjunction with a Flat Route to remove the flat defender from the route-side space.

The quarterback must shift his eyes to the Curl Route as he resets in the pocket. His focus must be on the route-side space of the Route Break. The cornerback and outside linebacker are typically the primary defenders who threaten to CAP the Curl Route. The quarterback must read the dominant position and hip angles of each defender to determine if they are in position to CAP the route. If the route-space is UNCAPPED, then the quarterback throws on a line at 10 yards. If it is CAPPED, then he will reset to the next route in the progression.

The Curl Route is the keynote route in the Hank concept. (FIG. 74)

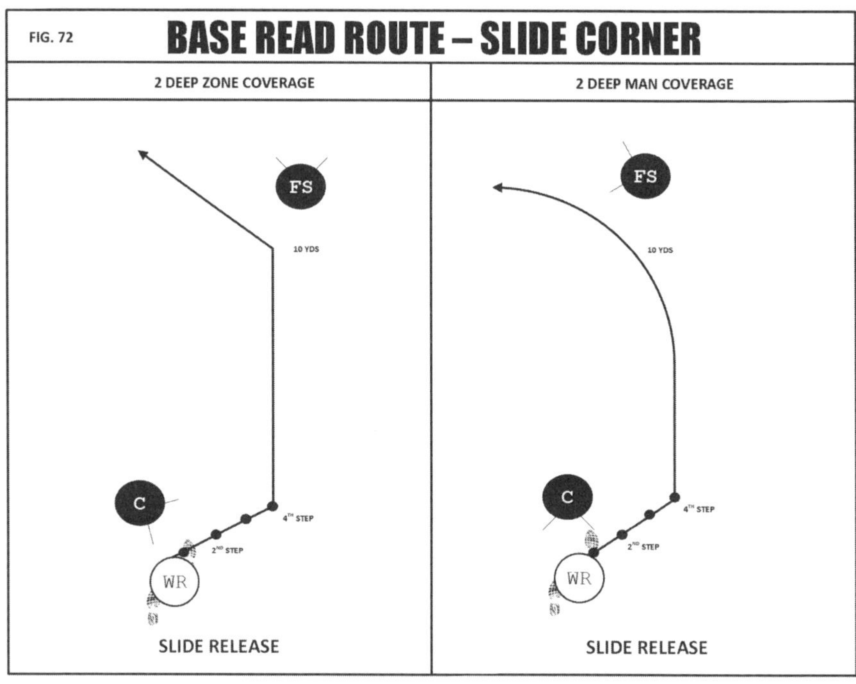
FIG. 72
BASE READ ROUTE – SLIDE CORNER
2 DEEP ZONE COVERAGE
2 DEEP MAN COVERAGE
FS
10 YDS
C
4TH STEP
2ND STEP
WR
SLIDE RELEASE
FS
10 YDS
C
4TH STEP
2ND STEP
WR
SLIDE RELEASE

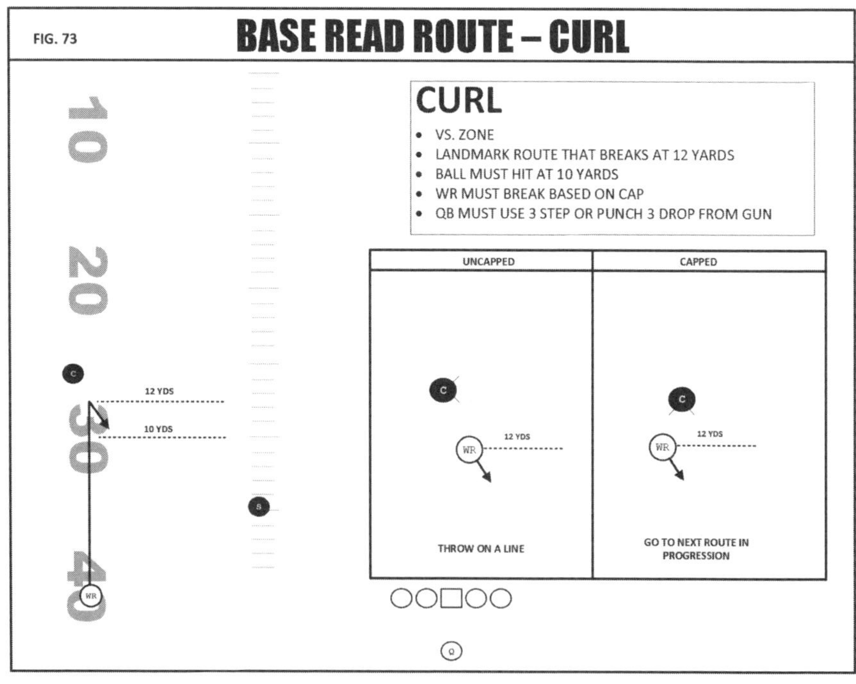
FIG. 73
BASE READ ROUTE – CURL
CURL
• VS. ZONE
• LANDMARK ROUTE THAT BREAKS AT 12 YARDS
• BALL MUST HIT AT 10 YARDS
• WR MUST BREAK BASED ON CAP
• QB MUST USE 3 STEP OR PUNCH 3 DROP FROM GUN
10
20
30
40
C
12 YDS
10 YDS
S
WR
UNCAPPED
CAPPED
C
WR
12 YDS
THROW ON A LINE
C
WR
12 YDS
GO TO NEXT ROUTE IN PROGRESSION

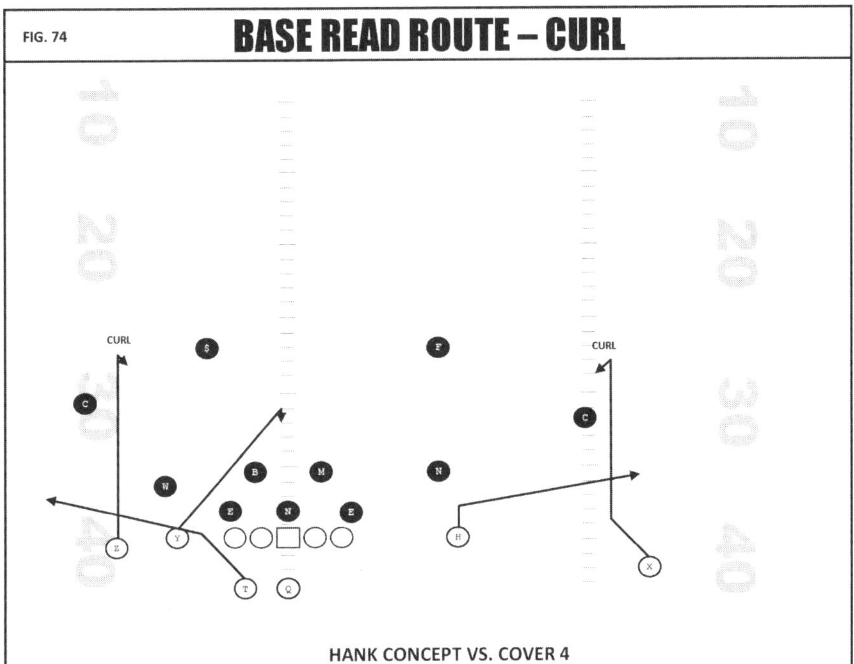

FIG. 74 **BASE READ ROUTE – CURL**

HANK CONCEPT VS. COVER 4

Hank is the West Coast offensive term for a Dual Curl-Flat concept to each side of route-space that is anchored by a Rhythm Spot Route over the center. The horizontal stretch created by the Spot and Flat Route provide time and space for the Read Curl Route to break open into UN-CAPPED space.

The receiver running the Curl Route must first explode off the line of scrimmage attacking the deep-zone defender. (FIG. 75)

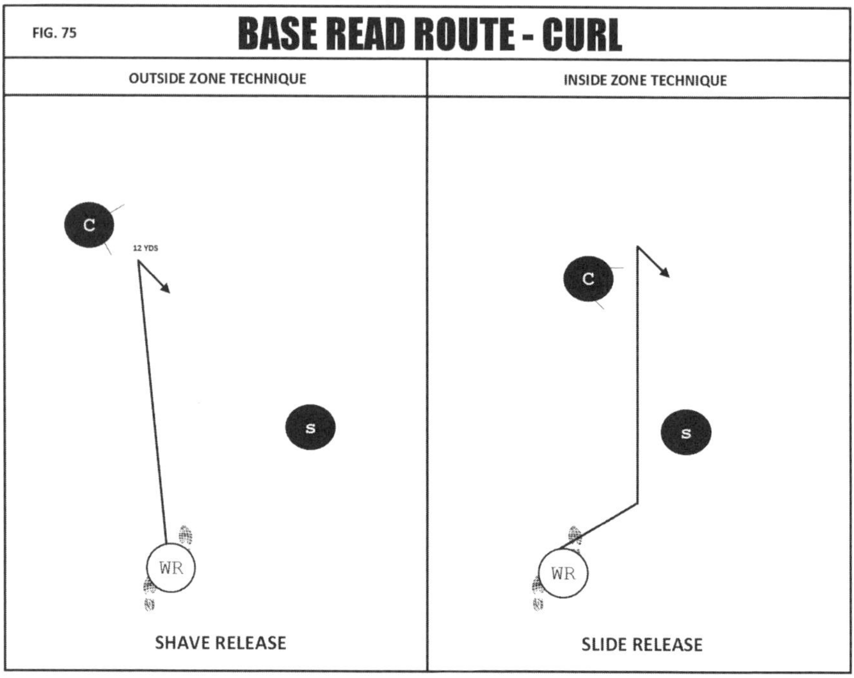

FIG. 75

BASE READ ROUTE - CURL

OUTSIDE ZONE TECHNIQUE	INSIDE ZONE TECHNIQUE
C 12 YDS S WR	C S WR
SHAVE RELEASE	SLIDE RELEASE

A Shave Release is used to attack the inside shoulder of an outside-leveraged deep defender. The receiver pushes vertical to 12 yards, then foot-fires and sticks on the break. On the break point, the receiver works downhill to 10 yards. A Flat Route is used to control the flat defender.

A defender playing with inside-zone technique owns the route-side space of the Curl pre-snap. A Slide Release can be used in this situation to attack the technique. The receiver will Slide inside 4-steps to get inside leverage, then push vertical to 12 yards and break back to 10 yards. The Slide Release also makes it easier for the Curl Route to get over the top of the flat defender. This allows for an easier throw and catch away from a CAP threat.

CHAPTER 6

Understanding the Vertical Read Routes

UNDERSTANDING THE VERTICAL READ ROUTES

The 5 Base Read Route family primarily attacks intermediate space. However, the Base Read Route family also contains a sub-group that attacks vertical space. This sup-group is called Vertical Read Routes. Vertical Read Routes break open in the same time frame as the Base Reads (2.2-2.6 seconds). The difference is that Vertical Routes are double-move routes that attack vertical-space. Vertical Reads are designed, explosive play routes that counter aggressive defenders who attempt to CAP break moves.

Vertical Reads are also good for attacking a defender who has an athletic advantage over a receiver. If a defender is CAPPING a Base Rhythm or Read Route, then a Vertical Read Route provides a sound alternative.

Out-and-Up Route: The route is run off 4 vertical steps and 3 out-breaking steps. The ball must hit between 30-35 yards from the line of scrimmage. The Out-and-Up Route protects against defenders who are over-aggressive on outside breaking routes. If a defender is consistently CAPPING outside horizontal space, then the Out-and-Up is a good complement route to use. (Fig. 76)

Many double-move routes like the Out-and-Up require a pump-fake. A pump-fake is the separating of the hands, and movement of the throwing arm forward, to act like the ball is about to be thrown. A pump-fake should be used based on the type of coverage being played by defenders.

For example, if the defense is playing Man Coverage, then a pump is not as effective and wastes critical time. In Man Coverage, the defender's eyes are not on the quarterback, so the pump-fake is less effective. Against Man Coverage, the quarterback would benefit more by looking for a Rhythm Route first, then coming to the Out-and-Up as a Read Route.

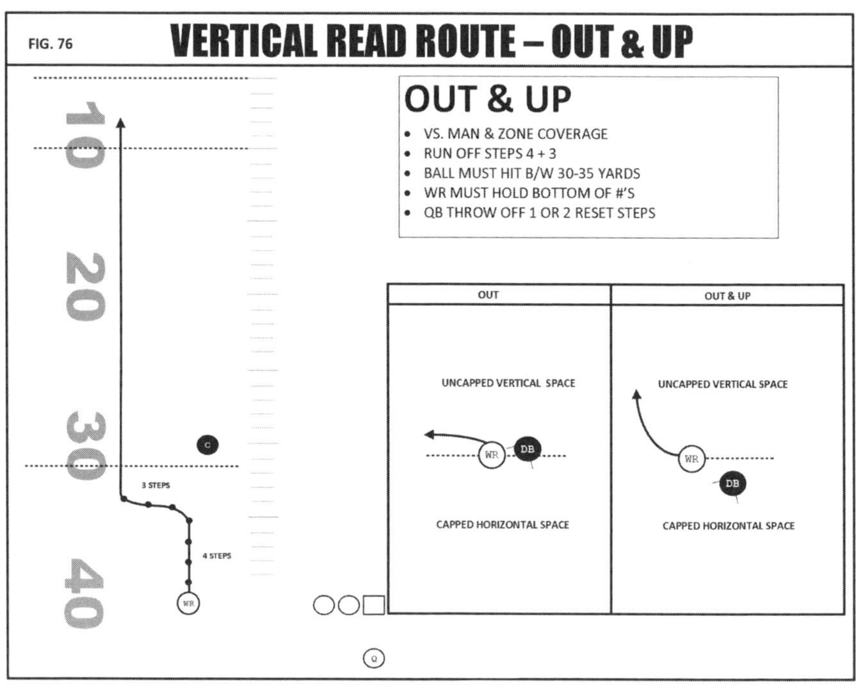

FIG. 76
VERTICAL READ ROUTE – OUT & UP
OUT & UP
• VS. MAN & ZONE COVERAGE
• RUN OFF STEPS 4 + 3
• BALL MUST HIT B/W 30-35 YARDS
• WR MUST HOLD BOTTOM OF #'S
• QB THROW OFF 1 OR 2 RESET STEPS
OUT
OUT & UP
UNCAPPED VERTICAL SPACE
UNCAPPED VERTICAL SPACE
CAPPED HORIZONTAL SPACE
CAPPED HORIZONTAL SPACE
3 STEPS
4 STEPS

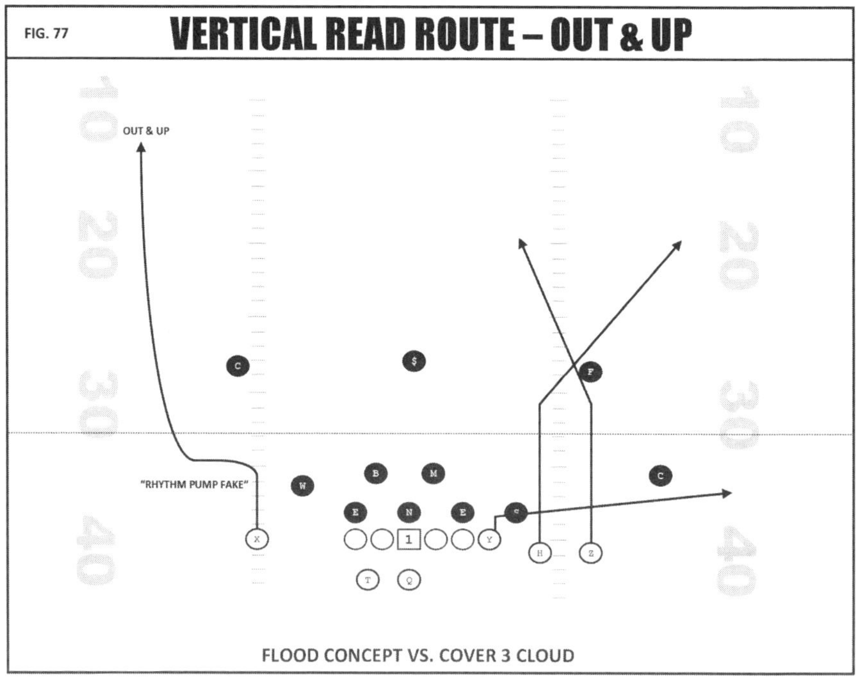

FIG. 77
VERTICAL READ ROUTE – OUT & UP
OUT & UP
"RHYTHM PUMP FAKE"
FLOOD CONCEPT VS. COVER 3 CLOUD

The pump-fake is more effective against Zone Coverage. The eyes of defenders are on the quarterback in Zone Coverage. This increases the chances that they will take the fake and UNCAP vertical space. A pump-fake against Zone Coverage would replace the Rhythm Route option in a progression. If the pump-fake on Rhythm did not generate an UNCAPPED look, then the quarterback would reset to the Read Route in the progression. (FIG. 77)

The Out & Up is used here on the backside of a standard Flood concept.

The receiver running the Out-and-Up Route must also determine the defensive coverage used pre-snap. (FIG. 78)

Against Man Coverage, the receiver takes 4 steps vertical, then breaks on the quick-out for 3 steps. On the 3rd step of the out-break, the receiver sticks his outside foot in the ground and gets vertical. The receiver must attempt to hold as much outside-space as possible to create throw space for the quarterback.

The receiver must increase his vertical stem against Zone Coverage. If the defender is at or above the hard-deck at 7 yards, then he must

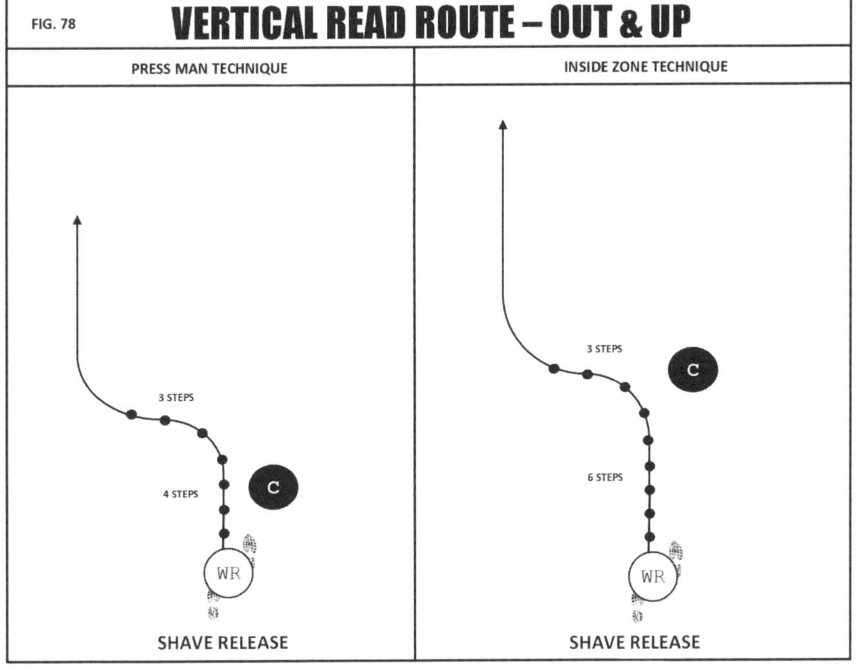

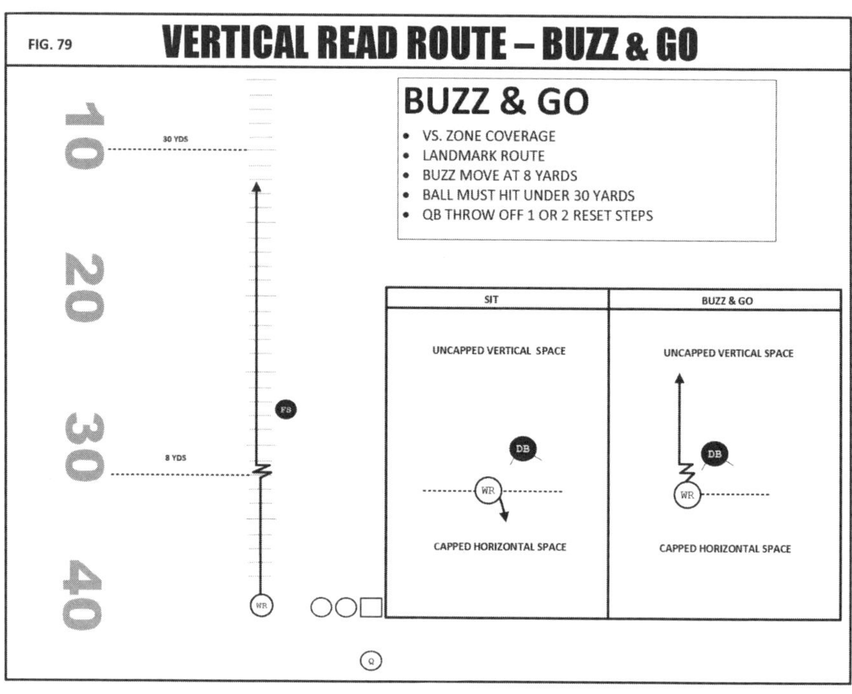

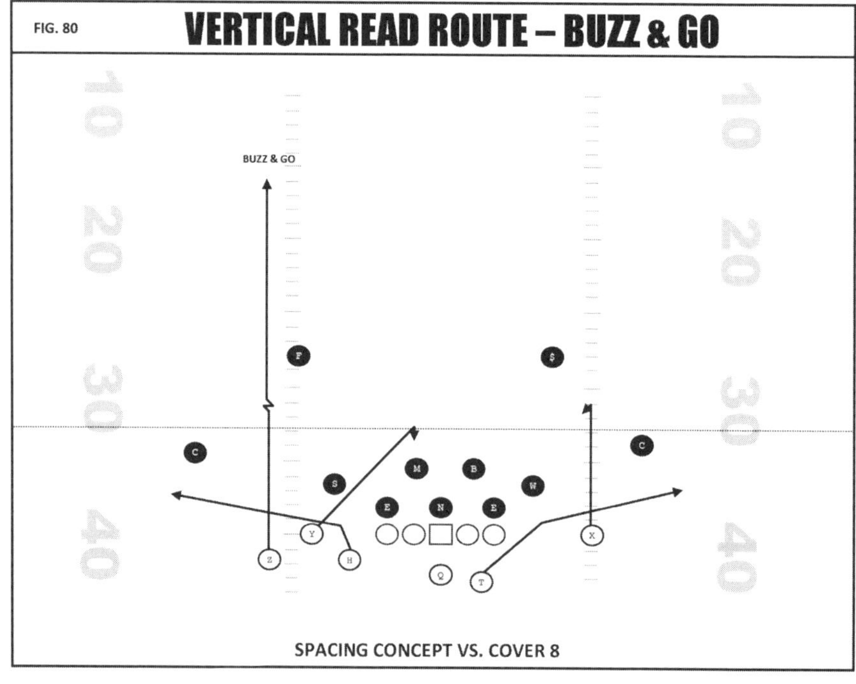

SPACING CONCEPT VS. COVER 8

take 6 steps to close the cushion, then break out for 3 steps selling the out-break. If the cushion isn't closed, then the defender can recover against the out-fake and CAP vertical space.

Buzz-and-Go Route: The Buzz-and-Go Route is another Vertical Read Route. (FIG. 79)

The Buzz-and-Go is a deceptive route primarily used to attack over-aggressive safeties and corners playing Zone Coverage. This is a landmark route that decelerates at 8 yards. The deceleration is accomplished by sinking the hips and buzzing of the feet to simulate the break of a Snap Rhythm Route. The throw must hit under 30 yards due to the deceleration of the break. The receiver must decelerate then reaccelerate. This places a limit on how deep the route can be thrown to be in sync with the route mechanics.

The quarterback will determine if it is Man or Zone Coverage pre-snap. This will inform the decision to use the Buzz-and-Go as a Read Route or to pump-fake it as a Rhythm replacement in the progression. The Buzz-and-Go Route protects horizontal-breaking Snap Rhythm Routes that are being CAPPED by defenders. (FIG. 80)

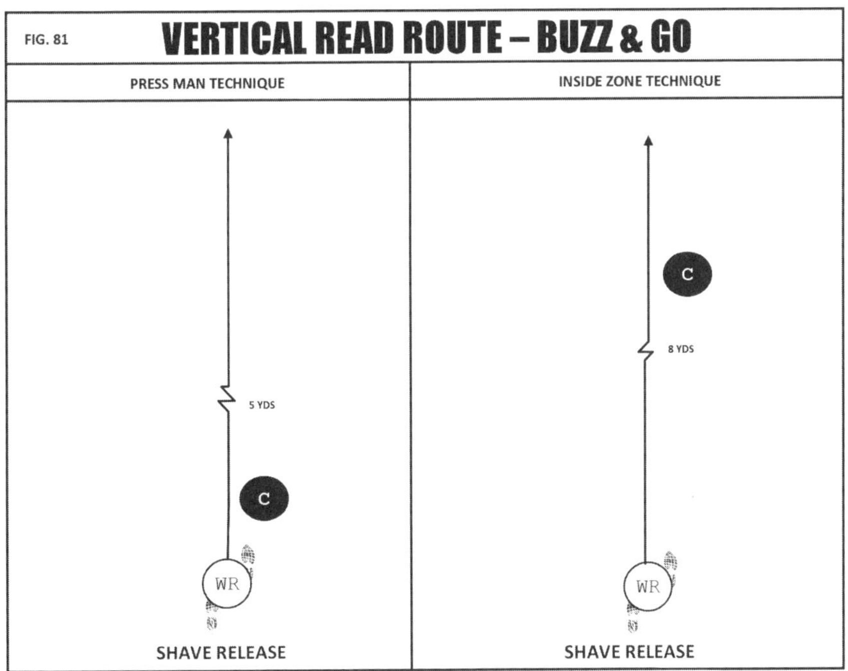

The Buzz-and-Go Route can be used to protect the Sit Route within the Spacing concept. When the free safety is aggressively attempting to CAP the Sit, then the Buzz-and-Go Route can counter the CAP move.

The Buzz-and-Go Route can execute the Buzz Move at a range of depths. The receiver's default rule on the Buzz Move is based on Man or Zone Coverage unless otherwise tagged. The receiver buzzes at 5 yards against Man Coverage, then reaccelerates to catch the ball. (FIG. 81)

The default depth against Zone Coverage is at 8 yards. This is the most consistent landmark to use against Zone Coverage. There are games that may require the Buzz adjustment to be made at 5, 10, 14 yards, or more. This is all based on the intermediate route breaks that the defensive is CAPPING or based on down and distance situations.

For example, on 3rd down and 10, the defense is more inclined to CAP routes breaking around 10 or more yards. In this case, running the Buzz-and-Go Route at 10 yards might be more favorable. Therefore, the Buzz-and-Go Route can be game-planned or tagged on the according route break depth.

Against Zone Coverage, the receiver must be reading for a collision by

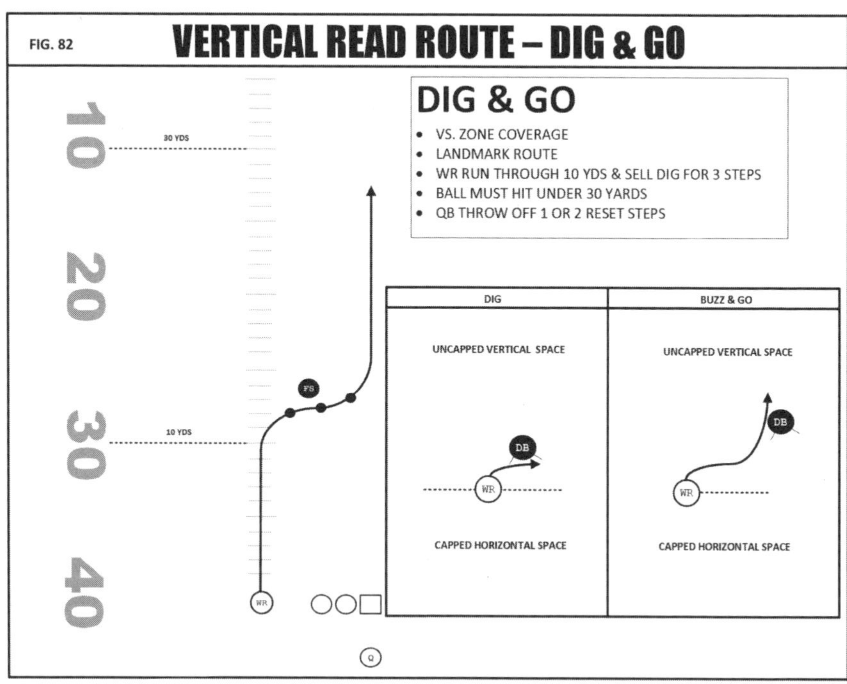

the defender. Most defenders are taught to run through a Buzz-and-Go Route to collision and CAP the vertical break. A receiver can defeat this action by using hand-strikes to relocate the collision attempt by the defender.

Dig-and-Go Route: The Dig-and-Go Route is a specialized Vertical Read Route primarily used to attack Zone Coverage. (FIG. 82)

The Dig-and-Go is used to counter an aggressive safety in a dominant position to CAP the Dig Route space. This is a landmark route run through 10 yards. The ball must hit under 30 yards due to the double-move timing of the route.

The Dig-and-Go can be used to take advantage of an aggressive CAPPING safety on the Dig Route within the Drive concept. (FIG. 83)

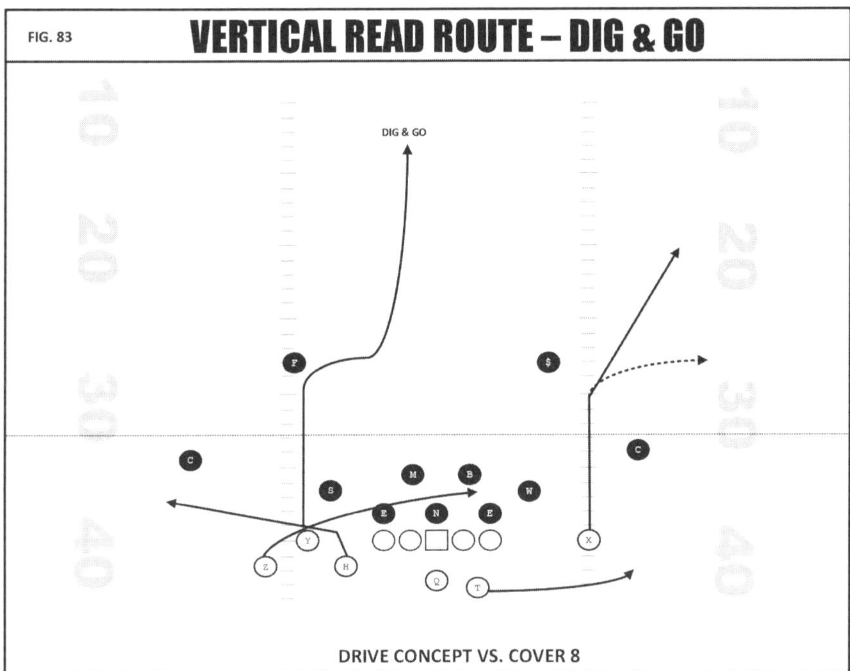

The quarterback determines, pre-snap, if he wants to use the Dig-and-Go as a Read Route or a Rhythm replacement with a pump-fake. Either way, on the Drop, the quarterback must confirm the defender is CAPPING the horizontal break-space of the Dig and UNCAPPED the vertical break-space of the Go. (FIG. 84)

The receiver must run through 10 yards to sell the vertical stem of the Dig Route. Getting through 10 yards in necessary to get beyond the

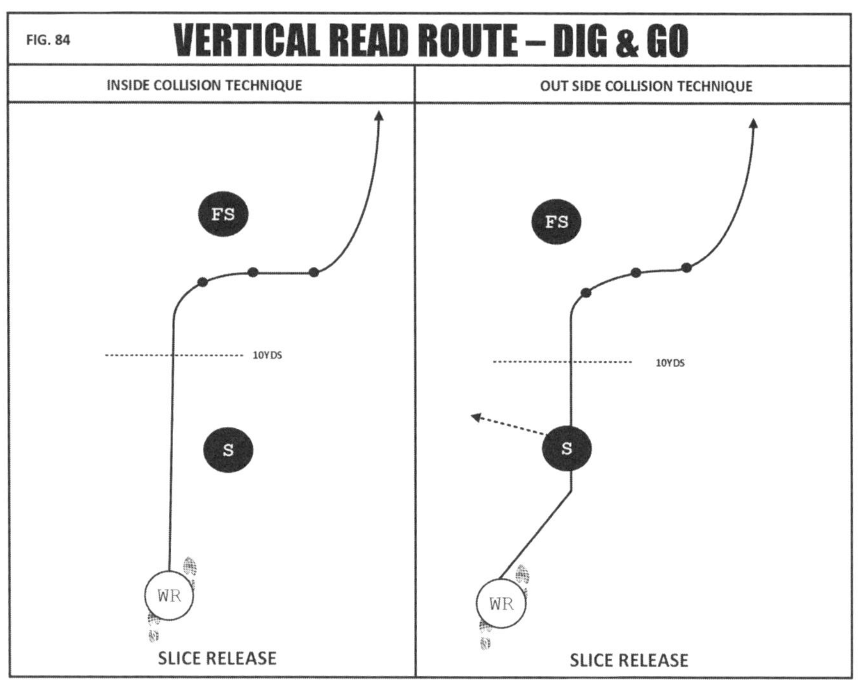
FIG. 84
VERTICAL READ ROUTE – DIG & GO
INSIDE COLLISION TECHNIQUE
OUT SIDE COLLISION TECHNIQUE
FS
10YDS
S
WR
SLICE RELEASE
FS
10YDS
S
WR
SLICE RELEASE

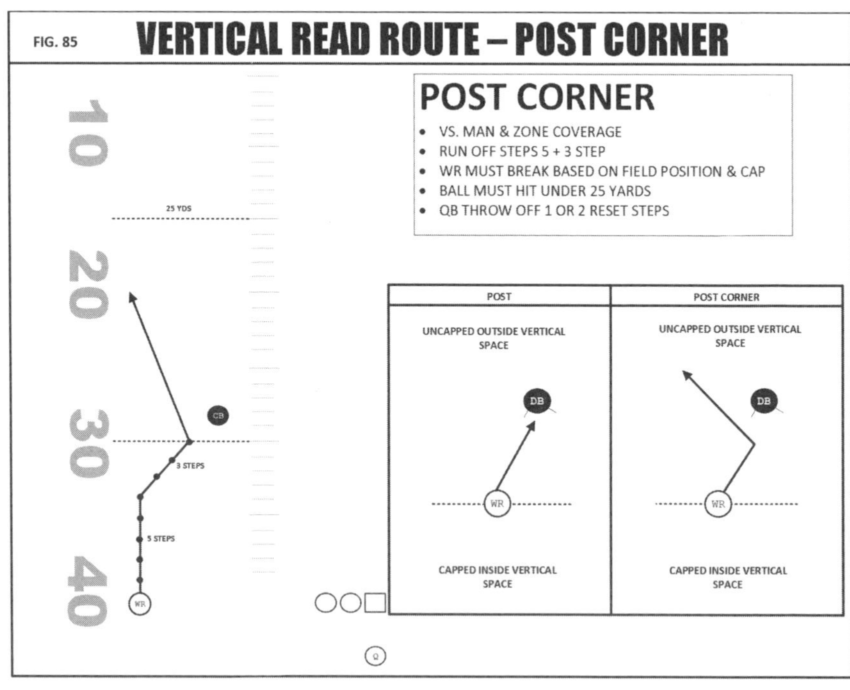
FIG. 85
VERTICAL READ ROUTE – POST CORNER
POST CORNER
• VS. MAN & ZONE COVERAGE
• RUN OFF STEPS 5 + 3 STEP
• WR MUST BREAK BASED ON FIELD POSITION & CAP
• BALL MUST HIT UNDER 25 YARDS
• QB THROW OFF 1 OR 2 RESET STEPS
10
20
30
40
25 YDS
CB
3 STEPS
5 STEPS
WR
Q
POST
UNCAPPED OUTSIDE VERTICAL SPACE
DB
WR
CAPPED INSIDE VERTICAL SPACE
POST CORNER
UNCAPPED OUTSIDE VERTICAL SPACE
DB
WR
CAPPED INSIDE VERTICAL SPACE

collision or carry of the linebackers, and to close the cushion of safeties. The Slice Release is optimal to use on the Dig-and-Go. This allows the receiver to take the easiest release to avoid collision and close the cushion on the safety as fast as possible.

After the receiver gets through 10 yards, then he will stick his outside foot in the ground and sell the Dig Break for 3 steps. On the 3rd step, he sticks his inside foot in the ground and breaks to the vertical space of the Go Route.

Post-Corner Route: The Post-Corner Route is a versatile Vertical Read Route used to attack both Man and Zone Coverage. (FIG. 85)

The Post-Corner Route is most effective when inside vertical-space is being CAPPED by a defender. The route is run off 5 vertical steps and 3 post-break steps. The receivers angle of attack out of the break is based on the field position of the rout and the CAP of the defender over it. The ball must hit under 25 yards. The Post-Corner Route is an excellent vertical Read Route that constrains a deep defender from CAPPING the Double-Post concept. (FIG. 86)

The quarterback must determine Man or Zone Coverage pre-snap to decide what progression to use post-snap. Against Zone Coverage, he can employ a Rhythm Replace pump-fake to entice the defender to

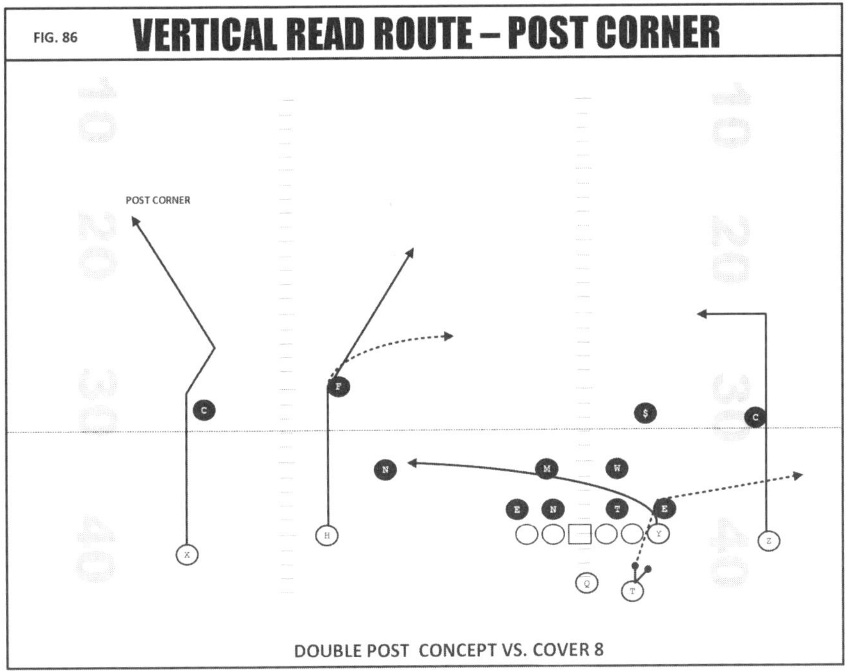

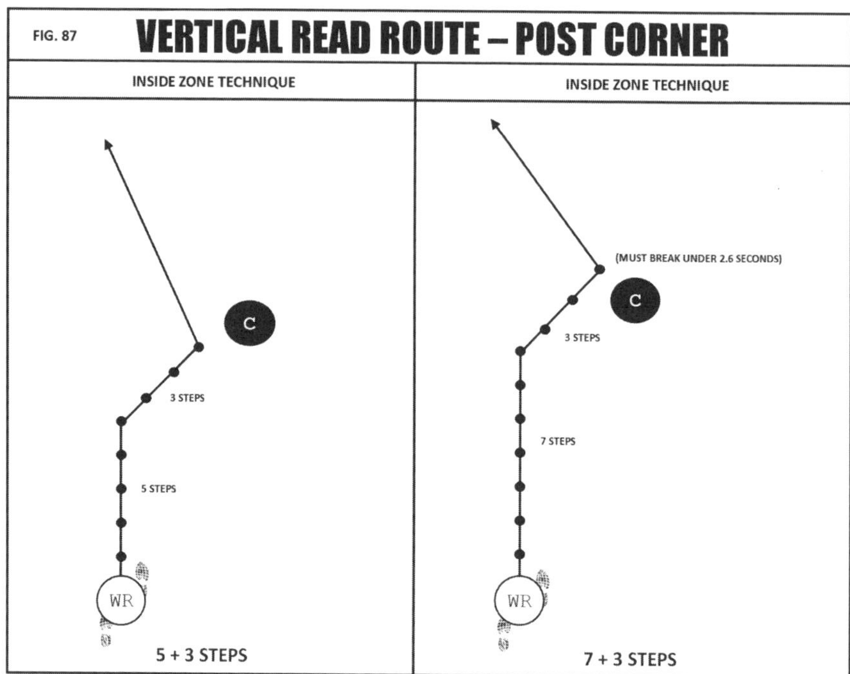

jump the Post Route. If the quarterback feels that the defender will take the fake without a pump-fake, then the Post-Corner will be used as a basic Read Route in the progression. Against Man Coverage there is no pump-fake needed due to the eyes of defenders not being on the quarterback. In this case, the Post-Corner Route would be used as a basic Read Route in the progression. (FIG. 87)

The baseline steps for a receiver running a Post-Corner is 5 vertical steps + 3 Post Break steps. This is a total of 8 steps that must be made between 2.2 – 2.6 seconds. Faster receivers may be able to take 7 vertical steps + 3 Post Break steps in under 2.6 seconds. We have found the baseline speed a receiver needs to execute a 7 + 3 step Post-Corner Route to be a sub-4.5 second forty-yard dash time. It is recommended to test receivers before the season to determine if they can make the top of the Post-Corner Route break in less than 2.6 seconds. Receivers who can will run 7 + 3 step Post-Corner Routes.

Receivers who cannot break the top of the Post-Corner Route in under 2.6 seconds will run 5 + 3 step Post-Corner Routes. Timing of double-move throws within the Drop timeline are more critical than the vertical threat of the route. If a coach desires the vertical threat is needed, then

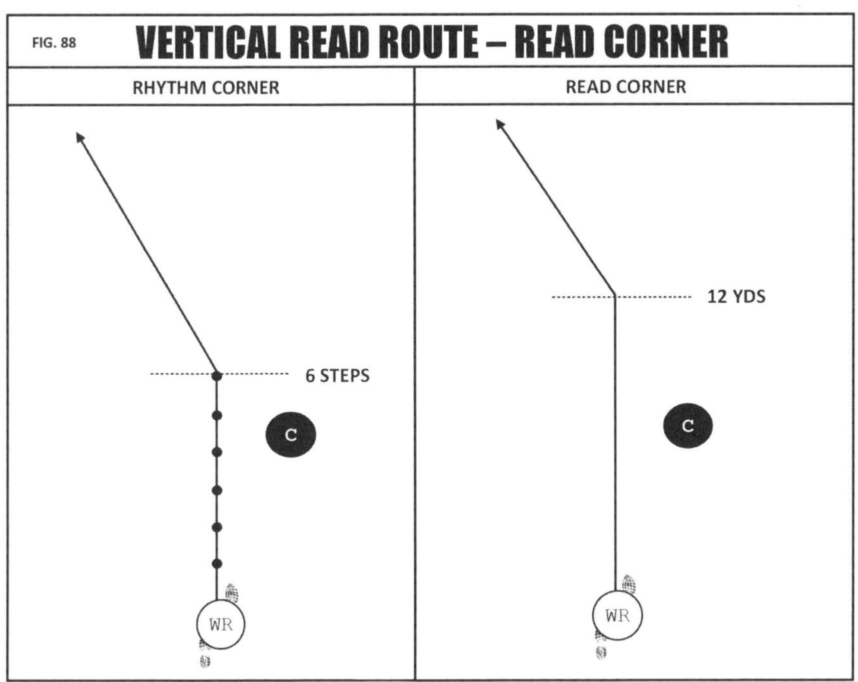
FIG. 88
VERTICAL READ ROUTE – READ CORNER
RHYTHM CORNER
READ CORNER
6 STEPS
C
WR
12 YDS
C
WR

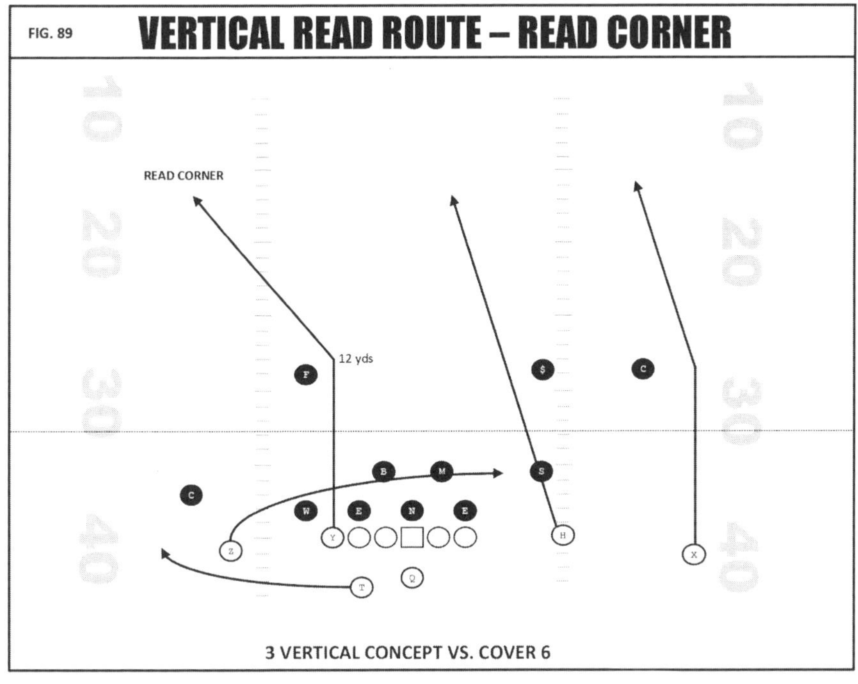
FIG. 89
VERTICAL READ ROUTE – READ CORNER
READ CORNER
12 yds
F
$
C
B
M
S
C
W
E
N
E
Y
H
Z
X
T
Q
3 VERTICAL CONCEPT VS. COVER 6

the timeline can be manipulated by adding extra protection or pocket movement. This can increase the Drop timeline and allow slower receivers to still run the Post-Corner Route at 7 + 3 steps.

The receiver must break the route to the front pylon of the end zone if the route originates beyond the 25-yard line. If the route begins inside the red Zone, it will break towards the back pylon of the end zone. The break of the route will snap flat to attack horizontal space if it is CAPPED by a defender who is over and outside of the route-side space. (FIG. 88)

There is also another variation of a Vertical Corner Route with Read Route timing. It is called a Read Corner. A Read Corner is a Corner Route that elongates its vertical stem to break at a minimum of 12 yards. Rhythm Corner Routes break on 6 steps at 1.8-seconds of time. A Read Corner Route breaks at 12 yards, which is beyond the 1.8-second Rhythm timeline.

The elongated stem of the Read Corner allows more time for a receiver to close the cushion of soft Zone defenders. It also provides the quarterback the ability to use the route as a Read Route in a progression. The 3-Vertical concept shows an example. (FIG. 89)

Corner-Post Route: The Corner-Post Route is another versatile Vertical Read Route used to attack both Man and Zone Coverage. (FIG. 90)

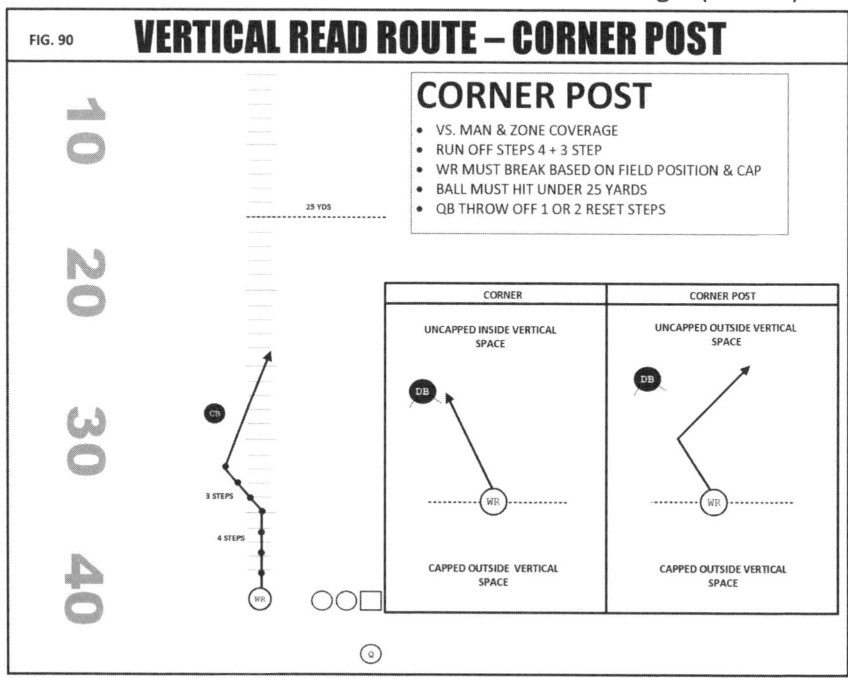

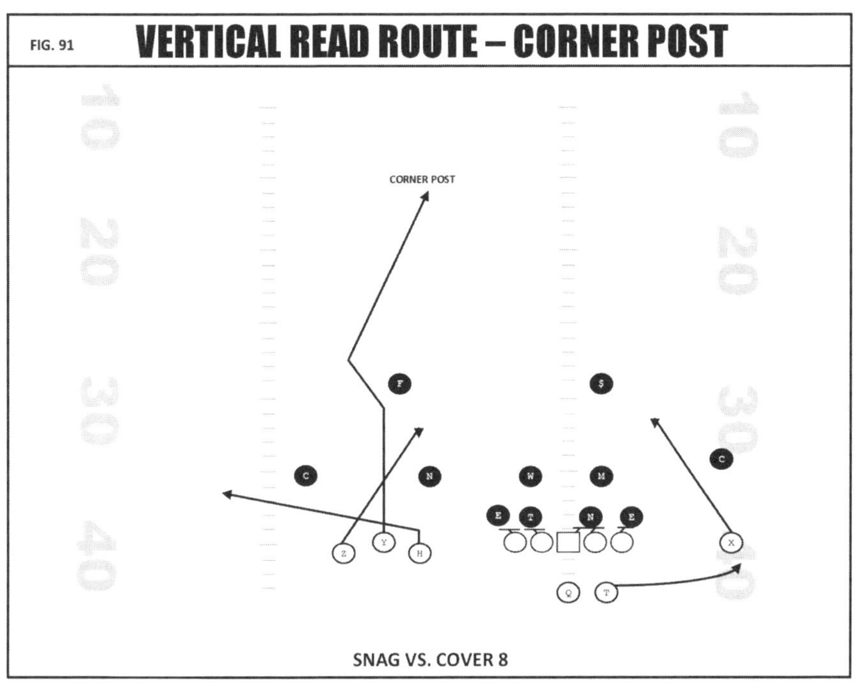
FIG. 91
VERTICAL READ ROUTE – CORNER POST
CORNER POST
SNAG VS. COVER 8

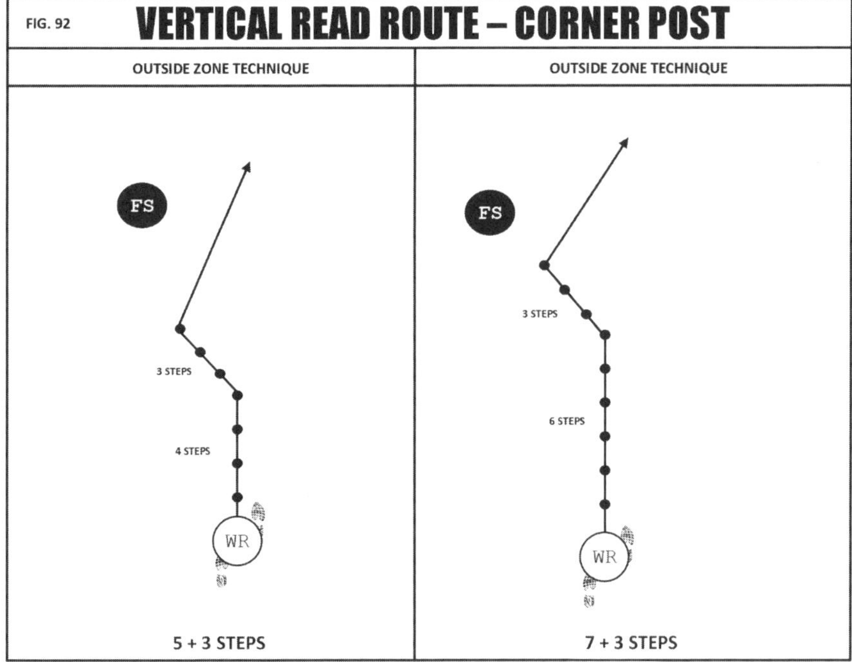
FIG. 92
VERTICAL READ ROUTE – CORNER POST
OUTSIDE ZONE TECHNIQUE
OUTSIDE ZONE TECHNIQUE
FS
3 STEPS
4 STEPS
WR
5 + 3 STEPS
FS
3 STEPS
6 STEPS
WR
7 + 3 STEPS

The Corner-Post is used to attack defenders who are CAPPING outside vertical route-space. The corner Post is run off 4 vertical steps and 3 corner break steps. The receiver's angle of attack out of the break is based on field position and the CAP of the defender over it. (FIG. 91)

The Snag concept can benefit from using the Corner-Post Route as a constraint on the free safety that is consistently CAPPING the Corner Route.

The quarterback will determine, pre-snap, if the defense is playing Man or Zone Coverage. Against Zone Coverage, the quarterback will decide if a Rhythm Replace pump-fake is needed, or if he will use the Corner-Post as a Read Route in the progression. Against Man Coverage, the Corner-Post will be a Read Route in the progression.

The baseline steps for the Corner-Post is 4 vertical steps + 3 corner break steps. (FIG. 92)

This is a total of 7 steps that the receiver should make between 2.2-2.6 seconds. If a receiver is a sub-4.5 second 40-yard dash runner, then he may be able to take 6 vertical steps + 3 corner break steps on the Corner-Post Route in fewer than 2.6 seconds. If this can be accomplished within the Read Route timeframe, then 6 vertical steps will create a bigger

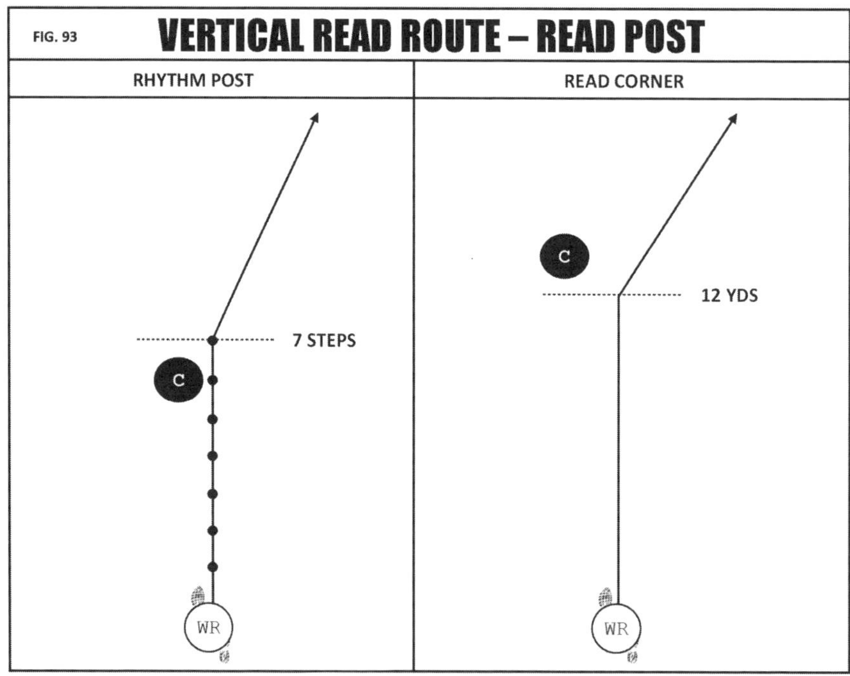

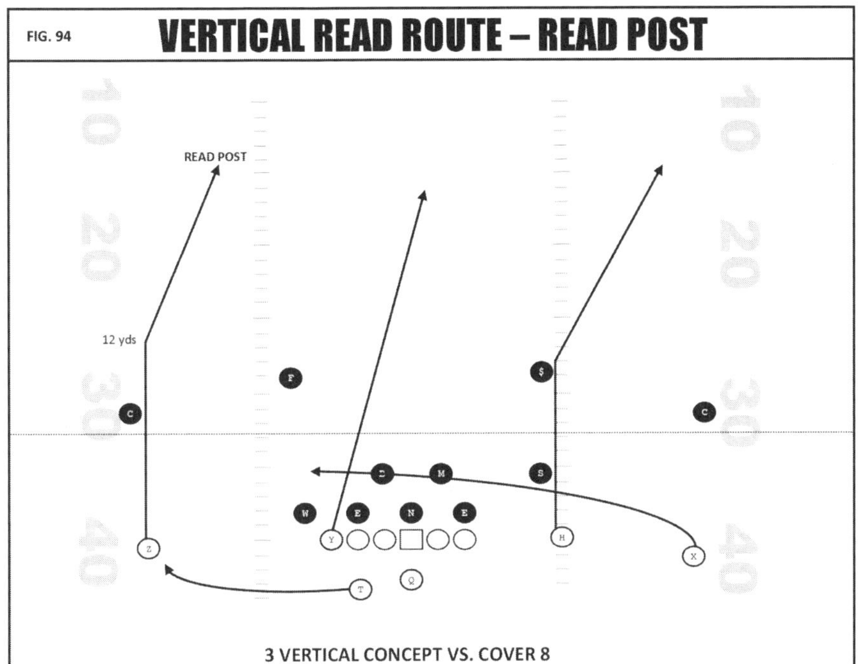

vertical-space threat on the defender. Once again, a coach can manipulate the timeline with extra protection or pocket movement. This will allow extra Drop time for a slower receiver to execute the vertical 6 + 3 step Corner-Post Route break.

Receivers who break the CAP of the defense must keep the break skinny to maximize the vertical space for the quarterback on the throw. If a defender is CAPPING the route-side space of the Post Break, then the receiver can win back the horizontal space by snapping the Post Break flat. The quarterback must read the CAP, as well, to determine the deep or flat throw that needs to be made.

A Post can also be transformed into a Vertical Read Route by elongating its stem. (FIG. 93)

The Rhythm Post is a 7-Step Route that breaks open in 1.8 seconds. Taking the route stem to a minimum of 12 yards moves the route beyond the Rhythm threshold and places it in the Read family.

The 3-Vertical concept can benefit from this route adjustment. (FIG. 94)

Extending the Post stem to 12 yards can allow a receiver more time to close the Cushion on a soft-zone or pattern-reading defender.

CHAPTER 7

Understanding the 5 Base Rush Routes

RHYTHM READ

R4

RUSH RELEASE

UNDERSTANDING THE 5 BASE RUSH ROUTES

The third family of R4 routes are the Rush Route family. Rush Routes are routes that have universal properties. They can be hit at any point along the Drop timeline. Rush Routes can serve as Hot Routes in the face of pressure or can be used as a check-down at the end of a progression. Rush Routes have comparable properties to each other in that they attack flat-space under the hard-deck line of 7 yards. There are 5 Base Routes in the Rush Route family. They are the Hitch, Stick, Shallow, Quick-Out, and Slant.

Rush Routes provide situational solutions for Red Zone and Blitz downs. Rush Routes also work in conjunction with Read Routes to create stretches on dual-read and flat defenders. Quarterbacks should always have an awareness of where Rush Routes are within a concept and use those as safety nets in heavy Blitz or Zone- Drop situations. We coach the quarterback, "If you feel the Rush, throw the Rush." This means if a quarterback feels the Rush of pressure from the Blitz of defenders, then look to throw the Rush Route as a "hot" throw.

Rush Routes are commonly paired to create quick-game concepts or side-to-attack the defense in an accelerated manner. This requires the quarterback to be able to manipulate his footwork to time his feet with a quicker throw. Quarterbacks must also practice throwing Rush Routes off-platform in the face of pressure. Rush Routes provide shorter throws for the quarterback has a high probability of completion and helps maintain the confidence and timing necessary to operate a successful concept passing game.

Hitch Route: The Hitch Route is the first route installed in an offense for most quarterbacks and receivers. (FIG. 95)

The Hitch is a 5-yard route that is primarily used to attack Zone Coverage. The Hitch Route is run off 3 big steps + 2 small foot-fire steps. The ball must be thrown on a line and the receiver must attack the football out of the break.

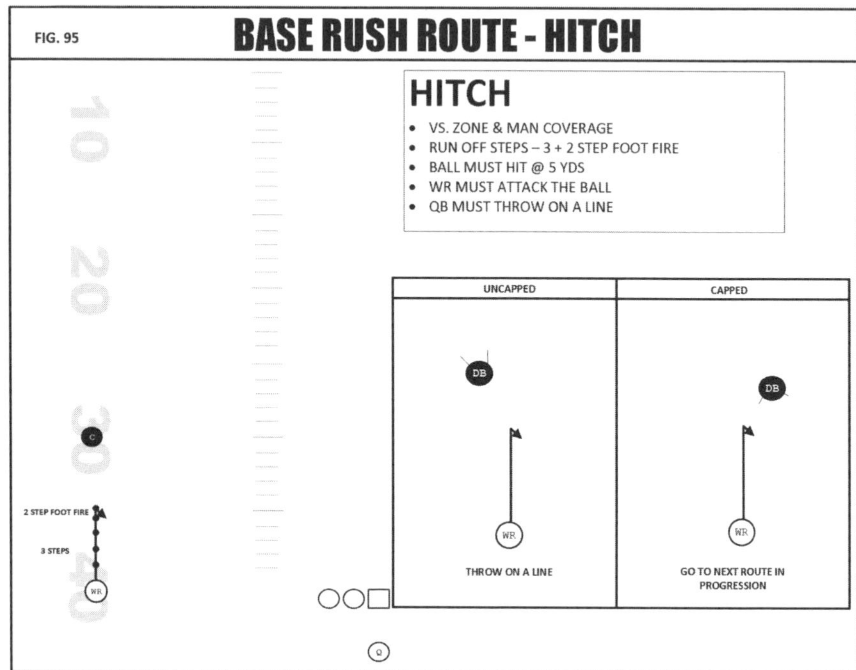

A quarterback throwing the Hitch Route must confirm the CAP of the route-side space on the Drop. If a defender is over and outside with a full-turned hip angle, then the route is UNCAPPED. As a defender moves more into an inside alignment and squares the hip angle, the CAP threat increases. Finally, the closure ability of the defender must be accounted for when throwing the Hitch Route. If the defender has a positive closure ability, then the Hitch should be confirmed as CAPPED by the quarterback.

Smash concepts are built on the Hitch Route. A Hitch Route combined with a Corner Route over the top creates a vertical stretch on a flat defender. (FIG. 96)

The Inside-Smash concept is an example of two Hitch Routes with a Corner Route by the #3 receiver breaking over the top. This is a valuable red Zone concept for many offenses.

The receiver can help UNCAP the hitch route-side space by creating a vertical threat on the stem of the route. This is used to attack a defender who is playing a soft-zone technique. His mindset should be focused on getting the defender to back-pedal and turn his hips toward the goal line. The receiver must be able to explode off the line of scrimmage

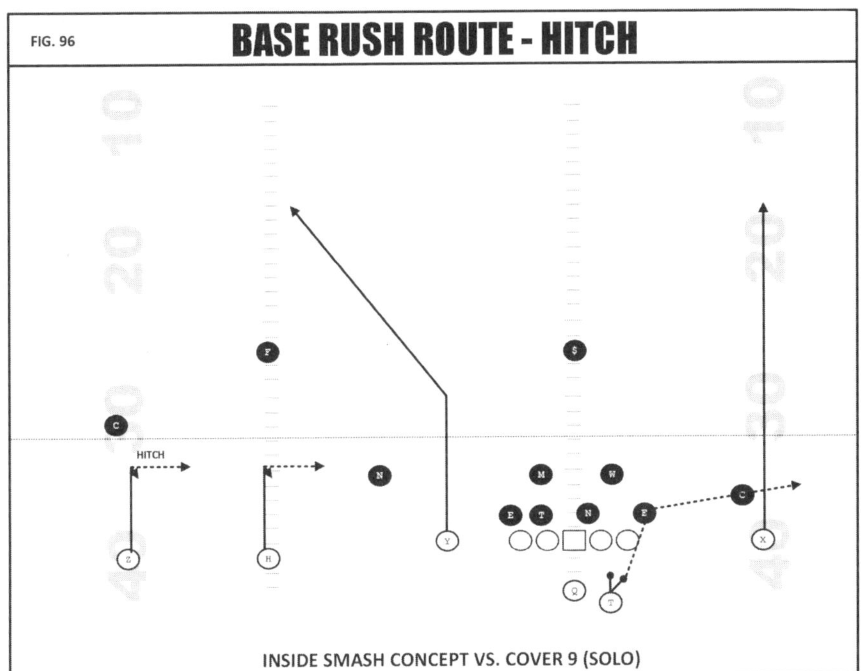

INSIDE SMASH CONCEPT VS. COVER 9 (SOLO)

with no false steps for 3 steps and come to an immediate stop in 2 small foot-fire steps. At the top of the 2nd small step, the receiver should stick the route with the instep of the foot and open his near hip toward the quarterback. (FIG. 97)

The receiver can overcome a CAPPED Hitch Route against an inside CAPPING Zone defender or and inside soft-man defender. This is done by converting the Route Break of the Hitch into continuous flat-break down the line at 5 yards. We call this a Fin Route. The Fin Route is a short name that comes from the break of the route being at five yards and working in. The route snaps the break at 90-degrees and helps win back the inside route-side space that an inside leveraged defender is trying to CAP.

Against a hard press-man defender, a receiver must take 3 steps and break with a flat speed cut to 5 yards. The aggressive speed cut is necessary to win back route-side space inside.

Stick Route: The Stick Route is a Rush Route run mainly by an inside receiver. The Stick Route is the cornerstone route of the Stick concept that is one of the most widely-used concepts in football. (FIG. 98)

FIG. 97

BASE RUSH ROUTE – HITCH

OUTSIDE ZONE TECHNIQUE	SOFT MAN TECHNIQUE	PRESS MAN TECHNIQUE
C 2 STEP FOOT FIRE 3 STEPS WR HITCH	C 2 STEP FOOT FIRE SETTLE B/W #'S & HASH 3 STEPS WR FIN	ACCELERATE C 3 STEPS WR FIN

FIG. 98

BASE RUSH ROUTE - STICK

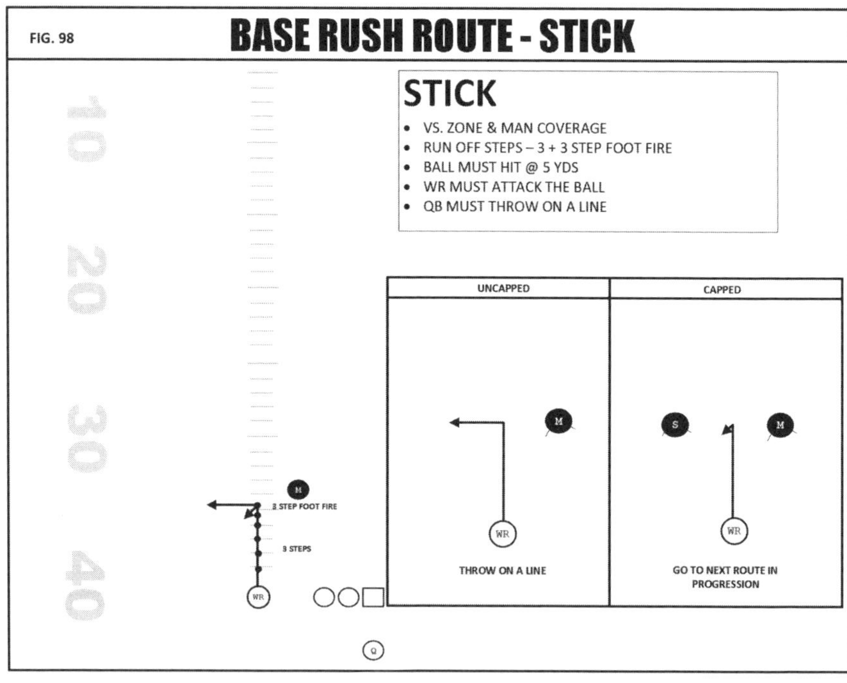

The Stick Route attacks both Man and Zone Coverage. The Stick differs from the Hitch by breaking out while the Hitch breaks in. Because of the break, the Stick Route is run off 3 vertical steps + 3 foot-fire steps. The ball must hit at 5 yards on a line.

The quarterback must confirm if the Stick Route is CAPPED or UNCAPPED. If there is no defender threat or the angle of the defender's hips are away from the break point, then the route is UNCAPPED. The coverage, hip angle, and closure ability of the inside defender most also be considered when confirming the CAP of the Stick Route. A middle linebacker who excels in these areas can undercut the Stick Route and CAP it.

The Stick concept is commonly associated with 3 x 1 formations. (FIG. 99)

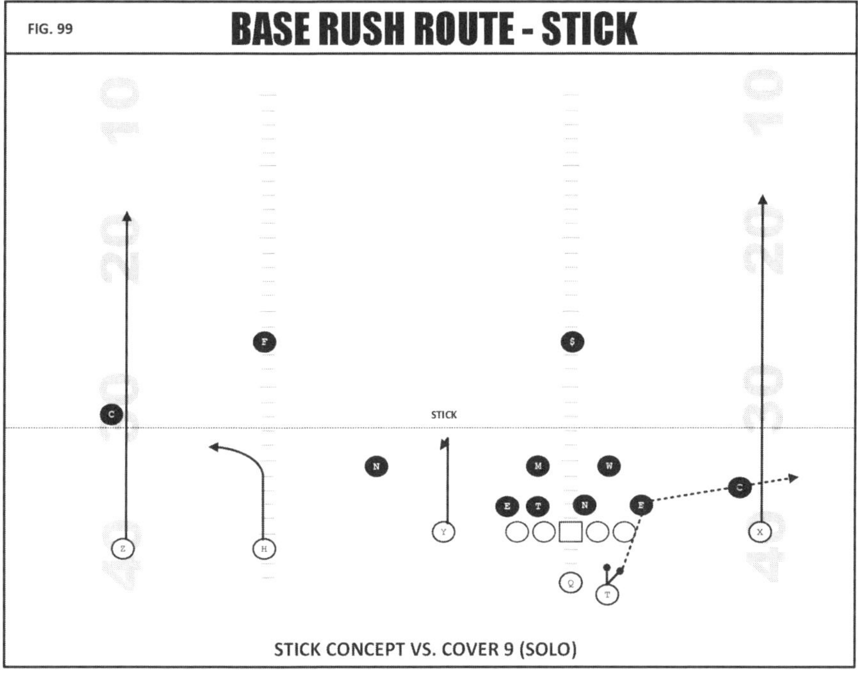

STICK CONCEPT VS. COVER 9 (SOLO)

The receiver can help overcome CAP situations by exploding off the line of scrimmage and creating a Vertical Route threat. (FIG. 100)

This can force the Mike to Drop to get in position to cover and carry the perceived Vertical Route threat. The receiver will take 3 foot-fire stick steps and break out, then settle to maximize open space between the middle and Sam linebacker.

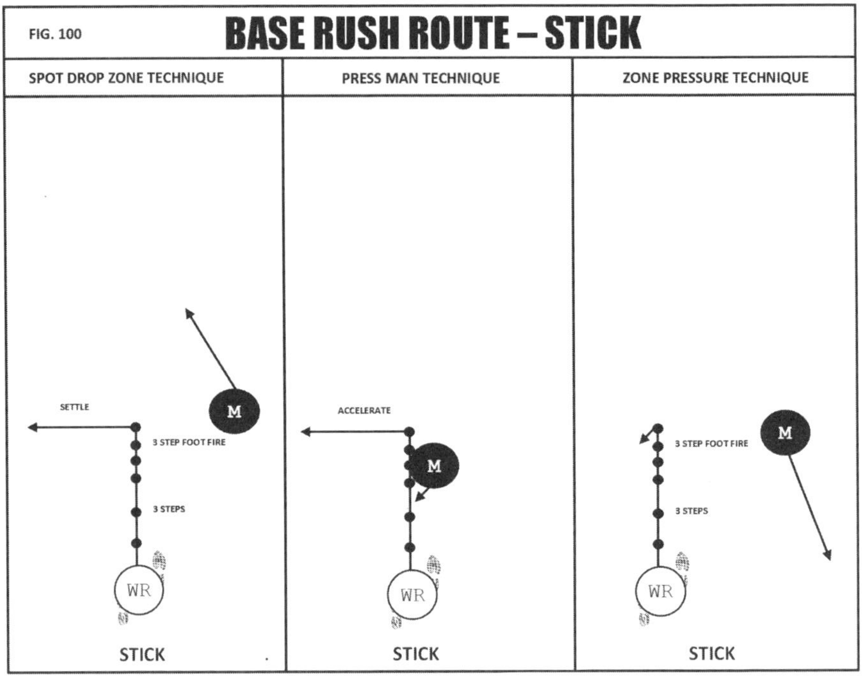

FIG. 100 **BASE RUSH ROUTE – STICK**

SPOT DROP ZONE TECHNIQUE	PRESS MAN TECHNIQUE	ZONE PRESSURE TECHNIQUE
SETTLE M 3 STEP FOOT FIRE 3 STEPS WR	ACCELERATE M WR	3 STEP FOOT FIRE M 3 STEPS WR
STICK	STICK	STICK

Against press-man technique, the receiver will take the same steps. On the final stick step, the receiver will lean into the press-man defender and explode out, pushing off with his near elbow to create separation from the defender. The receiver will accelerate out of the break and will not slow down on the route.

The receiver will adjust the route break against a perceived Zone pressure from the middle or sam linebacker. Against a Blitz, the receiver will turn out immediately after the 3-step foot-fire stick to position himself for a "hot" throw by the quarterback.

Shallow Route: The Shallow Route is another Rush Route used mainly by an outside receiver. The Shallow Route is the cornerstone route of the Shallow concept. (FIG. 101)

The route provides immediate stress on the defense by crossing the centerline to gain a Man advantage to a side of space. The Shallow provides versatility to concepts by attacking both Man and Zone Coverages. Shallow Routes are often paired with Dig Routes to create high-to-low stress on linebackers.

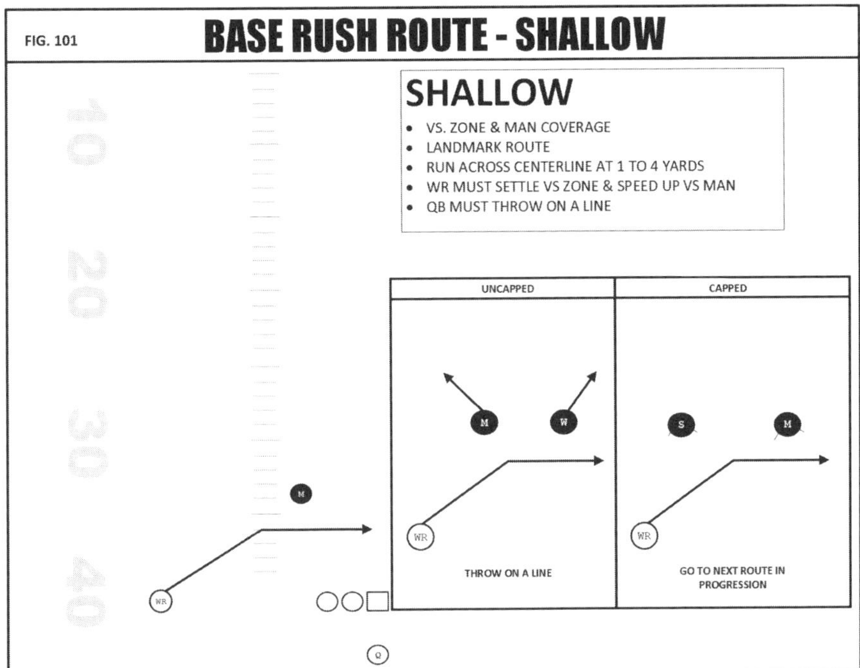

Shallow Routes are landmark routes that attack at 1 to 4 yards of depth across the line of scrimmage. Against Man Coverage, Shallow Routes keep on running. Against Zone Coverage, Shallow Routes will settle into space.

The Drive concept is developed by using the Shallow Route in conjunction with a Dig Route to create a high-to-low stretch on middle linebackers. (FIG. 102)

The quarterback can use the shallow as a "hot" throw against pressure or a check down at the end of a progression. Zone Dropping linebackers give confirmation to the quarterback that the Shallow is UNCAPPED. Linebackers with a square hip angle are in a better position to CAP the Shallow space. Quarterbacks must practice throwing Shallows under pressure over defensive lineman with extension and body-turn that gets the nose of the ball to turn over underneath the linebackers. Quarterbacks must also practice throwing the Shallow Routes between defenders. (FIG. 103)

Receivers adjust their depth of the Shallow based on the coverage used to defend them. Against Zone Coverage, a receiver pushes diagonal to 4-yards from the line of scrimmage, then break across the center-line

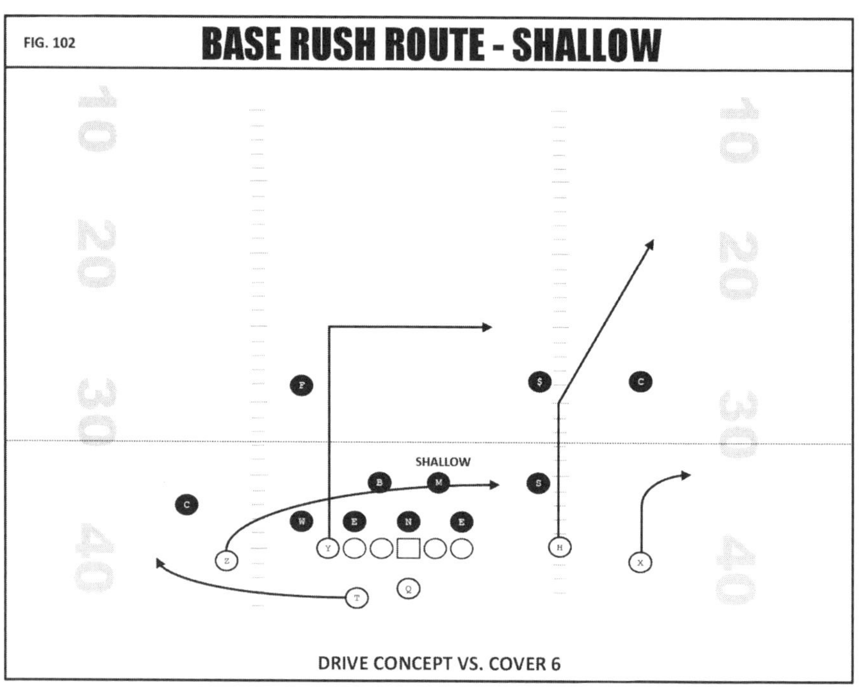
FIG. 102
BASE RUSH ROUTE - SHALLOW
SHALLOW
DRIVE CONCEPT VS. COVER 6

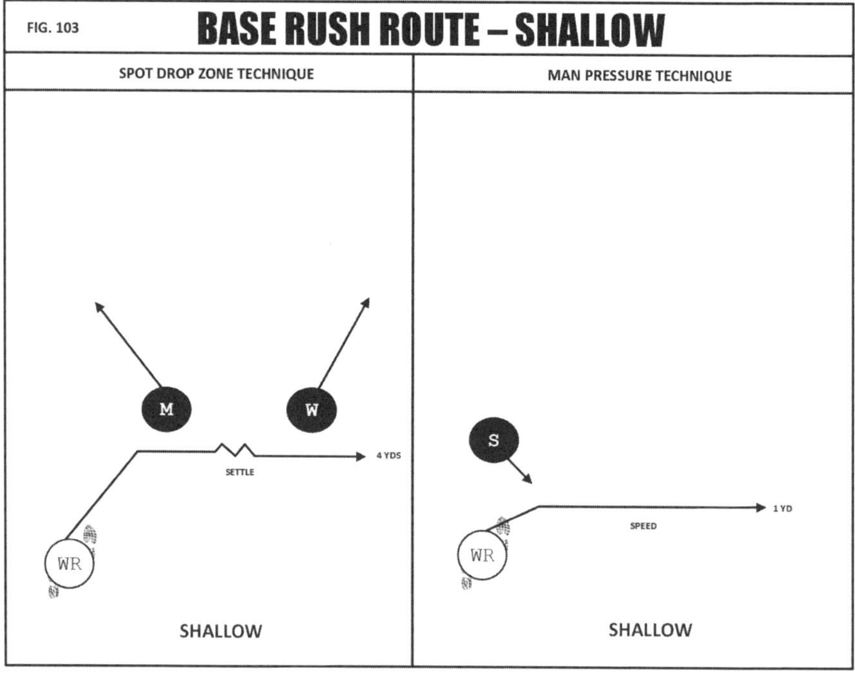
FIG. 103
BASE RUSH ROUTE – SHALLOW
SPOT DROP ZONE TECHNIQUE
MAN PRESSURE TECHNIQUE
M
W
4 YDS
SETTLE
WR
SHALLOW
S
1 YD
SPEED
WR
SHALLOW

to settle into UNCAPPED space. Attacking Zone-Dropping linebackers at 4 yards forces the linebackers to make a quicker declaration on the space they are going to cover.

Against Man Coverage, a receiver immediately attacks inside no deeper than 1 yard from the line of scrimmage and keeps running to stay in front of the Man defender. Attacking Man defenders at 1 yard helps reduce the collision at the line of scrimmage and increases the ability for a defender to get in position to CAP route-side space of the Shallow.

Quick-Out Route: The Quick-Out is a Rush Route that can be used to attack both Man and Zone Coverage. The Quick-Out is used in many concepts in football. (FIG. 104)

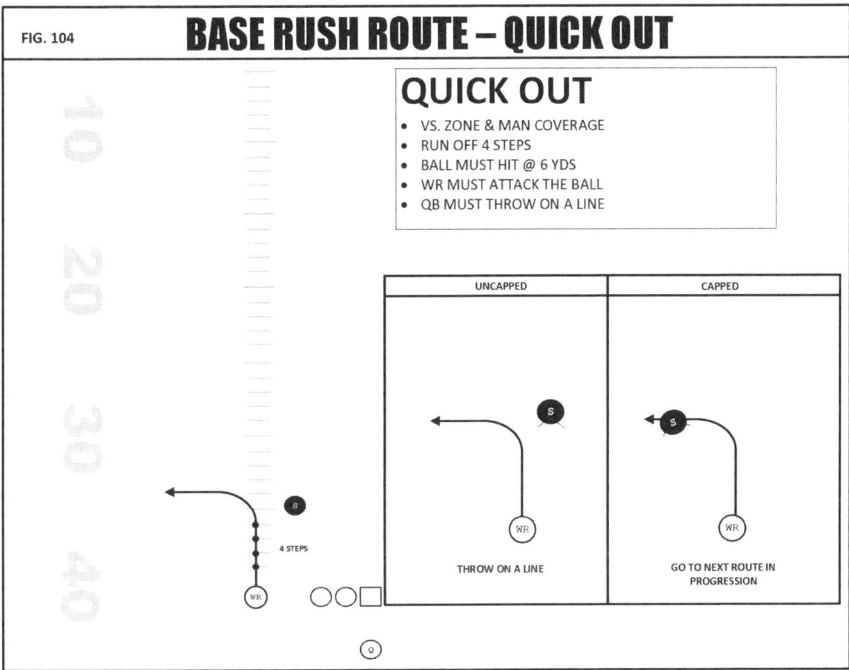

The immediate stretch to attack the flat space creates stress on the defense and requires defenders to adjust coverage to take away an easy high-percentage throw. The Quick-Out is run off 4 steps. The ball must be hit at 6 yards and thrown on a line.

The Y-Cross concept uses the Quick-Out as "Hot" Route or Trigger Route to create a high-to-low stretch on linebackers with the Climb (Cross) Route. (FIG. 105)

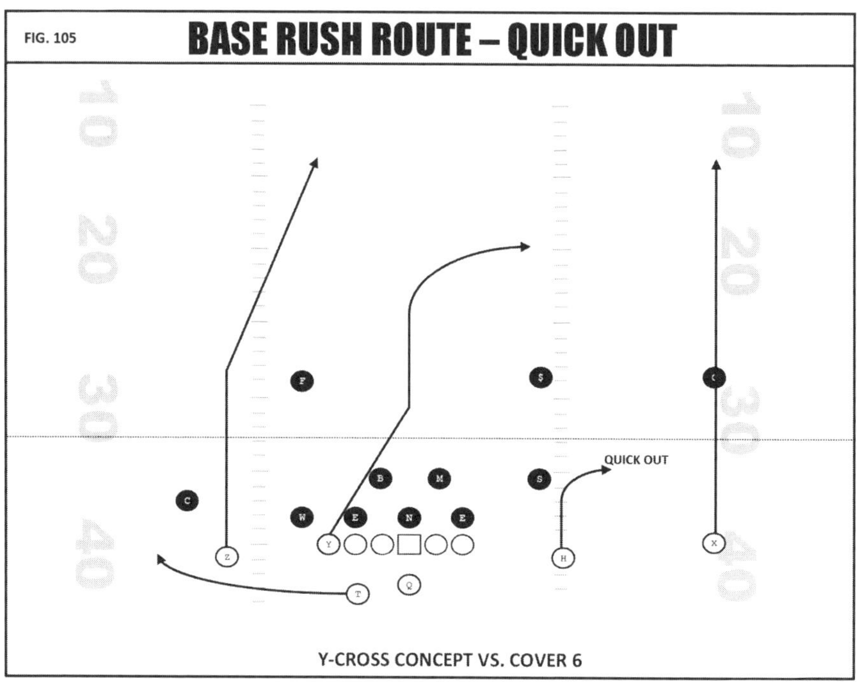

The quarterback throwing the Quick-Out must make a read like the Stick Route. The difference between the Stick and the Quick-Out is that the Quick-Out does not foot the feet before the break. The break of the route is a speed-break into space. If there is no defender in a dominant position outside the Quick-Out, then the route is UNCAPPED. However, if a defender is over-and-outside with a square or Zone hip-angle then the route-side space is CAPPED. The quarterback must also confirm the position of the inside defender. An inside defender with positive closure ability and man-turned hip-angle can undercut the Quick-Out for an interception. This must be taken into consideration. (FIG. 106)

To overcome some of these CAP issues, a receiver can settle out of the Quick-Out break and square towards the quarterback. This would be an example for use against a Cover-2 adjustment by a cornerback. Another route option against a Man defender is to adjust the 4-Step Quick-Out into a 2-Step Arrow Route. An Arrow Route is the term used for a 2-Step out-breaking route. The 2-Step Arrow gets a receiver outside faster against an inside-leveraged receiver and places a faster flat-stretch on the defense. The Arrow Route is great to use in Man and tight-field Zone situations.

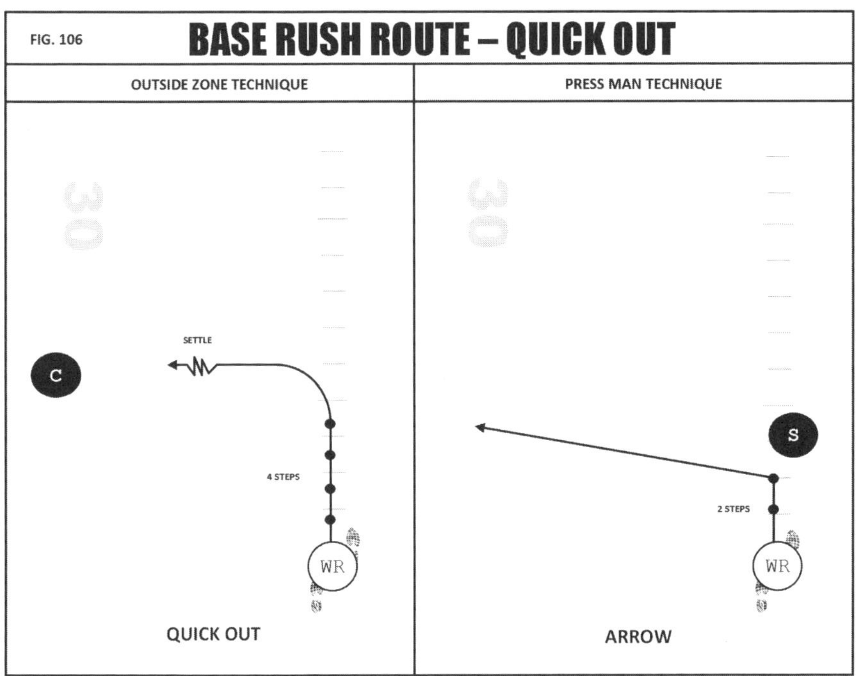
FIG. 106
BASE RUSH ROUTE – QUICK OUT
OUTSIDE ZONE TECHNIQUE
PRESS MAN TECHNIQUE
SETTLE
C
4 STEPS
WR
QUICK OUT
S
2 STEPS
WR
ARROW

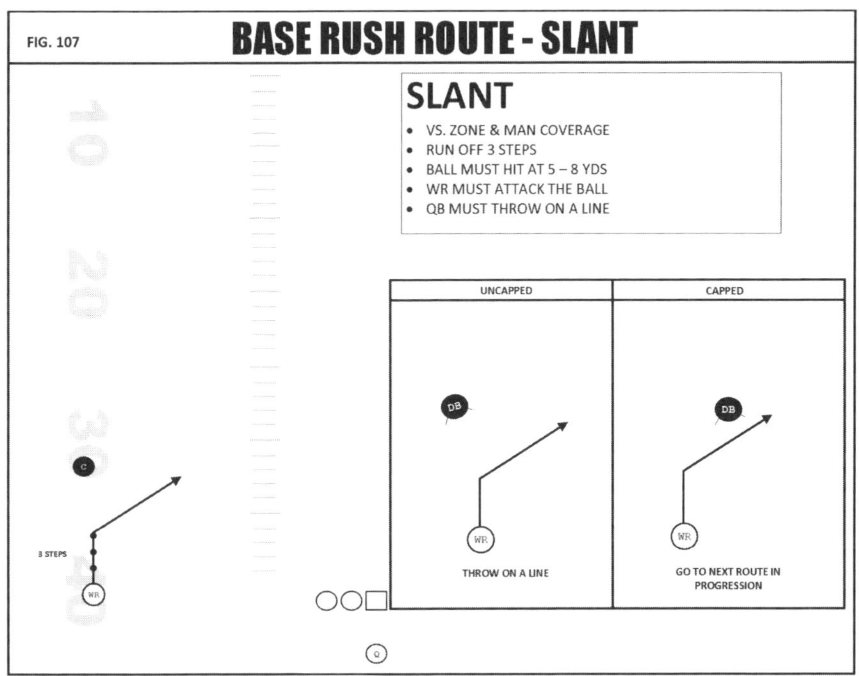
FIG. 107
BASE RUSH ROUTE - SLANT
SLANT
VS. ZONE & MAN COVERAGE
RUN OFF 3 STEPS
BALL MUST HIT AT 5 – 8 YDS
WR MUST ATTACK THE BALL
QB MUST THROW ON A LINE
UNCAPPED
CAPPED
DB
WR
THROW ON A LINE
DB
WR
GO TO NEXT ROUTE IN PROGRESSION
C
3 STEPS
WR
Q

Slant Route: The Slant Route is one of the most difficult routes to cover in football. (FIG. 107)

The Slant is used to attack both Man and Zone Coverage. The Slant Route is run off 3 steps. The goal of the route is to own inside-space against a defender. The ball should hit between 5 and 8 yards. The Slant Route breaking over the middle poses a high risk to the offense. If the ball is high or tipped, then an interception is common. This risk requires that the Slant Route must be thrown no higher than the chest level of the receiver.

The Slant Route can be infused to any pass concept to create an immediate space-threat to be defended. (FIG. 108)

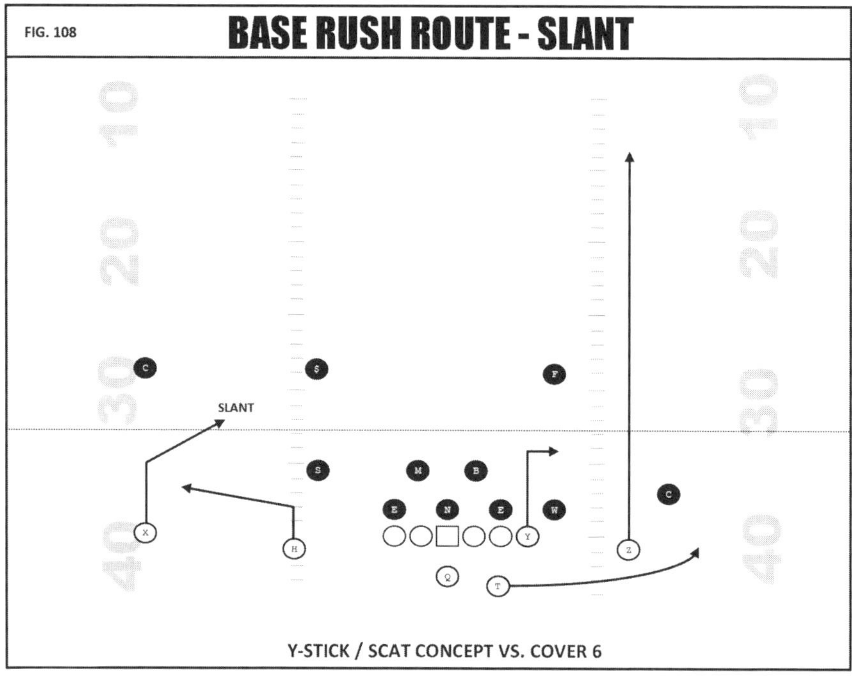

EXAMPLE: In this concept the Slant Route is used as part of a backside Scat concept that is attached to a frontside Y-stick concept. The Slant provides a priority threat to be defender in Zone Coverage. It also poses a potential 1-on-1 mismatch issue against Man Coverage.

The quarterback must speed up his footwork to adjust for the quick timing break of the Slant Route.

The quarterback must also confirm that the route-side space of the Slant is UNCAPPED before he makes the throw. A defender who is over and inside with a Zone or square-hip angle on the Slant is CAPPED. (FIG. 109)

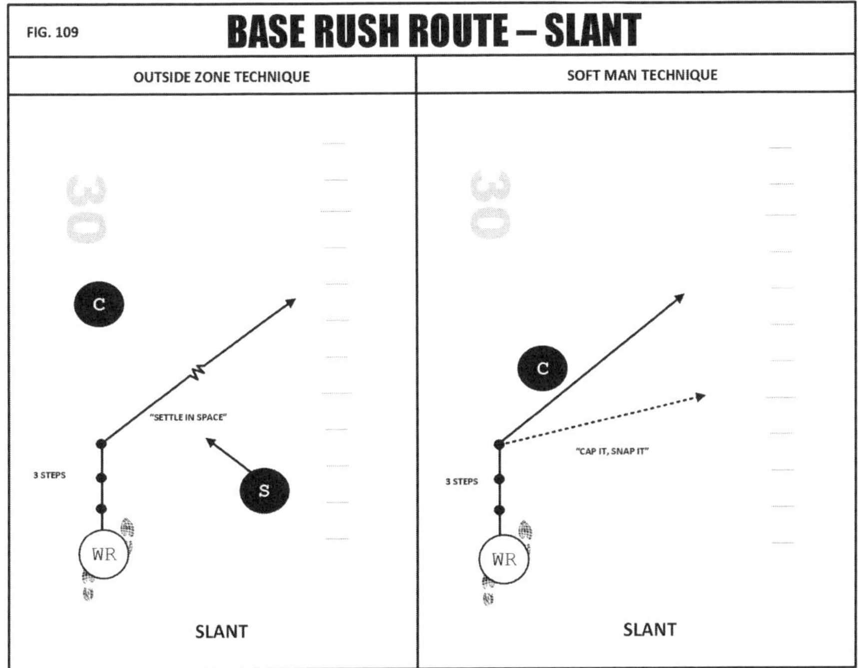

Receivers must explode off the ball and create a vertical threat against a secondary defender. Against Zone Coverage, they must break on the 3rd step at an attack angle high enough to get over a flat defending linebacker. As they clear the linebacker they must settle into space ready to receive the ball. The angle of attack out of the break will adjust flatter based on the leverage position of the secondary defender over the receiver.

If a receiver is running a Slant Route against a Man or Zone defender with a dominant inside-position then the Slant Route will break no further that 90-degrees to win back that inside routes-side space. Throwing the Slant against these two types of situations should be practiced regularly.

CHAPTER 8

Understanding Hybrid Rush Routes

UNDERSTANDING HYBRID RUSH ROUTES

Rush Routes are the most versatile family of routes in football. Their universal properties allow them to be thrown at any point in the timeline. This provides fluidity for a unique sub-group of Rush Routes that can also be thrown with Read Route timing. We call this sub-group Hybrid Rush Routes. Hybrid Rush Routes can be used as a Rush route or Read Route in a progression.

Hybrid Rush Routes have mixtures of both Rush route and Read Route properties. Routes with Read properties allow them to be thrown with Read timing. Some examples of these properties are Rush Routes that have double-moves within them. Having two moves within one route produces Read timing. There are also some Rush Routes that have the option for two different breaks based on defensive actions. The ability to move in multiple directions can place the Rush Route in the Read route category for timing. Another Hybrid Rush Route mixture is a route that can adjust the stem to break at, or between, the hard-deck line of 7-10-yards. This extended depth-break just around the hard-deck line can place the Rush Route in the Read Route timeline family.

Hybrid Rush Routes increase the functional strength of concepts by providing better options to defensive actions without having to create new plays. Understanding their properties and how you can place them within a progression is critical to creating more adaptability to your offense.

Slant Return Route: The Slant Return is a Hybrid Rush Route that attack both Man and Zone Coverage. (FIG. 110)

The Slant Return contains Read properties because it has two break moves within the route. The Slant Return also has Rush properties because it attacks the flat space and can be thrown as a check-down in the Drop timeline. The Slant Return Route is thrown off 3 vertical + 4 slant-break steps. The wide-receiver must sell the slant-break and the ball must hit at 6 yards.

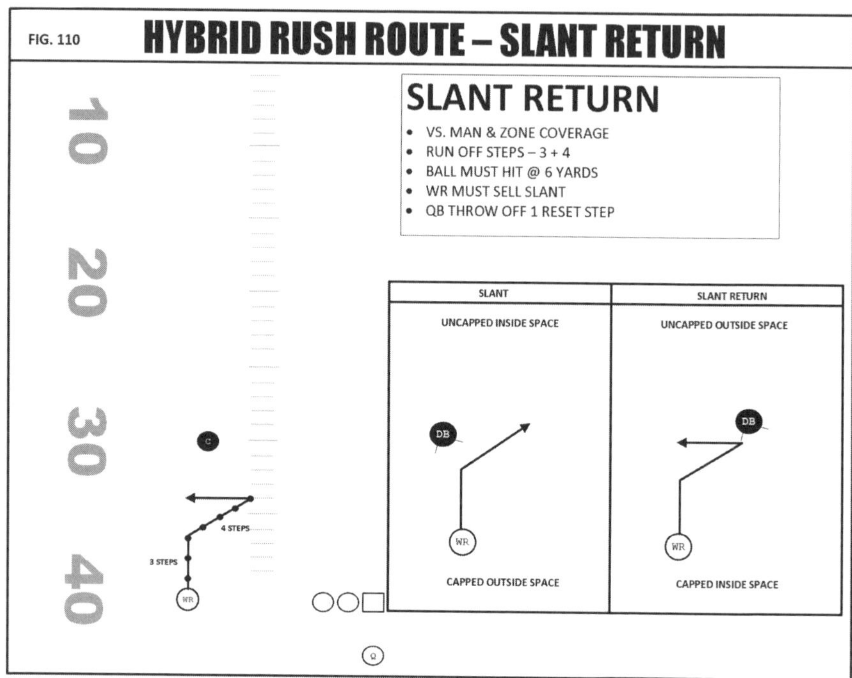

The Slant Return Route protects the Slant Route. If the Slant Route is CAPPED by a defender, then the Slant Return Route is the complement to counter the CAP. A quarterback must confirm that the defender is over-and-inside with a Zone hip-angle before throwing the Slant Return. Against Zone, he can use a pump-fake to influence the defender to CAP the slant.

The Slant Return protects the Slant Route against an aggressive CAPPING defender. (FIG. 111)

In this Y-Stick Double-Slant concept, the Hybrid Slant Return is used as a check down Rush Route. Using the 3-Quicks Rule and the Rhythm-Side Rule, the progression would be: Rhythm – Stick, Read – Inside Slant, Rush – Slant Return.

The Hybrid Slant Return can also be used as a Read Route in a progression. (FIG. 112)

In the Smash Shallow concept, the progression would be to Rhythm – Corner, Read – Slant Return, and Rush – Shallow and then release.

The receiver running the Slant Return Route must determine if the defense

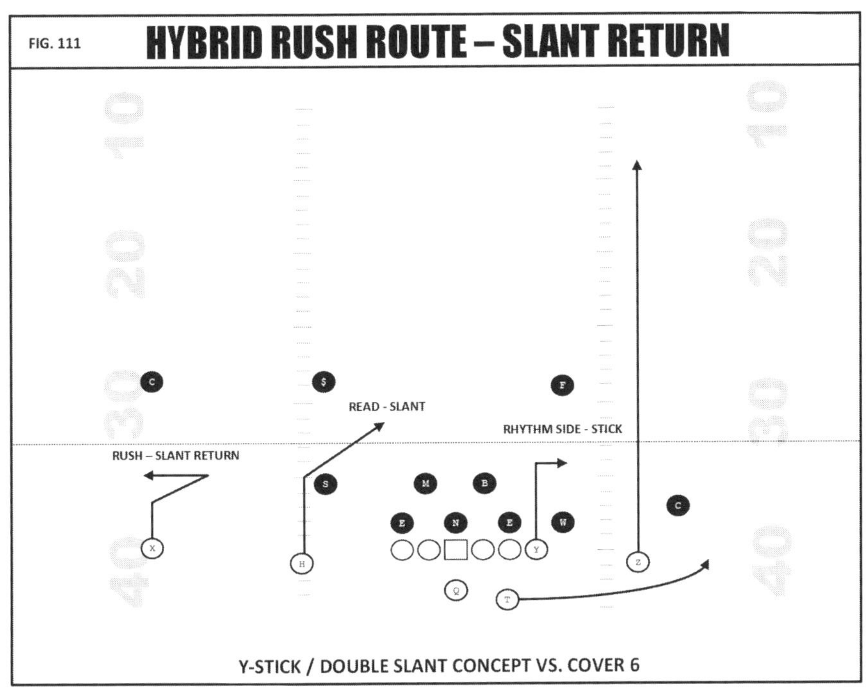
FIG. 111
HYBRID RUSH ROUTE – SLANT RETURN
READ - SLANT
RHYTHM SIDE - STICK
RUSH – SLANT RETURN
Y-STICK / DOUBLE SLANT CONCEPT VS. COVER 6

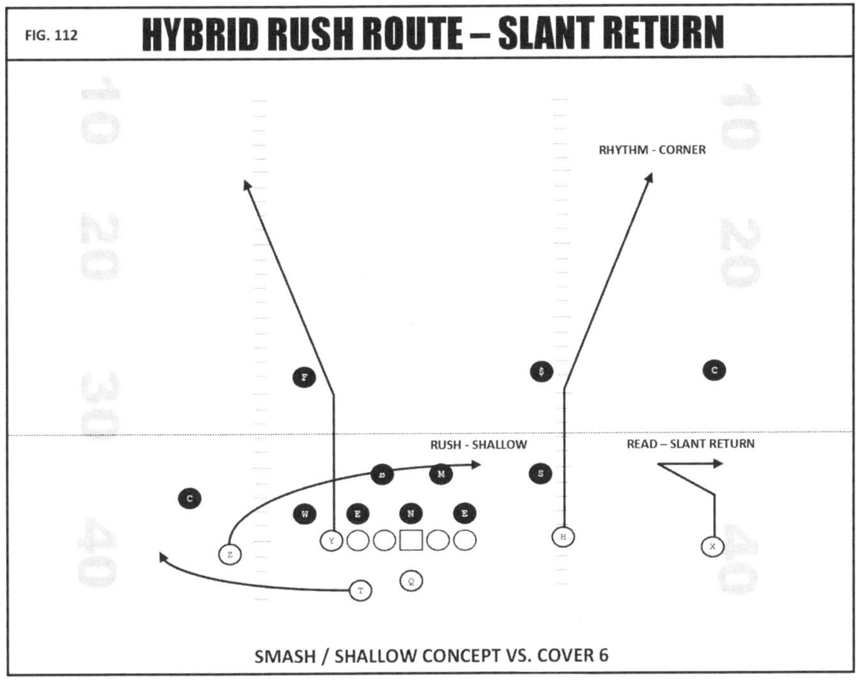
FIG. 112
HYBRID RUSH ROUTE – SLANT RETURN
RHYTHM - CORNER
RUSH - SHALLOW
READ – SLANT RETURN
SMASH / SHALLOW CONCEPT VS. COVER 6

is playing Man or Zone Coverage. Against Zone Coverage, the receiver takes 3 vertical steps to threaten the defender. On the 3rd step, the receiver breaks on the Slant. The receiver will sell the slant for 4 steps, sticking his foot in the ground and breaking back toward the sidelines. The receiver must stay flat and not drift for depth on the break. This prevents the defender from under-cutting the route as he attempts to recover. (FIG. 113)

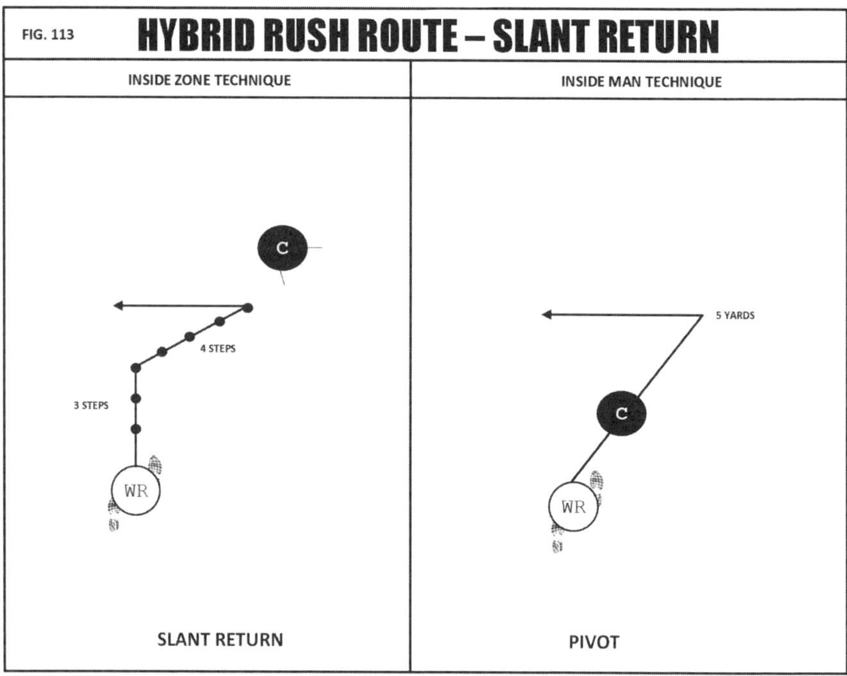

Against Man Coverage, the receiver must adjust his route stem. A press-man defender can impede the vertical stem and double-move break of the Slant Return. The receiver runs a Pivot Route instead. A Pivot Route takes an immediate inside-release to 5 yards. The receiver sticks his foot in the ground and breaks flat, holding the break line at 5 yards.

Pivot Route: The pivot route is a great route versus Man but is also good against Zone. (FIG. 114)

The Pivot Route is a landmark route that can adjust its break and depth based on post-snap defender reactions. This route requires a receiver to process the coverage and make the proper stem, and break based on the real-time reaction of the defense. These break rules are designed

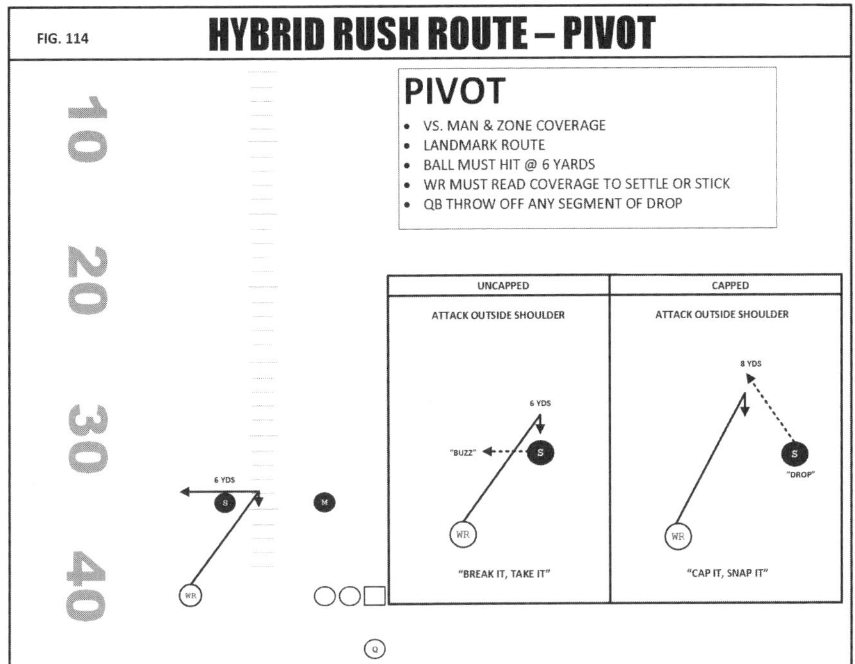

to counter the different movements of linebackers in Zone Coverage. The quarterback must also be able to process these movement rules for the route as well. The depth and decision-making of the break can place the route at different points in the timeline.

The Snag concept is assembled around the Pivot Route. The Hybrid Rush Pivot Route provides versatility within the Snag concept. This is executed by the Pivot Route's ability to adjust its break based on the post-snap reactions of the defense. (FIG. 115)

EXAMPLE: Against Zone Coverage, the quarterback can go through his base Rhythm progression and ***Rhythm – Corner, Read – Pivot, and Rush – Arrow.***

Zone Coverage provides time for the Pivot Route to find UNCAPPED space between defenders. This extra time allows the Hybrid Pivot Rush Route to be used as a Read Route in the progression time line.

If the defense decides to bring a Man Blitz, then the Pivot Route will adjust with an immediate stick and accelerate out of the break to run away from the Man defender. Against this look, the quarterback can go straight to the best mismatched Pivot Route and use it as a Quick-Game Rush Route in the progression.

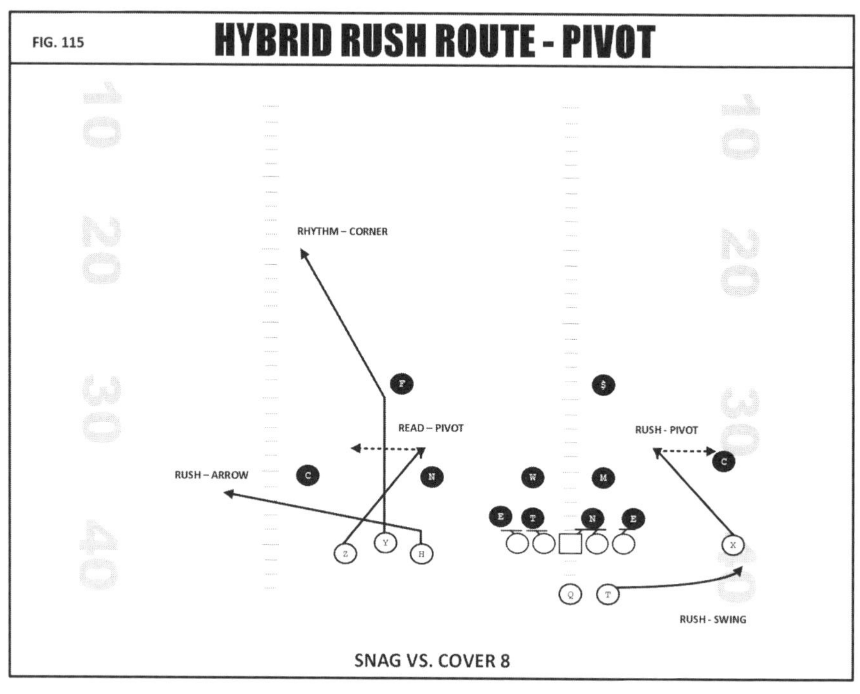
FIG. 115
HYBRID RUSH ROUTE - PIVOT
RHYTHM – CORNER
READ – PIVOT
RUSH – ARROW
RUSH - PIVOT
RUSH - SWING
F
$
C
N
W
M
E
T
N
E
C
Z
Y
H
X
Q
T
SNAG VS. COVER 8

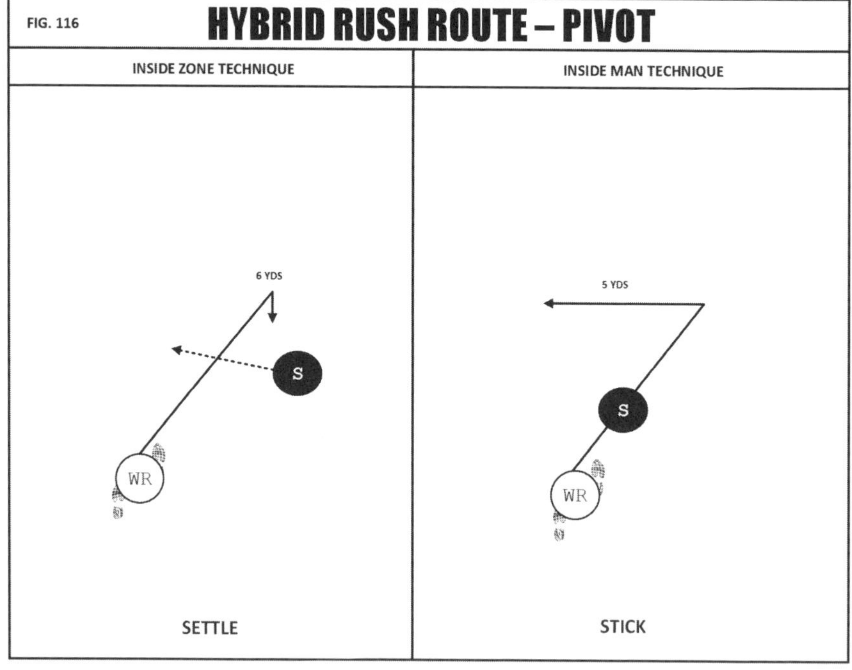
FIG. 116
HYBRID RUSH ROUTE – PIVOT
INSIDE ZONE TECHNIQUE
INSIDE MAN TECHNIQUE
6 YDS
S
WR
SETTLE
5 YDS
S
WR
STICK

The receiver's general rule at the line-o-scrimmage is to determine Man or Zone Coverage. (FIG. 116)

Against Zone Coverage, he must next locate the apex defender. The apex defender is the first linebacker who is outside the end-man on the line of scrimmage and inside the next eligible receiver. The Pivot Route running will attack the outside shoulder of the apex linebacker and attempt to get over the top of that linebacker to settle on the other side of his hip. If the apex linebacker Drops over 8 yards, then the receiver will settle the Pivot Route in front of him instead of getting over the top of him.

Against Man Coverage, the receiver takes the easiest release against the Man defender and runs inside to a depth of 5 yards. The receiver then sticks his foot in the ground and breaks out at 5 yards, holding the break-line.

Cruise Route: The Cruise Route is a Hybrid Rush Route that attacks both Man and Zone Coverages. (FIG. 117)

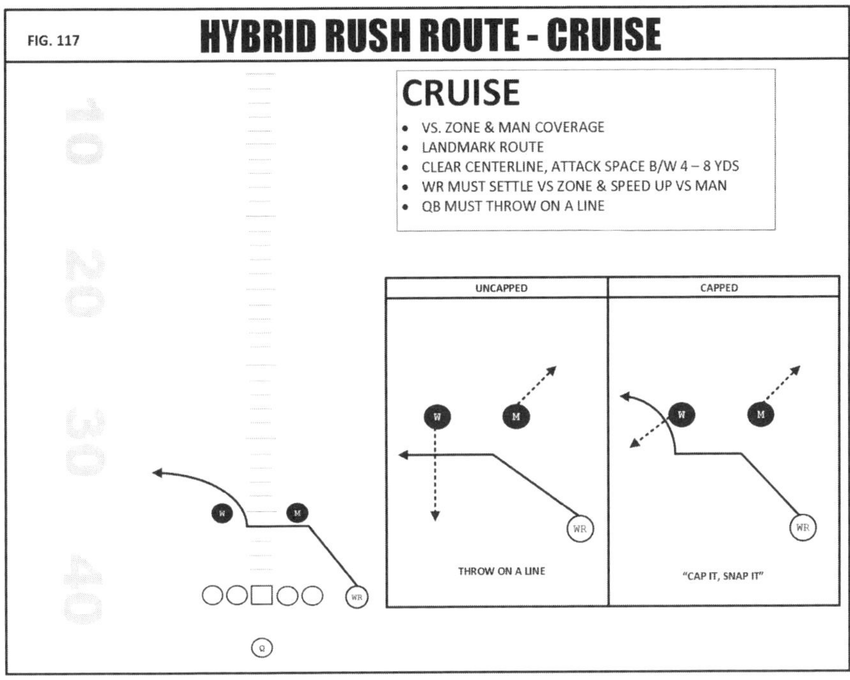

The Cruise is like the Shallow Route but can adjust the depth of the break beyond 4 yards, giving it Read Route properties. The Cruise Route clears the centerline and attacks space between 4 – 8 yards. The Cruise

Route allows a receiver freedom to search for space if a defender is CAPPING the beginning of the route. The Cruise Route must settle in Zone Coverage and keep moving in Man Coverage.

This weakside Flood concept out of a tight-end trips nub formation shows an example of the Cruise Route in action. (FIG. 118)

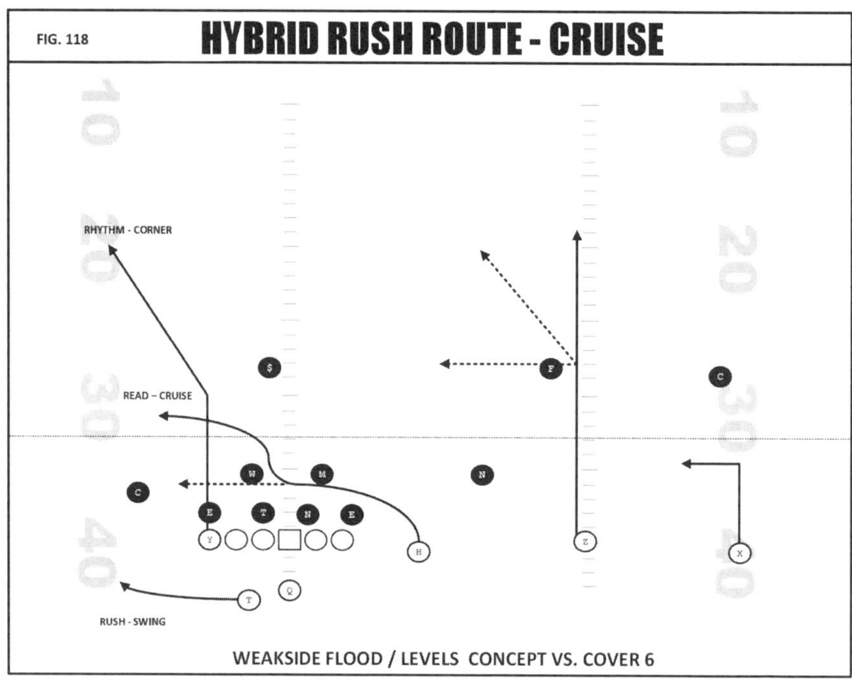

Against Zone Coverage, the quarterback would: ***Rhythm – Corner, Read – Cruise, Rush – Swing and then release.***

If the defense brought any interior pressure with the Mike or Will linebacker, then the Cruise Route would convert to a Rush Shallow Route. The quarterback could then throw the Rush Shallow Route as a "hot."

Against Zone Coverage, the receiver attacks the centerline at a depth of 4 yards. The receiver determines whether to settle or stair-step to the next level based on the CAP of the inside linebackers. If the linebackers split and Drops into hook Zones, then the receiver will settle. If the linebackers attempt to collision and CAP, then the receiver will stair-step to UNCAPPED space around the hard-deck line between 7-10 yards. (FIG. 119)

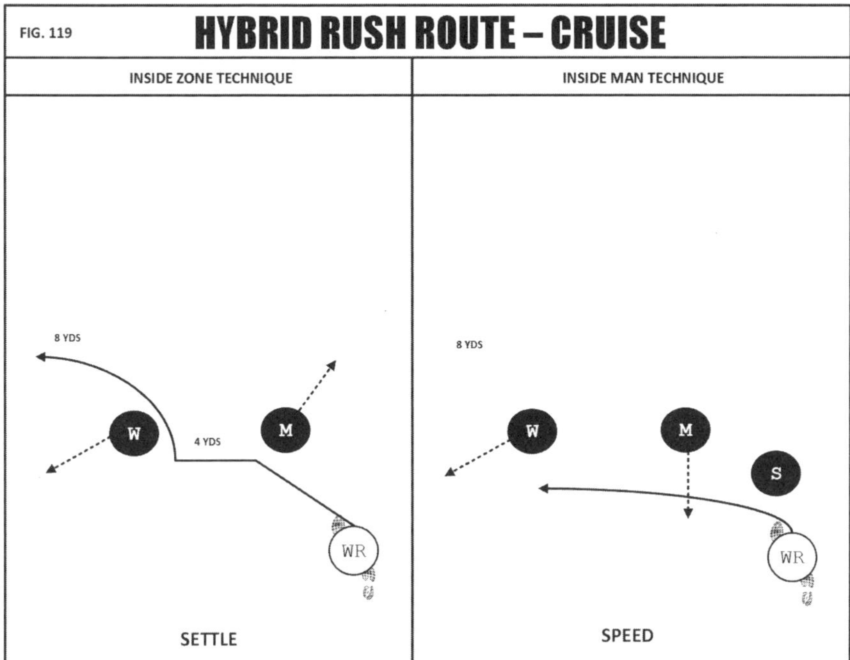

Against Man Coverage, the receiver takes an immediate inside release and runs a Shallow no deeper than 1 yard from the line of scrimmage. The receiver maintains his speed all the way across the centerline as he attempts to create separation from the Man defender.

Whip Route: The Whip Route is a Hybrid Rush Route that attacks both Man and Zone Coverage. (FIG. 120)

The Whip Route is run off 4 vertical + 4 out-break steps. The ball must hit at 6 yards against Man Coverage and no more than 8 yards against Zone Coverage. The Whip Route protects the quick-out that is consistently being CAPPED by an outside-leveraged defender. There are certain defensive coverages that align an apex player or rotated safety with outside leverage over an inside receiver. The Whip is a good route to use to attack this technique.

The Whip Route is mostly used as a tag adjustment off combos that use a Quick-Out Route. For example, the Fade-Out combination creates the initial stretch to create space within the Y-Cross concept. (FIG. 121)

The Whip Route can provide a space-advantage opportunity for defenders who are CAPPING the quick out, post-snap.

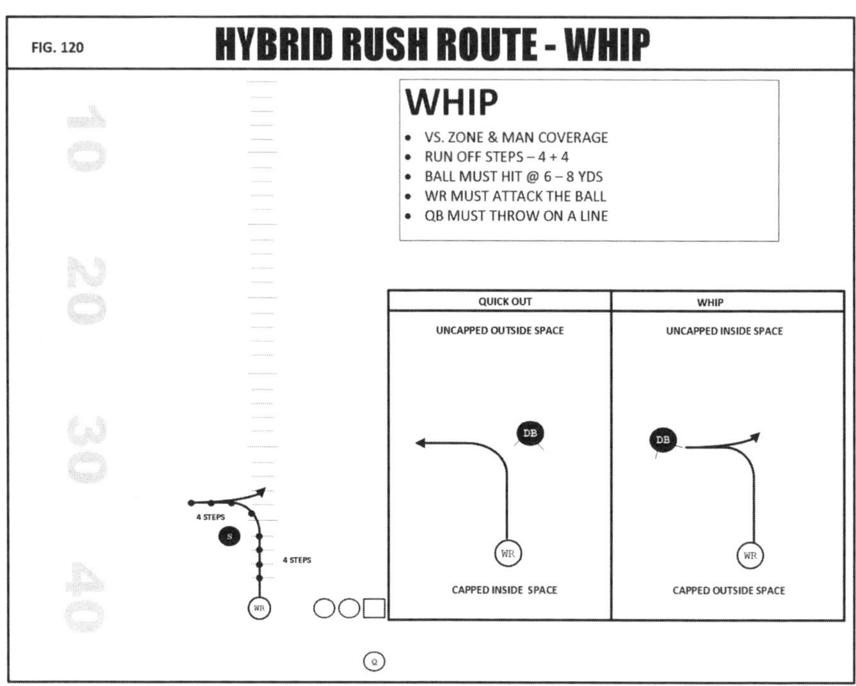

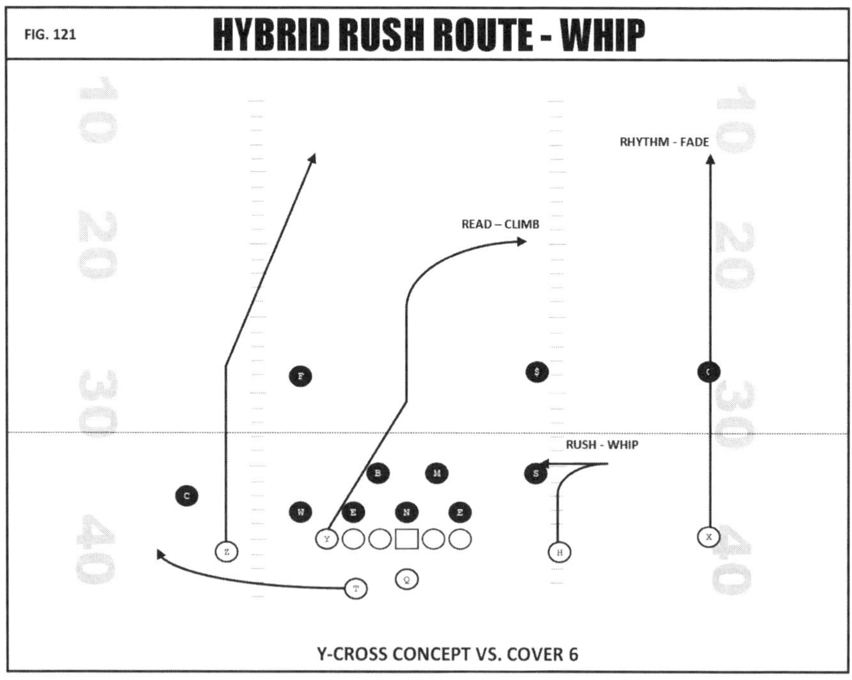

Y-CROSS CONCEPT VS. COVER 6

The receiver running the Whip Route against a Zone defender attacks vertical for 4 steps. The receiver breaks out on the 4th step, selling the Quick-Out Route. On the 4th step of the Quick-Out Break, the receiver again sticks his foot in the ground and breaks back inside, working to UNCAPPED space. The receiver has more freedom to work from 6-8 yards on the in-break of the whip route against Zone Coverage. (FIG. 122)

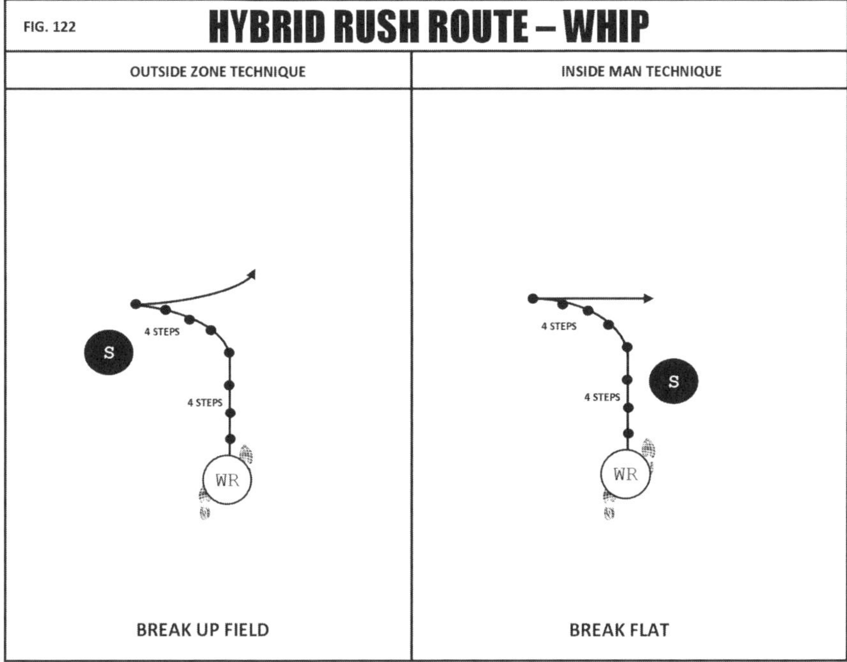

Against Man Coverage, the receiver takes the same steps but must break flat at 6 yards, holding the break-line to prevent the Man defender from under-cutting the route on the recovery.

Jerk Route: The Jerk Route is A Hybrid Rush Route that is good against both Man and Zone Coverage. (FIG. 123)

The Jerk Route is a landmark route with different break depths based on post-snap defender reactions. The Jerk Route is like the Pivot Route but adjusts its breaks to attack inside-space instead of outside-space. The Jerk Route protects the Pivot Route against defenders who are pushing the under coverage toward the pivot to Flood flat-space coverage to a side.

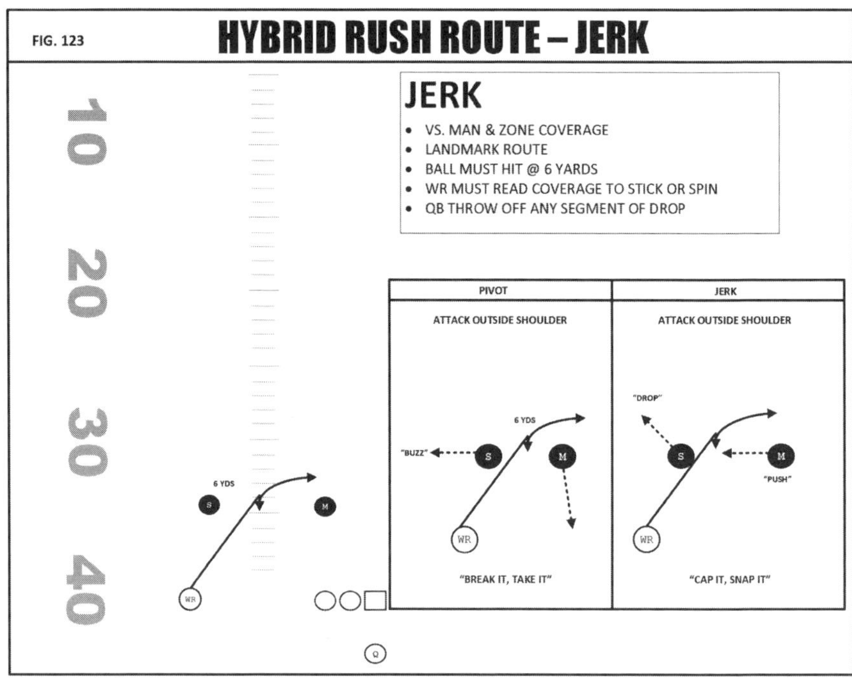
FIG. 123
HYBRID RUSH ROUTE – JERK
JERK
VS. MAN & ZONE COVERAGE
LANDMARK ROUTE
BALL MUST HIT @ 6 YARDS
WR MUST READ COVERAGE TO STICK OR SPIN
QB THROW OFF ANY SEGMENT OF DROP
PIVOT
ATTACK OUTSIDE SHOULDER
"BUZZ"
6 YDS
"BREAK IT, TAKE IT"
JERK
ATTACK OUTSIDE SHOULDER
"DROP"
"PUSH"
"CAP IT, SNAP IT"
6 YDS
10
20
30
40

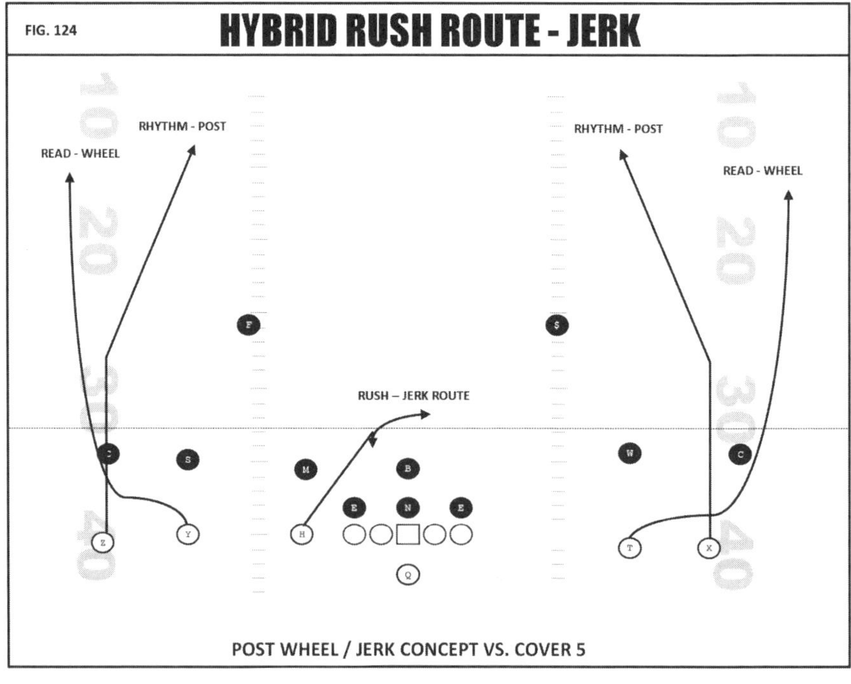
FIG. 124
HYBRID RUSH ROUTE - JERK
READ - WHEEL
RHYTHM - POST
RUSH – JERK ROUTE
RHYTHM - POST
READ - WHEEL
POST WHEEL / JERK CONCEPT VS. COVER 5

The Jerk Route can be incorporated into many concepts. (FIG. 124)

Using it within a 5-wide empty formation is common. This formation places the Jerk Route running against a middle linebacker, which poses a mismatch against most defenses. The primary Rhythm progression in this concept would be to ***Rhythm – Best Post, Read – Wheel, Rush – Jerk, and then release.***

A receiver running the Jerk Route starts the stem, attacking the outside shoulder of the first linebacker inside of him. If the linebacker buzzes flat, then the receiver works over the top of him and settles to UN-CAPPED space on the other side of the hip. If the linebackers are pushing the under-coverage, then the receiver will Jerk the route over the top of the 2nd linebacker and settle to UNCAPPED space on the other side of him. This requires Read timing, so the receiver can set up the route and determine the best space to attack. (FIG. 125)

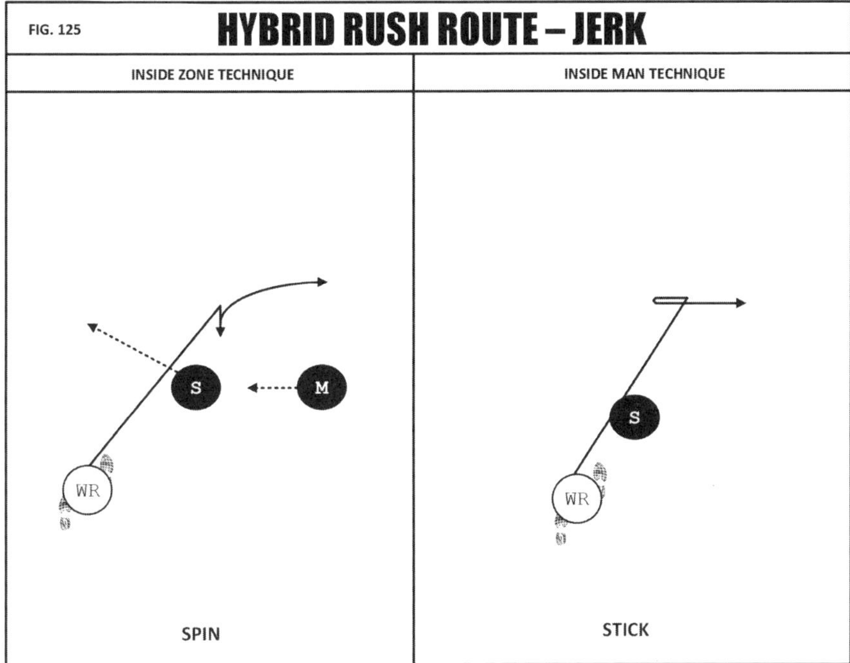

The Jerk Route is also an effective route to use against a Man defender who is over-aggressive with CAPPING the first break of a route. For example, if a receiver is running a Pivot Route against Man Coverage, and the defender is aggressive on the break-out of the Pivot and is under-cutting the route, then the Jerk Route will counter the CAP. The receiver running the Jerk against Man will take the easiest release, attacking at an inside-break to 5 yards. At the break-point, the receiver works out to simulate a Pivot Route. As the defender attempts to undercut the Pivot Route break, then the receiver sticks his outside foot in the ground and breaks across the defender's face to attack the UNCAPPED space inside.

CHAPTER 9

Understanding Release Routes

UNDERSTANDING RELEASE ROUTES

The release phase of the R4 process was built to provide exit strategies for the quarterback. The strategies are comprised of instinctive moves on how to avoid defensive pocket-pressure, as well as how to extend the timeline on plays in which all route-space was CAPPED for the initial progression. Over time, the release phase evolved to form a family of release routes that are designed to fit outside the normal time constraints of the Rhythm, Read and Rush Route families.

Release routes break over 15 yards, have more than 2 moves, or contains break designs that are more favorable with movement outside the pocket. The release route family requires an extended timeline to maximize the route design. Most release routes will require a gap escape, pocket movement like bootleg or sprint out, or 8-9 Man pass protection.

Hitch and Go Comeback Route: The Hitch and Go Comeback is an example of a release route. This route breaks over 15 yards and requires more than 2.6 seconds of time to develop on a normal Drop timeline. The Hitch and Go Comeback attacks both Man and Zone Coverage. This route is effective against defenders who are less likely to bite on a double move and risk getting beat deep vertically. The Hitch and Go Comeback will break at 20 yards. The ball must be thrown on a line and hit at 18 yards. (FIG. 126)

The Hitch and Go Comeback can be inserted in variety of ways to advance a concept. One way is to provide a release route option if the base progression of a concept is CAPPED. For example, if a quarterback is progressing through a ***Rhythm – Cross, Read – Slide Corner, and Rush – Arrow*** and confirms all are CAPPED, then he will gap escape away from the routes and look for the ***Release – Hitch and Go Comeback Route.*** The double move and extended depth of the route break syncs with the release of the quarterback outside the pocket.

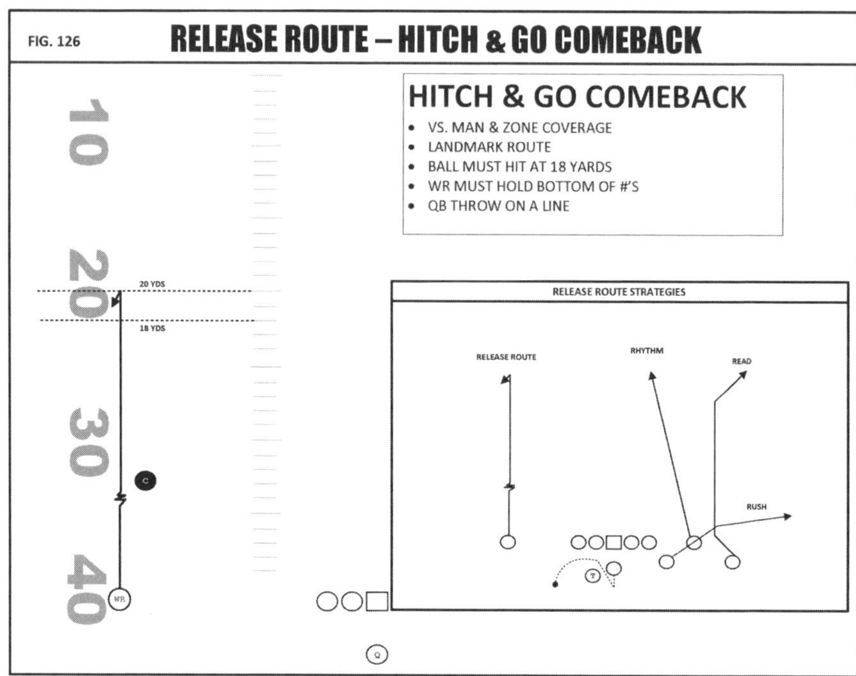

Deep Dig, Curl, or Comeback: The Deep Dig, Curl, or Comeback are three types of intermediate route that go behind the intermediate route depth and break on the timeline. These routes break from 18-25 yards based on the concept design employed by the coach. (FIG. 127)

One of the ways the Deep Dig, Curl or Comeback release routes can be used is in situational 3rd down and long concepts. For example, in this concept we will use a Dash half-roll protection to increase the timeline for the deep release routes to develop. The quarterback can Rhythm – Slide Corner because he has elongated the timeline with the half-roll. On the 5th step of the roll, the quarterback will ***Rhythm – Slide Corner.*** If the Slide Corner is CAPPED, he will then ***Release to the Deep Dig or Curl.*** The release phase informs the quarterback that he will have to move or gap escape in or out of the pocket to create time and space for the deep throw to be made.

Shallow Wheel Route: The Shallow Wheel Route is another example of a Release Route. This is a specialized route that is often run by a tight end as a throwback explosive play off sprint-out action. This route breaks over 15 yards and requires more than 2.6 seconds of time on the Drop timeline to develop. The route can also be used off bootleg

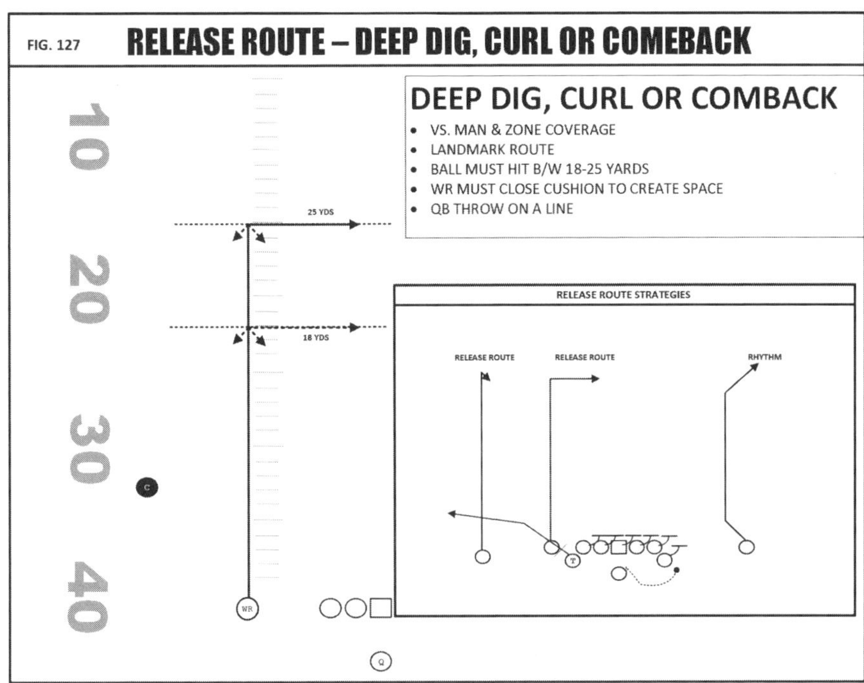

FIG. 127 **RELEASE ROUTE – DEEP DIG, CURL OR COMEBACK**

play-action, as well. The receiver running this route must break flat down the line of scrimmage. The goal is to step down and chip or rub the down defensive lineman to the inside to give the illusion of a run or pin block on the perimeter. The receiver will continue to work down the line until he crosses the centerline. After the receiver crosses the center line, he will gain depth toward the numbers and then turn up-field to run the wheel action of the route. (FIG. 128)

The quarterback who has a Shallow Wheel Route included in the concept will use it as a release option if his base routes in the progression are CAPPED. For example, if the quarterback is sprinting out to Snag concept, he will progress the ***Rhythm – Corner, to Read – Drag, to Rush – Pivot.*** If all those routes are CAPPED he will pull up and check backside for the ***Release – Shallow Wheel.*** Using sprint-out protection helps in extending the timeline and creating the space necessary for the Shallow Wheel to break the CAP of the defense.

Out and Up Comeback Route: The Out and Up Comeback Route is a release route that attacks both Man and Zone Coverage. This route has more than 2 route breaks, which requires additional time than the re-

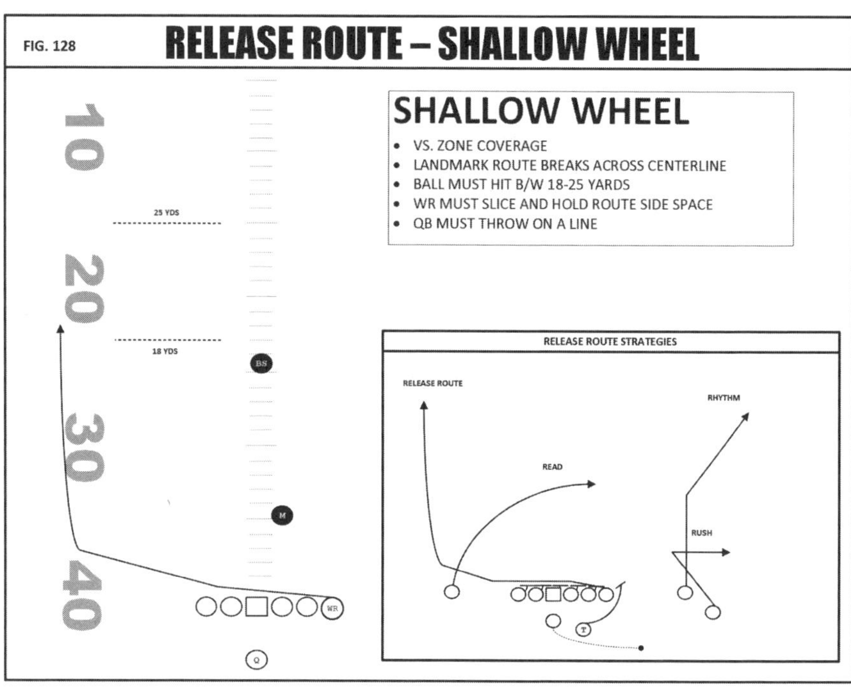
FIG. 128
RELEASE ROUTE – SHALLOW WHEEL
SHALLOW WHEEL
• VS. ZONE COVERAGE
• LANDMARK ROUTE BREAKS ACROSS CENTERLINE
• BALL MUST HIT B/W 18-25 YARDS
• WR MUST SLICE AND HOLD ROUTE SIDE SPACE
• QB MUST THROW ON A LINE
10
20
30
40
25 YDS
18 YDS
BS
M
WR
Q
RELEASE ROUTE STRATEGIES
RELEASE ROUTE
READ
RHYTHM
RUSH
T

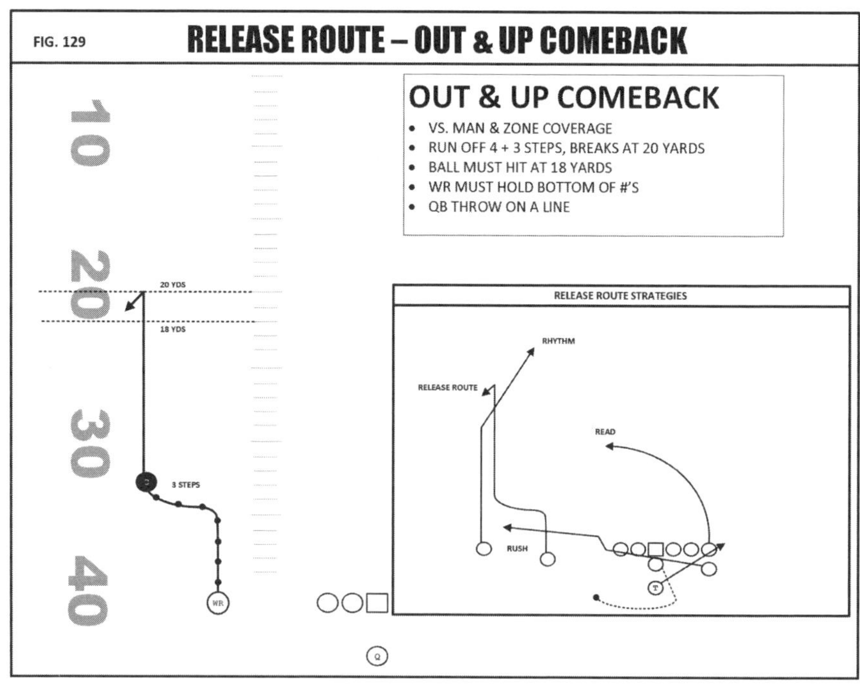
FIG. 129
RELEASE ROUTE – OUT & UP COMEBACK
OUT & UP COMEBACK
• VS. MAN & ZONE COVERAGE
• RUN OFF 4 + 3 STEPS, BREAKS AT 20 YARDS
• BALL MUST HIT AT 18 YARDS
• WR MUST HOLD BOTTOM OF #'S
• QB THROW ON A LINE
10
20
30
40
20 YDS
18 YDS
3 STEPS
WR
Q
RELEASE ROUTE STRATEGIES
RHYTHM
RELEASE ROUTE
READ
RUSH
T

lease move generates. The Out and Up Comeback is run off steps and breaks at a landmark of 20 yards. The ball must be thrown on a line at 18 yards. (FIG. 129)

The receiver will run 4 vertical steps and break for 3 steps on the out route. On the 3rd step of the out-break, the receiver will stick the outside foot in the ground and get vertical to 20 yards. At 20 yards, the receiver will foot-fire stick and break back to 18 yards and attack the ball.

The Out-and-Up Comeback can be used with max protection, different pocket movement protections or as a gap-escape release strategy. One example can be shown off a naked bootleg play-action. On this play, the quarterback is faking a wide Zone run to the right, and bootleg to the left. On the boot leg, the quarterback will go through his base progression. The Rhythm is the post, the read is the drag, and the Rush is the strike route in the flat. If all the routes in the base progression are CAPPED, then the quarterback can work the Out and Up Comeback as the release route. This is made possible by the extended timing and depth that the Out and Up Comeback takes to develop.

Release routes provide a designed route to throw to off-gap escapes that occur at the end of a CAPPED progression. They also add explosive play opportunities when attacked to max protection or pocket moving protections. There are other routes that can be added to this family, as long as they follow the rules of the route's break and timeline.

Post-Corner-Post Route: The Post-Corner-Post Route is a release route that attacks both Man and Zone Coverages. This route is another specialized route that requires release timing. The Post-Corner-Post has 3 route-breaks that place it over the standard Drop timeline. To increase time for this route to develop, the route will have to be used in a pocket movement protection or with extra blockers in protection. This Post-Corner-Post is run off steps and must be hit over 35 yards. (FIG. 130)

The receiver must be able to accelerate out of breaks and take the proper steps to set up route-side space. The receiver will push vertical for 5 steps, break in on the Post for 3 steps, then break out on a corner for 3 steps, and finally break on the Post route. The angle of attack on the final Post Break is relative to the CAP of the defender.

The quarterback must buy time for the Post-Corner-Post Route to develop. One way to do this is by using an 8- or 9-man pass protection off play-action. In this example, an 8-man pass protection is being used off a Zone fake. The quarterback will progress the Rhythm – Corner first. If the Rhythm Corner is CAPPED, then the quarterback will release to the Post-Corner-Post Route. The quarterback must step up in the pocket, or buy the extra time needed, to throw the release route.

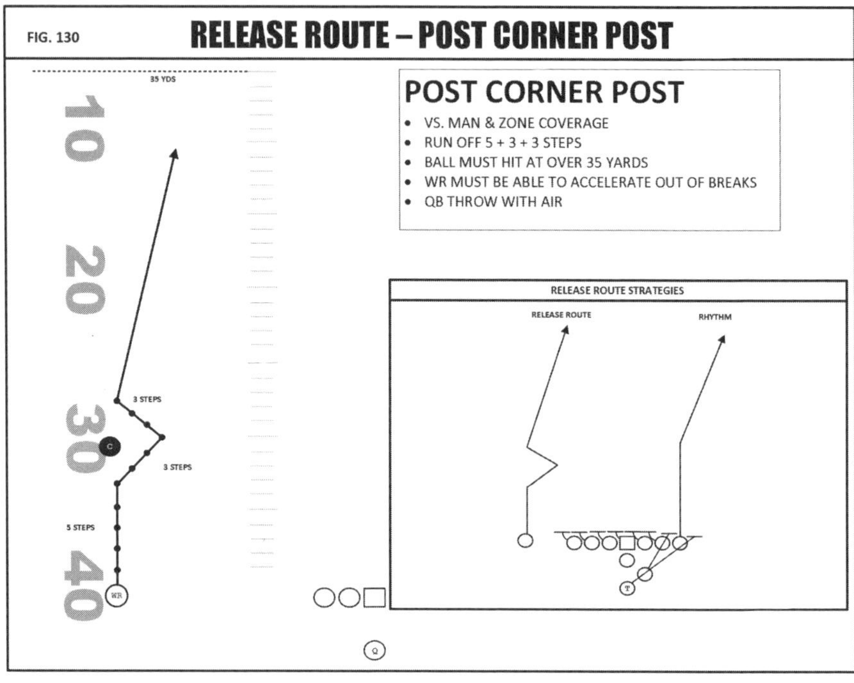

CHAPTER 10

R4 Progression Platforms

RHYTHM • READ • RELEASE • RUSH

R4

R4 PROGRESSION PLATFORMS

The Marines' strategy for MOUT and CQB prior to 2004 was to use speed and surprise with a top-down approach. Throwing a grappling hook and climbing to the top, repelling down from a helicopter to the top, and jumping from an adjacent building to the top, were all early top-to-down methods of entry into a defended building. The problem: This top-to-down mindset didn't adhere to the changing environment and adapting enemy in Iraq.

Heavy gear and snipers negated the rope-climb tactic. RPGs and other rockets inhibited the repelling techniques. And when the enemy started shooting out the ceilings of the buildings they occupied, the jumping from one building to the next didn't work either. The enemy was using the top-to-down entry tactics against them. They were forcing them to come through the front door where all their firepower was focused. When you face an enemy that knows where you will enter, and they are willing to die for that... well that doesn't usually end well.

This was the turning point for the Marines and Special Forces in Iraq in 2004. They quickly learned that attacking defended space in close-quarters required the ability to use different progressions of entry. If the same progression to enter a room was used, then the enemy would adapt and use that progression against them. This realization created a context for new CQB tactics that had previously not been considered.

The U.S. Military would go back to the drawing board and develop new entry progressions that never looked the same to the enemy. Sometimes the Marines would enter a building from the top-down. The next time they would enter from the bottom-up. Then to throw the enemy off, they would use explosives to create a side entry. It wasn't just the type of entry approach that changed, it was also the order and pathways team members used to move through close-quarter spaces.

The Special Forces created different movement patterns and techniques to protect blind sides and potential weaknesses that were different from the traditional 4-man stack patterns. If the soldiers stayed within the rules of space and time, the strategy of creating different entry patterns was endless. This created a new weapon of adaptability that changed the tide of war in the Middle East.

Inspired by the best, this same adaptation was infused into the passing game with R4. Most of the intermediate passing game was tied to a top-down progression approach. Some coaches preferred a bottom-up progression approach. Other coaches wanted a single-side space approach by focusing on 2 routes attacking a single defender. As the Military discovered in Iraq, no matter what method you use, if you cannot adapt and create versatility with simplicity, then the advantage goes to the enemy.

Understanding the relationships of route timing and space non-negotiables allows coaches to accelerate their ability to create and call concepts that best attack a defensive coverage. The real magic behind a great concept is how you teach your quarterback to progress through it. The bottom line is that the highest need of the quarterback is to have a reads

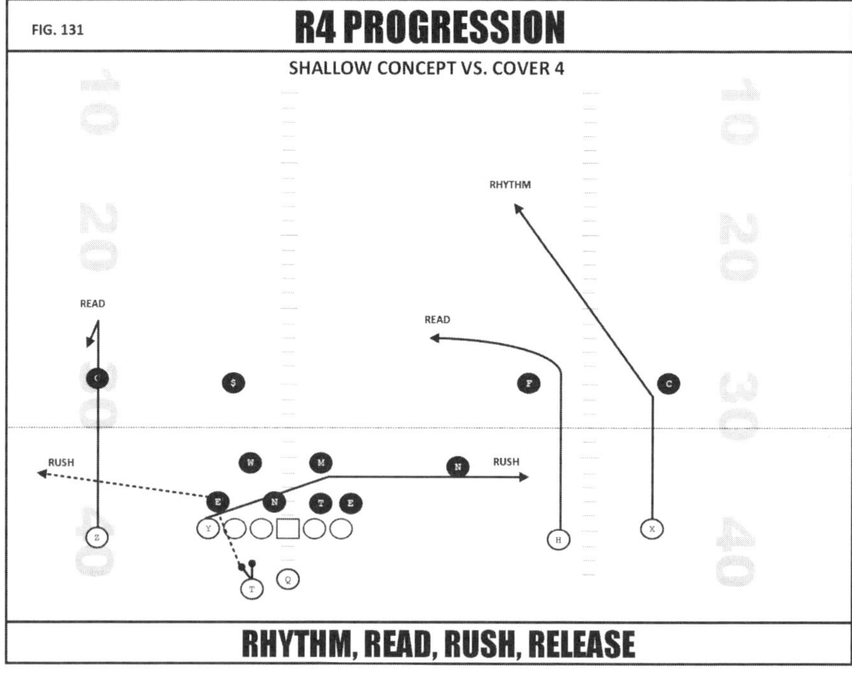

and recognition system that allows him to navigate through concepts in different ways with a simple set of rules in real-time. The R4 system provides that for any quarterback in any offense.

Navigating a quarterback through a progression of a concept is much easier when the "why" behind route relationships is known. Let's use this Air Raid shallow concept as an example. Based on the route family structure, we navigate through the concept in a Rhythm, Read and Rush progression due to the route-break timing. The defense's highest priority on a given pass play is to not get beat deep.

Therefore, the goal for the offense is to have the ability to take advantage of attacking vertical space when it is UNCAPPED. This forces the progression priority of the concept to Rhythm the post, then Read the dig, and Rush the shallow route. If those routes were CAPPED, we would next Release to the backside of the concept. If the quarterback felt the Rush, then he would throw the Rush shallow route as a hot. (FIG. 131)

Contrast reading the shallow concept against the way the Air Raid purists run it. Coaches within the Air Raid system "Peek" at the post-route pre-snap. The quarterback must determine if he likes the Post before the play begins. This greatly reduces the power of generating explosive plays, especially in pattern-reading, or disguising defenses that will adjust post-snap. From there the quarterback is taught to read the apex defender and progress in this order: 1- "hot route," 2-Dig, 3-Shallow, 4-Shoot, 5-Comeback. (FIG. 132)

Progressing through five routes within a 3-second Drop timeline is next to impossible, visually speaking. Saccadic eye movement (eye tracking from one object to another) from the best visual athletes occurs around .20 tenths of a second. This is the same time it takes to reset the feet in the pocket. This means that a quarterback that takes a Drop to process the defensive coverage and first route in a progression, followed by two resets steps, has time to navigate three route-spaces in less than three seconds. This is the problem with the Air Raid progression of the shallow concept. The progression teaching doesn't work with the physiology of the quarterback. As coaches, we want all the answers built into one progression in less than 3 seconds. But scientifically, that can't be done.

This is the dilemma that traps many coaches. It is the feeling of needing more plays or route options within plays to keep the defense from zeroing in on the concept that is being called. If the defense knows the

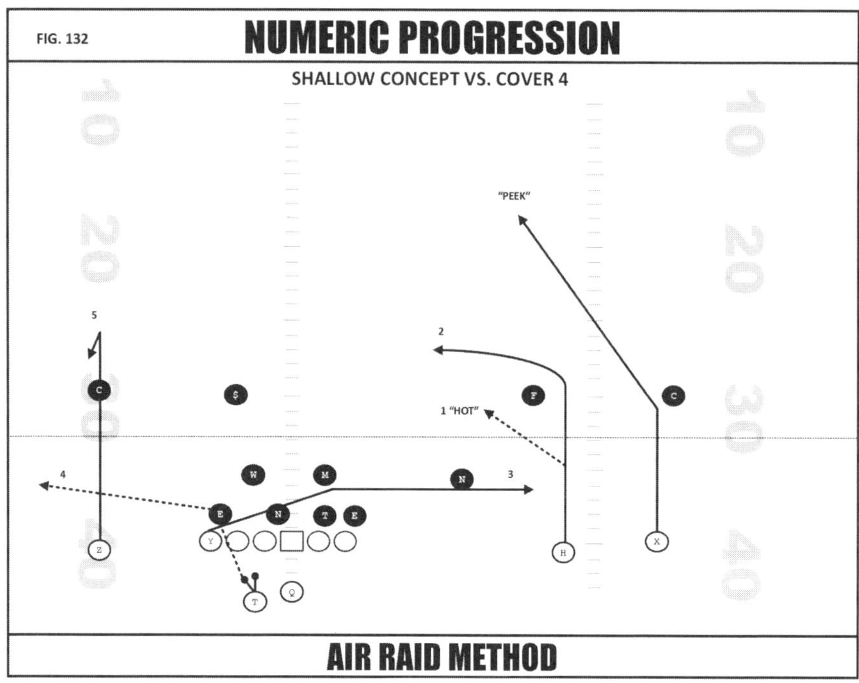

concept and the progression, then they can use those methods against the offense. This begs the question: How do coaches increase adaptability without adding more concepts? How do coaches communicate the best progression to use on a concept while maintaining the non-negotiable timing required by the quarterback's eyes and feet with the route breaks? This is the highest need of the modern passing game. It is creating adaptability within a concept. The key is doing it with simplicity that can operate under pressure. This is difficult to do unless you have a foundational structure rooted in the non-negotiables of football, along with a common language to accelerate it under pressure.

This dilemma gave rise to the creation of the R4 progression platforms. R4 progression platforms provide coaches and players the foundation to quickly adapt concepts under pressure. R4 progression platforms provide an organization structure that is set up with the same Rhythm, Read, Rush and Release containers as the route families. The Rhythm, Read, Rush and Release progression platforms define the "why" behind the progression. It also creates a context for adaptability with simplicity by communicating the intent behind the progression used.

RHYTHM PROGRESSION: Every pass concept has a design that is created to attack a specific coverage weakness or conflict-defender to a side of space. The highest defensive weakness determines the base progression. For example, the Air Raid shallow concept is a high-low Flood concept that is designed to attack a 2-high safety defense to a 3rd of the field. The Post and Dig create a high-low stretch on the quarters-safety and the Dig and Shallow create stretch on the apex linebacker. Therefore, we define the Post, Dig and Shallow as the Rhythm progression for the Air Raid shallow concept. The Rhythm progression is the primary progression for a concept based on the rational of core routes to attack a specific coverage. (FIG. 133)

> *The **Rhythm Progression** is the primary progression for a concept based on the rational of care routes to attack a specific coverage.*

When installing concepts with players in Spring ball or before the season, it is important to first implement only the Rhythm progression. Do not

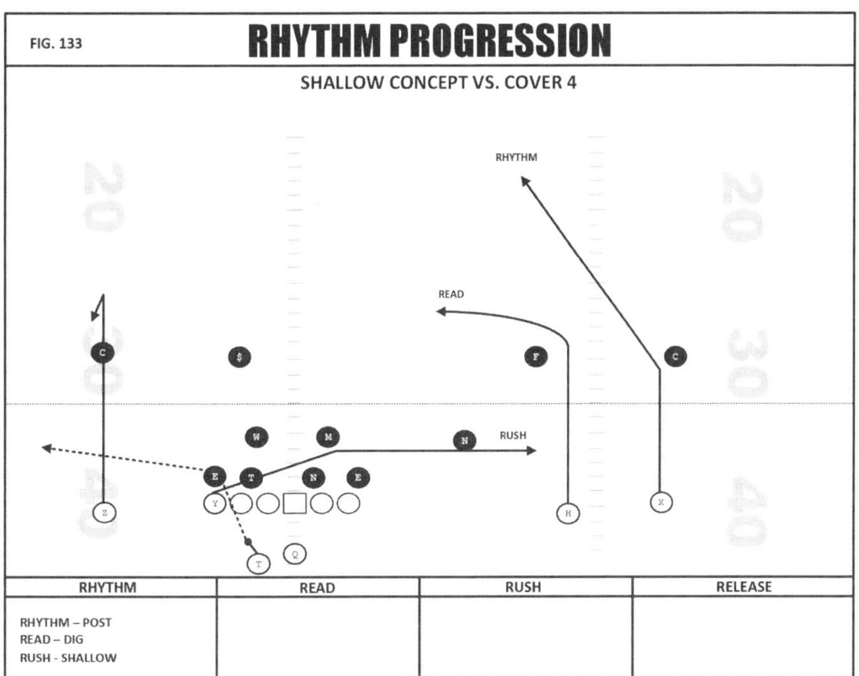

install or cover other progression options within a concept until they master the mechanics and method behind the primary progression of the play.

READ PROGRESSION: The goal for any pass concept should be to acquire the ability to attack the full field. While most plays do this, they lack the tools to teach the quarterback how to get to different parts of the field in-Rhythm under pressure.

> *A **Read Progression** is a secondary progression that attacks a different side of space or the most anticipated coverage adjustment to CAP the primary progression.*

EXAMPLE: We have called the Air Raid Shallow concept in the game and our box coach is watching the backside of the concept. He sees that the comeback route is UNCAPPED with the corner playing over and inside with a Cover-4 Zone technique. We can simply get our quarterback to that side of space by tagging or telling him to use a Read progression on the play. A Read Progression is a secondary progression that attacks a different side of space or the most

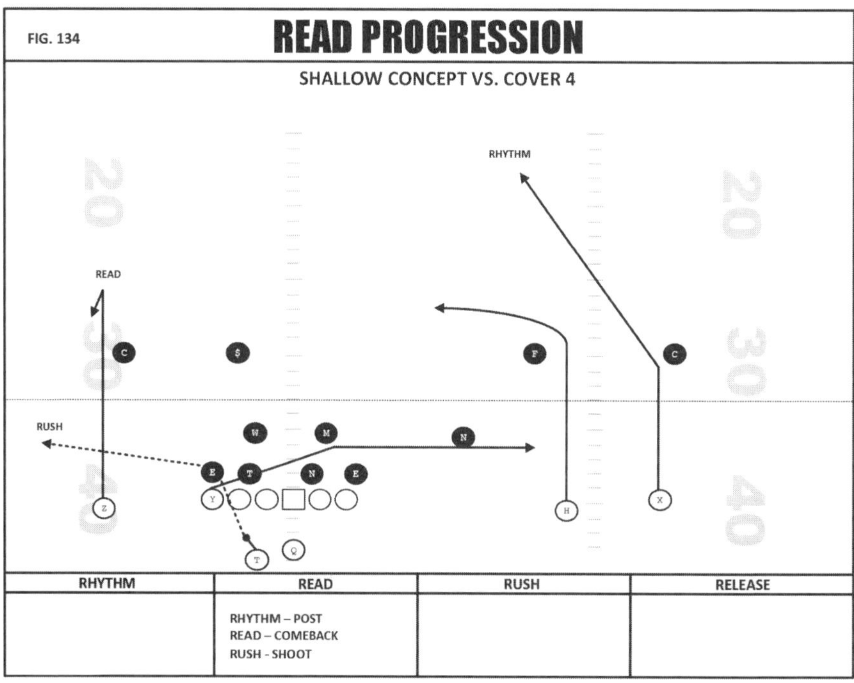

anticipated coverage adjustment to CAP the primary progression.

> A **Rush Progression** is an ancillary progression within a concept that elevates a Rush Route to replace a Rhythm Route in the progression.

A read progression for the Air Raid Shallow concept would be to progress the Rhythm – Post, Read-Comeback and Rush-Shoot route. (FIG. 134)

Another situation in which a read progression can be implemented is a pre-snap "check with me" situation, or a freeze-count situation where the quarterback and coach are trying to determine the base progression based on pre-snap defensive alignment. If the advantage is seen to the backside of the concept, then the coach can make a signal to the quarterback to use a Read progression instead of the Rhythm progression.

RUSH PROGRESSION: Another common situation that must be considered within concepts are how to handle Blitz pressure and Red Zone areas where vertical space is reduced. These situations require progressions that create horizontal stress and increase route availability below the

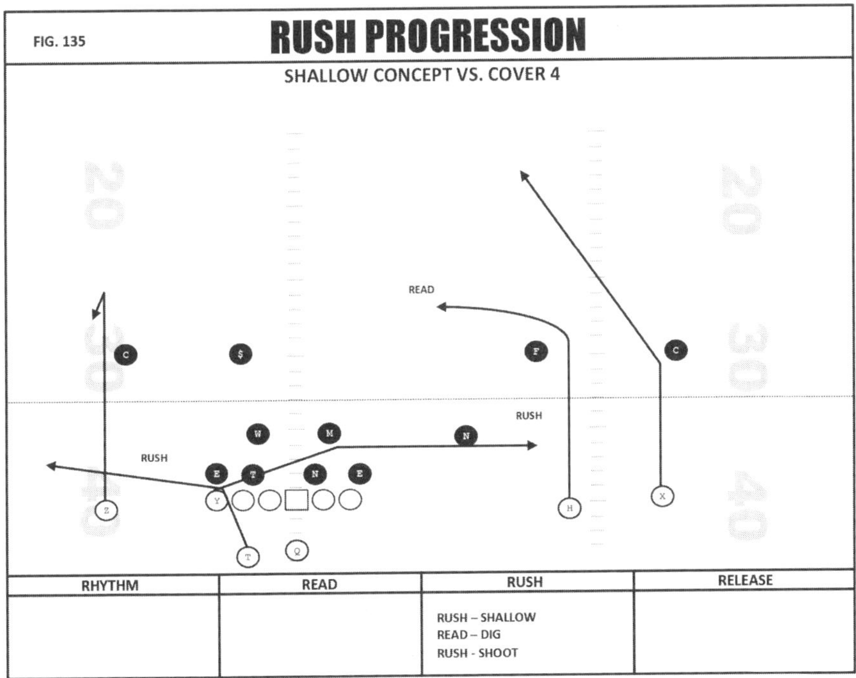

hard deck. Rush Progressions provide the platform for this to occur. A Rush Progression is an ancillary progression within a concept that elevates a Rush Route to replace a Rhythm Route in the progression. A Rush progression would progress starting with a Rush Route, to Read Route, to another Rush Route. (FIG. 135)

In the absence of 2 Rush Routes in the pass concept, a Rush progression platform could begin with a Rush Route, reset to a Read Route, and reset to another Read Route as a supplement to not having a second available Rush Route on the play. The 4-vertical concept would be an example of a scheme that uses a Rush progression with a Rush-Read-Read Route combination. We will discuss this in detail later.

> **The reason that a Rush Route can replace a Rhythm Route is because Rush Routes have universal properties that allow them to break open at any point in the timeline. Therefore, a Rush Route has break timing that corresponds with Rhythm Route breaks. This compatibility allows Rush Routes to replace Rhythm Routes in a progression and still maintain the same R4 timing as a base progression.**

Elevating the Rush Route to the first route in the progression places priority on a "hot" throw against an anticipated Blitz or can help to remove a defender faster to open a Read Route within the concept. A Rush progression creates a horizontal stretch on the defense, which can benefit red Zone situations or confidence building situations for a quarterback that may be struggling with his deep throws during a game. Rush progressions can also be used if there is a possible Blitz-threat tendency. If any of these situations are present, then after the play call we would tag, say or signal "Rush it" to our quarterback. This would alert him to use the Rush progression on that concept.

On the Air Raid Shallow concept, a Rush progression would alert the quarterback to elevate the Shallow Route 1st in the progression. The Rush progression would flow from a Rush-Shallow, to Read-Dig, to Rush-Shoot Route. This progression creates a maximum stress on the under coverage and allows the eyes to be in a better position to throw the shallow route "hot" in case of a Blitz.

RELEASE PROGRESSION: The final progression platform that we use with R4 is a Release Progression. A Release Progression is a game-planned or shot-play progression that is set up off defensive accelerator

*A **Release Progression** is a game-planned or shot-play progression that is set up off defensive accelerator reactions to a Rhythm, Read or Rush progressions.*

reactions to a Rhythm, Read or Rush progressions. Release progressions provide a one-off progression for concepts that are run more than once during a game. This is where the coach and players can get creative. (FIG. 136)

EXAMPLE: We have run the Air Raid Shallow concept twice in the game and hit the Dig on the first play, and Shallow on the second play, using a Primary Rhythm progression. On the backside, the Comeback Route has been seen twice by the boundary corner and we notice he is aggressively CAPPING the Comeback route on the break. The receiver running the comeback notices it, too. We have game-planned and practiced for this situation all week with the Release progression. The progression has informed the coaches and players to set it up and look for it during the game. The common language of R4 and the progression platform allows for easy communication to quickly take advantage of the defense.

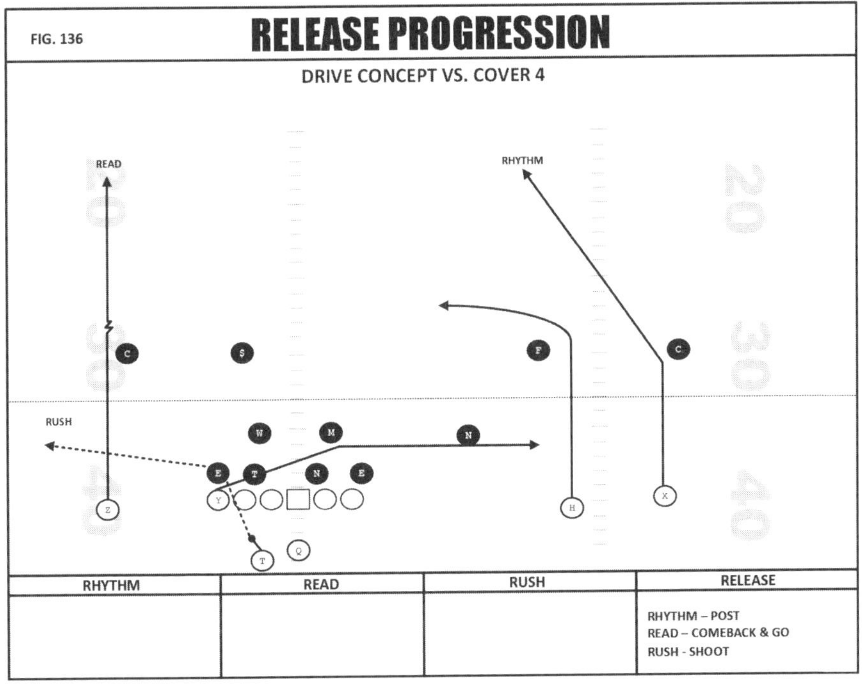

RHYTHM	READ	RUSH	RELEASE
			RHYTHM – POST READ – COMEBACK & GO RUSH - SHOOT

When the communication confirms that the comeback is being CAPPED, the coach can inform the quarterback by tagging the route adjustment on the play. The tagging of the route adjustment should inform the quarterback to use the Release progression. The progression would go as follows: ***Rhythm-Post, Read – Comeback and Go, Rush – Shoot.*** Release progressions are generally shot or situational route adjustments that are used only once during a game.

Many times, coaches get lost in the game-planning process, trying to overthink ways to attack the defense. The R4 progression platforms of Rhythm, Read, Rush and Release are designed to increase adaptability of concepts through simplicity. The platforms are present to provide guardrails to your decision-making so you will not get off-track.

The R4 progression platforms also allow the coach to increase versatility within a single concept. Having different ways to attack the defense with an existing play helps diminish the need for multiple different concepts to be taken into a game plan. The players and coaches can accelerate their decision-making and execution under pressure because they understand the network of progressions within a singular concept, along with the "why" they are needed.

It is important to note that not every concept will have a Rhythm, Read, Rush and Release progression. Some concepts are designed with a network of routes that only attack one specific coverage and do not allow them to fit within the context of all the R4 progression platforms.

R4 PROGRESSION PLATFORMS FOR THE DRIVE CONCEPT: Let's look at some other concepts to further show how R4 progression platforms increase adaptability within an existing concept. The Drive concept is a popular West Coast scheme made up of similar routes to the Air Raid shallow concept. There is one major distinction between the Air Raid Shallow concept and the West Coast Drive concept. The Shallow concept has the Dig and Shallow route breaking in *opposite* directions from the other. The Drive concept has the Dig and Shallow route breaking in the same direction as the other. (FIG. 137)

The West Coast method for progression through a Drive concept is like the Air Raid method in that the vertical routes are pre-snap Alert routes. The post-snap progression is reading the Shallow, to Dig, to Shoot Route. The Drive concept is a well-designed play that contains

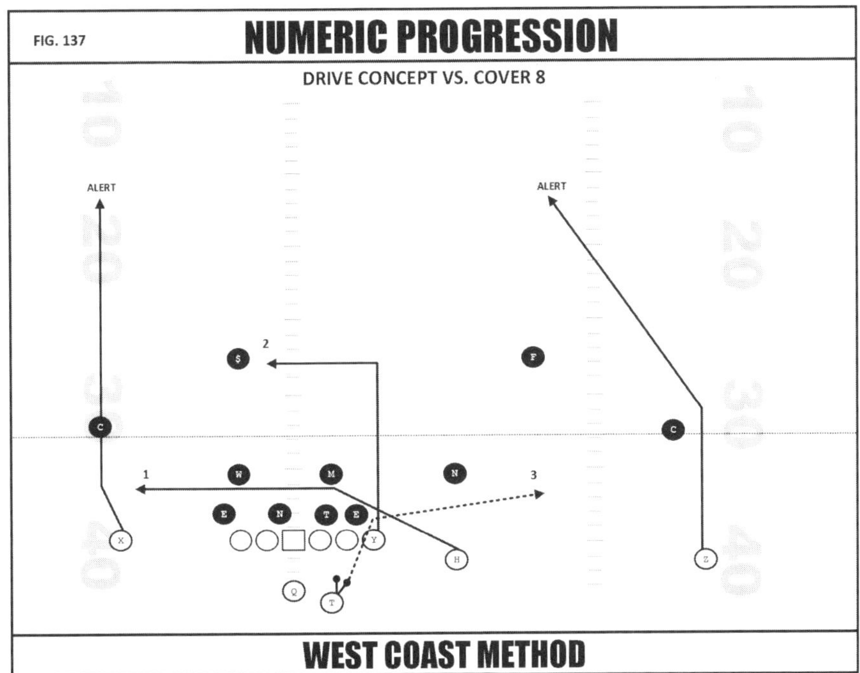

many progression possibilities. The R4 progression platforms create a simple workflow to organize the best navigation tools for the concept.

DRIVE CONCEPT – *RHYTHM PROGRESSION:* When determining the Rhythm progression for a concept, you must ask the question, "What is the main design of this concept used to attack?" The Drive concept is designed to create a high-low Flood to the weak side of a formation. This is effective since most defensive coverages rotate or push defenders towards the formational field side. The Dig and Shallow route breaking from the same side creates immediate stress on the boundary safety and inside linebackers. This stress helps to isolate the single side X receiver 1-on-1 with the boundary corner.

This 1-on-1 match-up is an important battle to win. The X receiver and the boundary corner are usually the best skill players on each side of the ball. Therefore, it is critical that the concepts used allow the X receiver different releases and route breaks to maximize the different coverages and techniques the defense will use to stop him. This need required us to manipulate the Drive concept to sync a progression that maximizes adaptability. (FIG. 138)

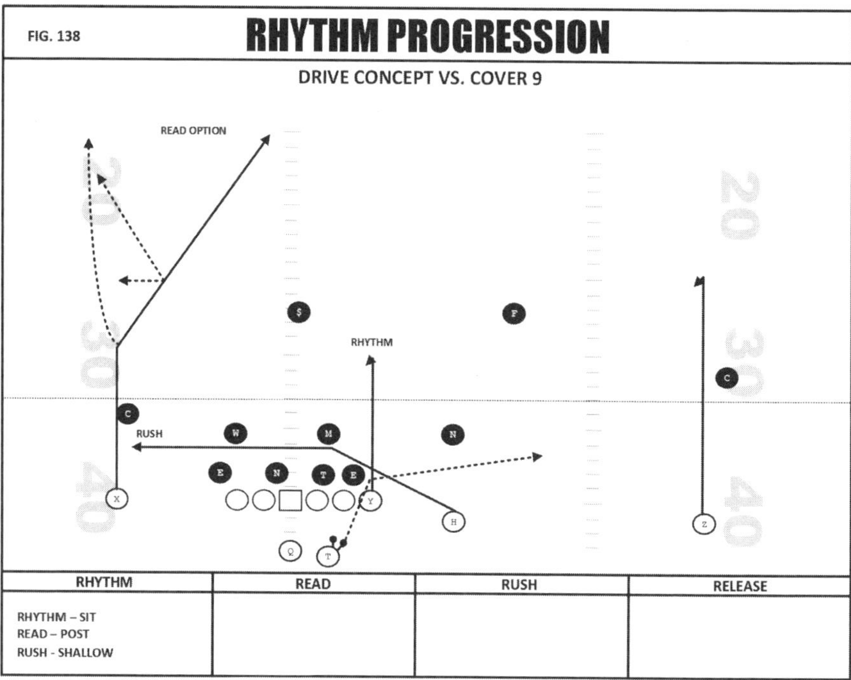

To do this, we supplemented a Rhythm-Sit Route to replace the Dig Route in the concept. This creates the same initial stretch of the Drive concept but allows us to first Rhythm the Sit. Rhythming the Sit route provides an interior Blitz-beater and forces the boundary safety to CAP-commit faster. This allows us to use the X receiver as a Read Option Route. The Base Route in this concept for the Read Option is a Read Post that breaks at 12 yards. We can tag different Read Route breaks like a Post-Corner or Post-Bench Route against defenders that are CAPPING inside-space. We can also tag other routes in the Read family like a Comeback. If the Read Route is CAPPED, then we work the Rush Shallow Route as a check down. The Rhythm progression for the ***Drive Concept is Rhythm – Sit, Read – Post, Rush – Shallow.***

Concepts built around a core receiver with multiple break options generates adaptability. The key to maintaining simplicity is keeping the same complementary routes and progression structure around the Read Option route. When installing Route Option concepts, it is best to begin by signaling or tagging the best anticipated route adjustment to the quarterback. The benefit of having the common language and sequential process of R4 is in the acceleration of coach and quarterback

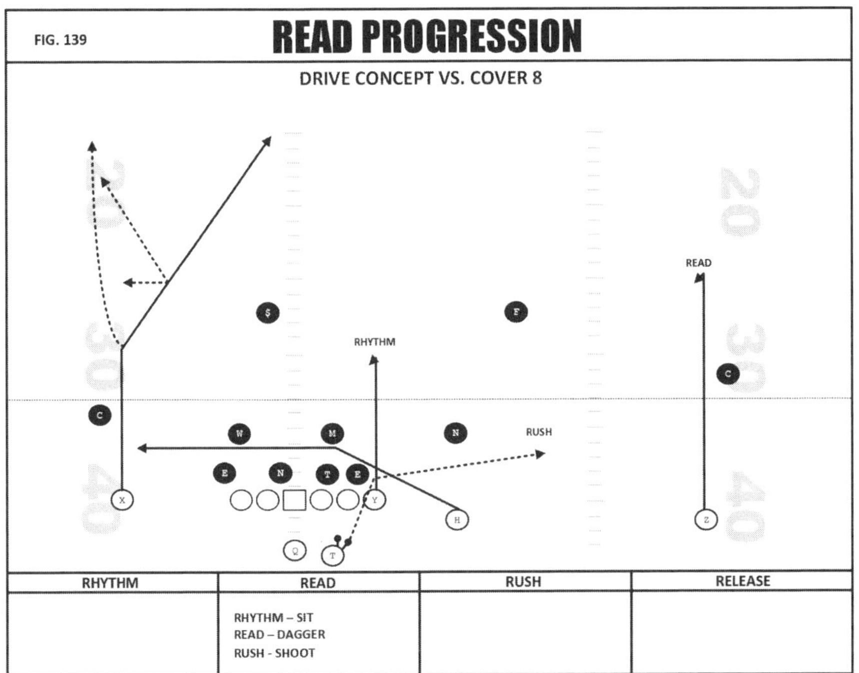

understanding the best route to call for specific situations. This allows coaches to gain the confidence to let the quarterback eventually make the call on his own.

DRIVE CONCEPT – *READ PROGRESSION:* The Read Progression counters the primary progression for the Drive concept. To stop the primary progression, the defense most call coverages that will gain the Man advantage back in their favor to the weak side. If this occurs when a Drive concept is called, then a secondary read progression can be more favorable. (FIG. 139)

The read progression for the quarterback on a Drive concept is the ***Rhythm – Sit, Read – Dagger, Rush – Shoot.*** The Dagger Route is an extended Curl Route that breaks at 15 yards. The read progression can be used as a bail out when an unanticipated overload to the weakside occurs on the play call. It can also be used when the field corner is leaving the dagger to the field UNCAPPED.

For example, during a game we are running the Drive concept and using the Rhythm progression, our box coach is watching the backside a seeing that the dagger route is UNCAPPED. We will use that information to inform and incorporate a read progression the next time we call the Drive concept.

DRIVE CONCEPT – *RUSH PROGRESSION:* The Rush progression for the Drive concept is to Rush – Shallow, Read – YOLO, Rush – Shoot. The Rush progression for the Drive concept is built around YOLO route. The YOLO route is a Y-Option route that allows the Y-receiver to break away from a CAPPING defender into the most UNCAPPED space. The YOLO route restores the Drive concept to its original West Coach design with the Dig route as a viable option break. The YOLO route allows the Y to Curl, Comeback or Break outside. This creates more versatility against defensive CAP adjustments seen post-snap. (FIG. 140)

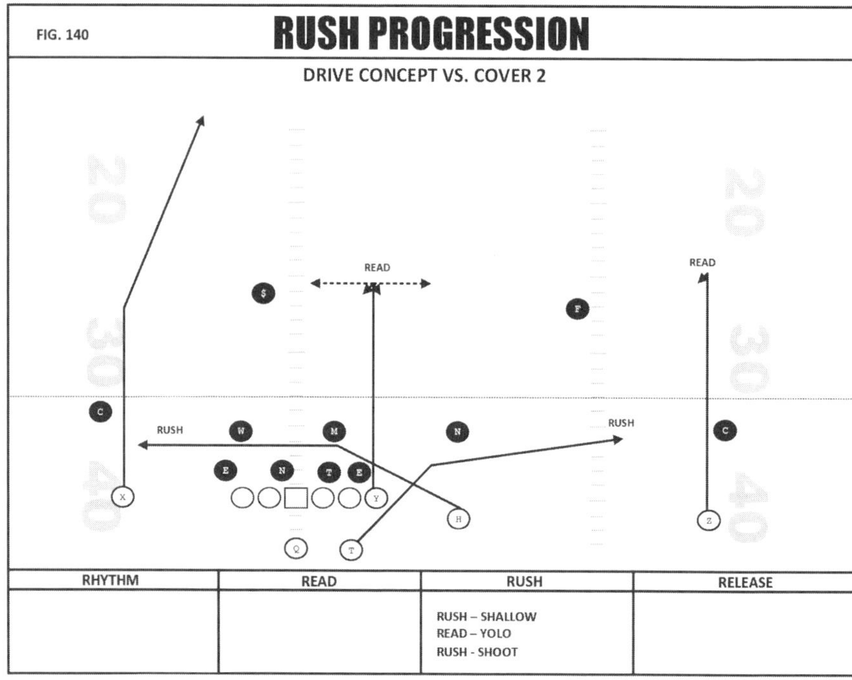

The Rush Progression for the Drive concept creates a horizontal stretch on the defense. This progression is good for situational Blitz and 3rd downs. The running back is a free-release on a Rush progression. The quarterback must practice throwing "hot" to the shallow and shoot against Blitzes.

DRIVE CONCEPT – *RELEASE PROGRESSION:* The Release Progression for the Drive concept can be game-planned to a what a coach feels gives him the best potential for an explosive play or completion on critical down. The default release progression for our Drive concept is a Wheel Tag to create a Post-wheel concept to the weak side of the formation. (FIG. 141)

The progression is ***Rhythm – Post, Read – Post or Wheel, Rush – Shallow.*** This release progression is good against defenses that have a linebacker manned up on a running back.

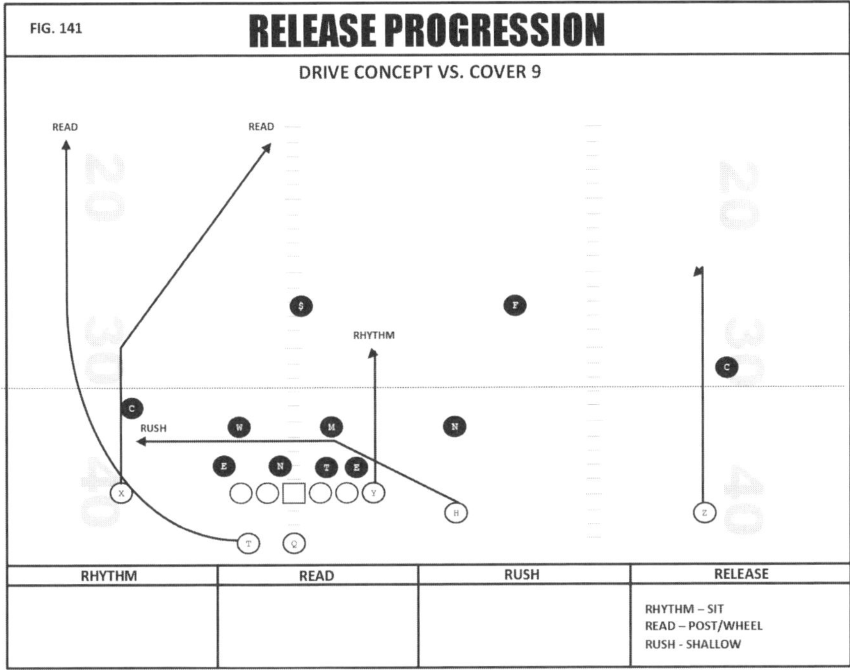

R4 PROGRESSION PLATFORMS FOR THE LEVELS CONCEPT: Vertical Space and time are limited in the Red Zone area and 3rd down situations. This requires route concepts that create quick horizontal full-field stretches. The routes must break open quickly versus Man and adapt to attack Zone. The vertical routes must be able to adjust to the confined space of the Red Zone. The Levels concept that is built on the R4 progression platform provides all the necessary requirements for these pressure-packed situations.

We will focus on the Levels concept out of a 3 x 1 formation. The Levels concept is centered around Dig and Fin route. The Read Dig and Rush Fin route combination creates a horizontal stretch on inside linebackers.

To increase versatility of the Read Dig, we changed the route into a Read Seam. The progression platform that is used controls what break the Read Seam Route will take. The Read Seam Route break can be signaled or tagged before the play to confirm the break. This tag adjustment provides the adaptability needed for multiple defender post-snap reactions.

LEVELS CONCEPT – *Rhythm Progression:* The Rhythm progression for the levels concept is the ***Rhythm – Fade, Read – Dig, Rush – Fin, then Release.*** (FIG. 142)

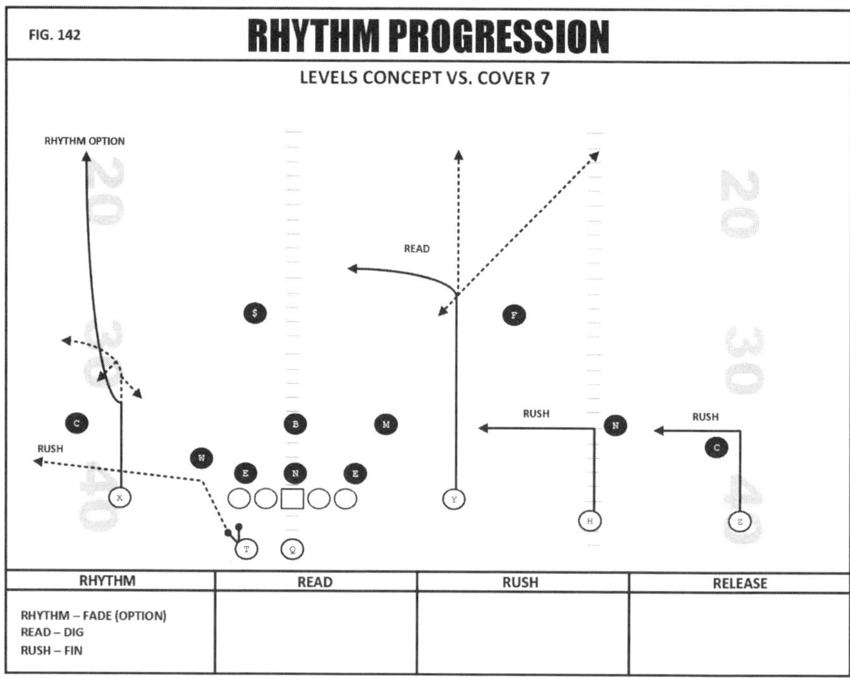

The Fade is a Rhythm-Option route. This means that the quarterback can signal any route that breaks on Rhythm. We generally keep this Rhythm option menu small and predetermined by game-plan. The theory behind the Rhythm-option route is to place the receiver into the best UNCAPPED space based on the CAP of the defender covering the single side receiver.

The Seam Read is run as a Read Dig when using the Rhythm progression. The Read Dig also has route break versatility. The dig can speed-cut at 15 yards or stick-and-settle at 15 yards. The style of break is predicated by the collision and CAP technique of the middle linebackers. The two

Fin routes will foot-fire-stick-and-settle in Zone Coverage and keep running against Man Coverage.

LEVELS CONCEPT – ***Read Progression:*** The Read progression for the Levels concept is built to attack the most anticipated adjustment to the Rhythm progression of the concept. The Levels concept is designed to put maximum strain on Zone Coverage. Therefore, the most common adjustment to defend it is by playing man. The threat of Man Coverage places the read progression of the levels concept to contain man-route beating adjustments. This is achieved by Rhythming the Seam or Corner route. Against Cover-0 the Rhythm will be a Seam. Against Cover-1 the Rhythm will be a corner. (FIG. 143)

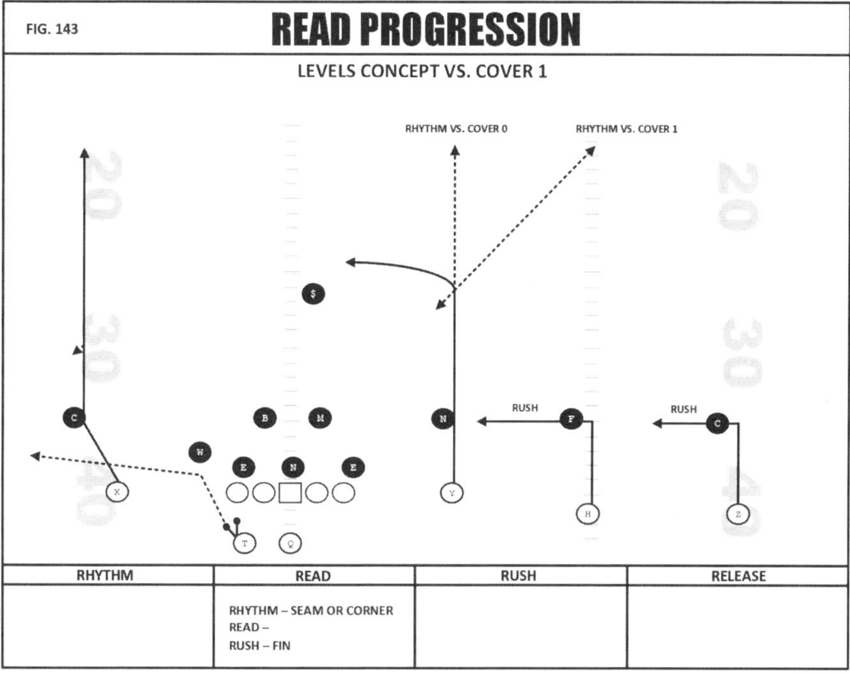

The secondary Read progression for the levels concept is to ***Rhythm – Seam, or Corner, Rush – Best Fin and then Release.*** A Rhythm and Rush Route progression is used against Man Coverage due to the time limits that Man Coverage establishes.

LEVELS CONCEPT – ***Rush Progression:*** The Rush progression for the levels concept is used when anticipating pressure situations. The

Read progression that was just covered answered Man pressure. Another style of pressure that a defense can employ is by Dropping eight defenders into Zone Coverage. This Drop-action of eight players creates pressure on the quarterback by reducing the route space available to him on the Drop. This strategy of defense requires precise throws on time. (FIG. 144)

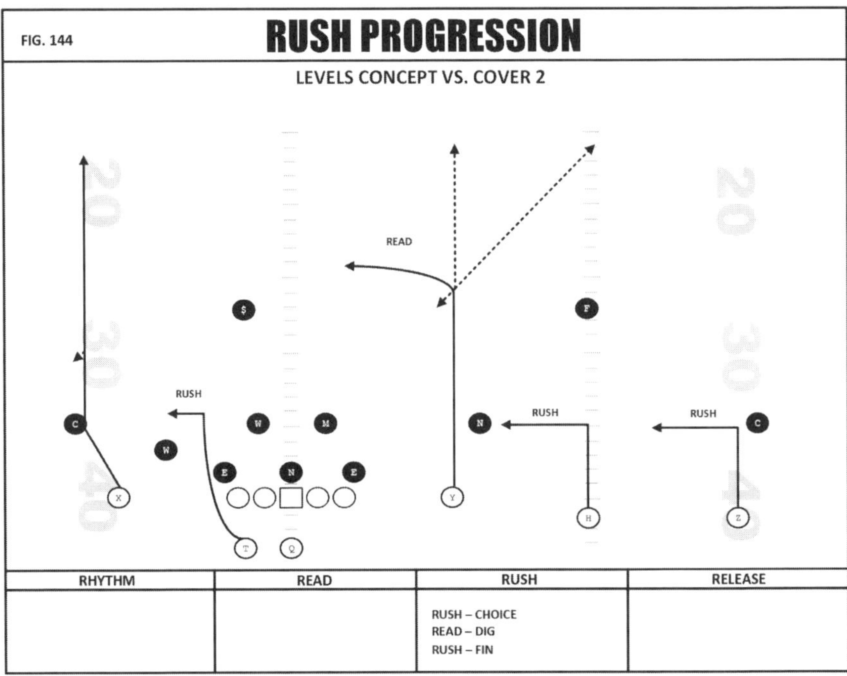

The Rush progression used to attack a Drop-8 Zone strategy is to free-release the running-back and elevate his route to first in the progression. The Rush progression for the Levels concept is to ***Rush – Choice, Read – Dig, and Rush – Best Fin and then Release.*** This style of progression places an immediate horizontal stretch on the defense and forces them to reveal the CAPPED and UNCAPPED space faster.

LEVELS CONCEPT – ***Release Progression:*** The release progression platform is designed to set up an explosive play off the Rhythm progression. One of the most common release progressions used with the levels concept is to tag the Read Dig into a Dig & Go. The release progression for the levels concept is the ***Rhythm – Fade, Read – Dig & Go, Rush – Best Fin and then Release.*** (FIG. 145)

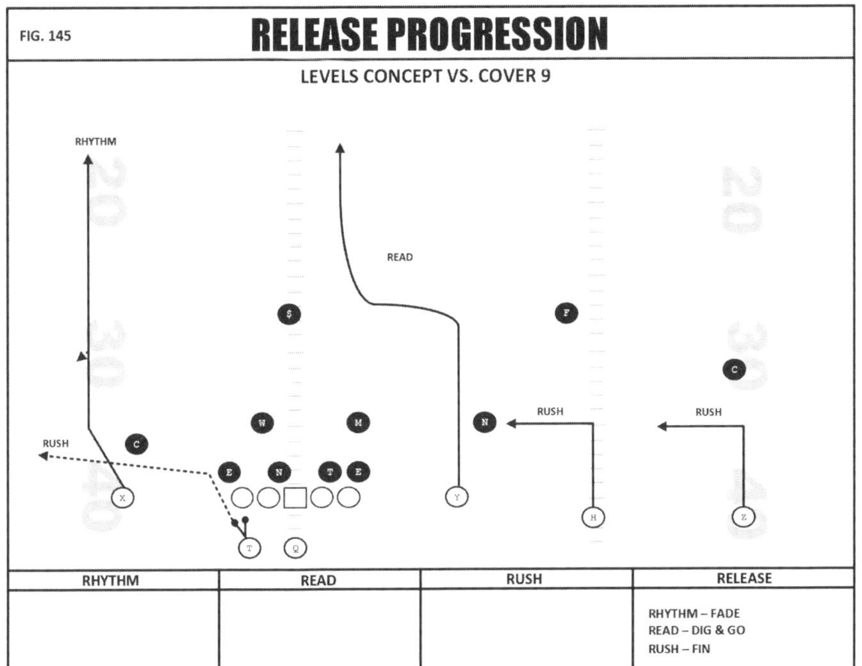

RHYTHM	READ	RUSH	RELEASE
			RHYTHM – FADE READ – DIG & GO RUSH – FIN

This is used against Zone Coverage teams who attempt to cross-key the boundary safety post-snap to CAP the #3 receiver running the Dig. The coaches should determine the best route tag or combination adjustment for the release progression platform. The main thing to remember is to formulate the progression around something that looks like the Rhythm progression and uses your best personnel mismatch.

R4 PROGRESSION PLATFORMS – RED TEAMING: The R4 progression platforms create the context that is missing in most game-planning war rooms. In the absence of game-planning guardrails, it is easy to get off-track in staff or install meetings. The key to accelerating decision-making under pressure is not by having all the answers to every situation. It is by having the best answer for the most anticipated situations. The R4 progression platforms provide the questions that matter most when determining the best concepts and progressions to use in a game.

Furthermore, the platform questions allow you to put on the defensive coordinator hat and see the game from that perspective. This is the purpose behind the military exercise called Red Teaming. Red Teaming is a war game simulation that allows a group of soldiers to practice their strategies against a veteran group of commanders who know your tactics better than you do. Red Teaming is essentially a what-if game that forces the players to build out a decision-making tree that can be used to accelerate better decisions when the real war occurs.

In the football world, the R4 progression platforms have pre-built the decision-making tree for coaches and players. The Rhythm, Read, Rush and Release platforms contain the questions that drive the decision-making answers. The questions are as follows: (Fig. 145a)

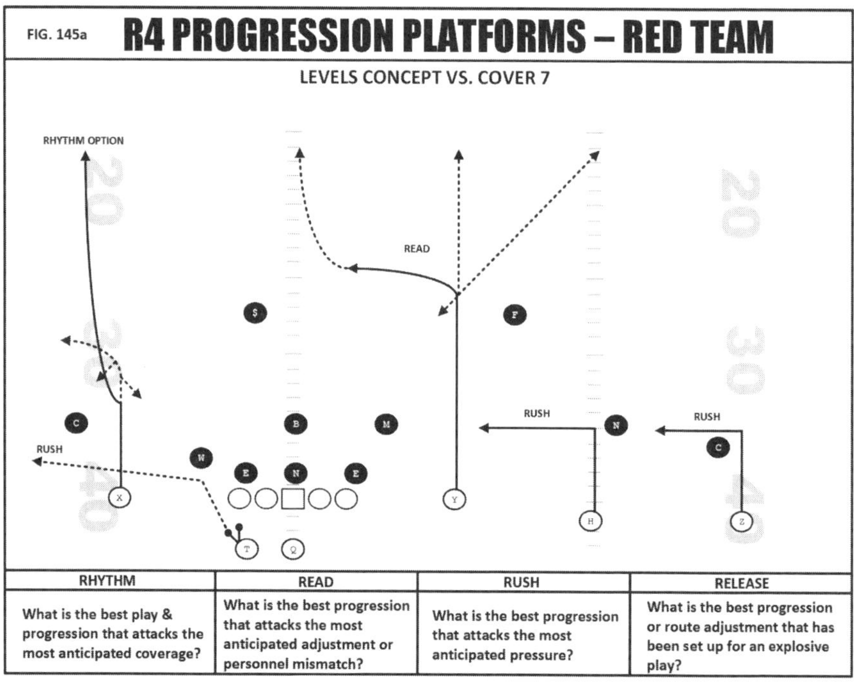

RHYTHM	READ	RUSH	RELEASE
What is the best play & progression that attacks the most anticipated coverage?	What is the best progression that attacks the most anticipated adjustment or personnel mismatch?	What is the best progression that attacks the most anticipated pressure?	What is the best progression or route adjustment that has been set up for an explosive play?

Rhythm Progression Platform – What is the best play and progression that attacks the most anticipated coverage?

Read Progression Platform – What is the best progression that attacks the most anticipated adjustment or personnel mismatch?

Rush Progression Platform – What is the best progression that attacks the most anticipated answer?

Release Progression Platform – What is the best progression or route adjustment that has been set up for an explosive play?

These questions allow the staff to Red Team their concepts and progressions over and over to decide what play, progression and adjustment will be needed against the highest priority threats of an upcoming opponent. They can essentially play the game before it has been played. The result is less time wasted in game-planning, more adaptability in concepts with simplicity, and more efficient meetings and practices with players. The R4 progression platforms create a storyboard that allows you to read the game-plan to your players as you are reading them a simple bed-time story.

Another benefit that the R4 progression platforms provide is that is allows coaches and players to game-plan their concepts situationally in the spring. An offense doesn't have to wait until the season to game-plan schemes and adjustments against different defensive looks and mis-matches. The offense can use the R4 progression platforms to Red Team concepts, and practice what their best play and adjustments would be by using the questions to guide the process. The result is accelerated decision-making that will be sustained under pressure through the confidence of the R4 common language and increased mental reps generated through Red Teaming.

CHAPTER 11

R4 Route Combination Rules

R4 ROUTE COMBINATION RULES

The inception of the R4 Passing System was built around 5-step intermediate concepts. The reason for this was because most 5-step concepts are built to create stretches using a Rhythm, Read and Rush Route. Introducing the R4 system using concepts that had a route from each family made it easier for coaches and players to understand the relationships of route progressions and timing. However, some intermediate concepts do not have a route represented from each family. Furthermore, there are many other types of pass concepts, such as Quick-Game, Play-Action, Sprint-Out/Bootlegs that have concepts built without routes represented from each family.

These different types of passing concepts along with the rise of RPO (Run-Pass Option) concepts required an understanding of routes on a deeper level. This brings us to the next phase of the R4 evolution... R4 route combination rules.

There are 3 core route combination rules that are used to increase versatility of pass concepts and navigate other concepts besides the intermediate passing game. They are:

1. 2-Rhythms Rule
2. Rhythm-Side Rule
3. 3-Man Quick Rule

The R4 route combination rules are undifferentiated by themselves, but they can be inserted into concepts to create specialized progressions. These specialized progressions enhance concepts and increase progression options. They also provide the ability for conceptual blending between different styles of concepts. Finally, they provide the ability to navigate different route combinations that do not flow in sync with a 5-step Drop timeline.

2-RHYTHMS RULE

The 2-Rhythms Rule states that any 2 Rhythm Routes that are adjacent to or cross with each other create Read Route timing. It's important to note that the Rhythm Route conversion to a Read Route can be made because Rhythms do not terminate in space (stop or decelerate) and therefore can be thrown off a reset step when shielded by a neighboring Rhythm. When using snap Rhythms (Rhythms that stop or decelerate by design), such as the Spot Route, it's important to automatically make it the first Rhythm in the progression. (FIG. 146)

*The **2-Rhythms Rule** states that any 2 Rhythm Routes that are adjacent to or cross with each other create Read Route timing.*

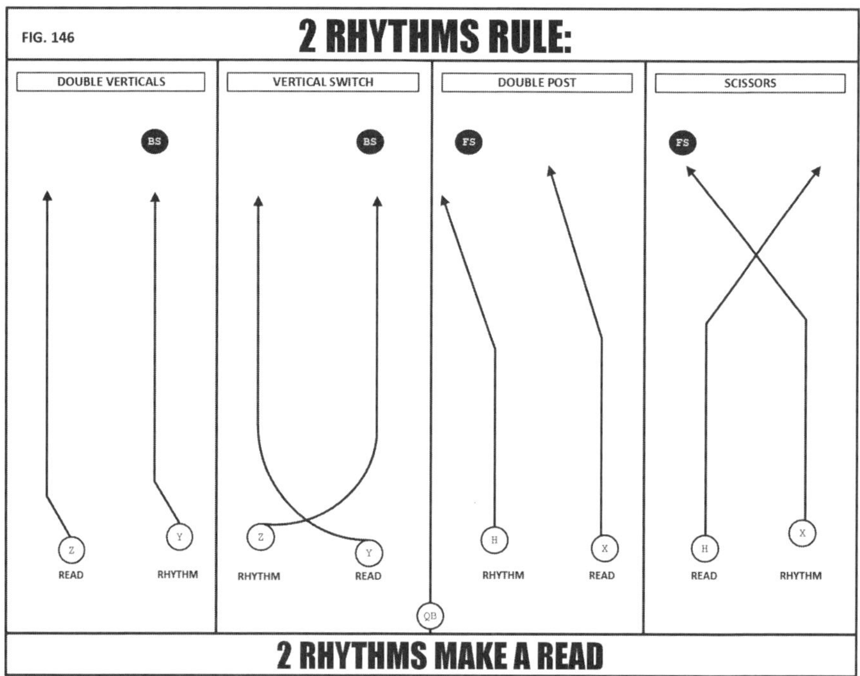

Placing a Rhythm Seam (inside) side-by-side with a Rhythm Fade (outside) forces a Cover-2 Safety to CAP one of the routes, thus isolating the other Rhythm against the corner; the quarterback can then throw off a reset step if he remains UNCAPPED. A quarterback who picks the Rhythm Seam by the inside receiver in his progression changes the Rhythm Fade by the outside receiver into a Read Route that would be thrown off a reset step.

The 2-Rhythms Rule can also be used to treat both Rhythms as a Read combination. This allows a quarterback to Rhythm a route elsewhere in the formation and reset his feet to the backside and treat the 2 adjacent Rhythms as Read Routes. This is particularly effective with Rhythm Route combinations that switch or exchange, like a Vertical-Switch or scissors combination.

2-RHYTHMS RULE: ***4-Vertical Concept – Rhythm Progression***

The 4-Vertical concept is a foundational intermediate passing game concept used in most offenses. The 2-Rhythms rule provides the teaching process needed to help the quarterback and coach navigate the 4-Vertical concept in a variety of ways. The R4 progression platforms will be used to show some examples. (FIG. 147)

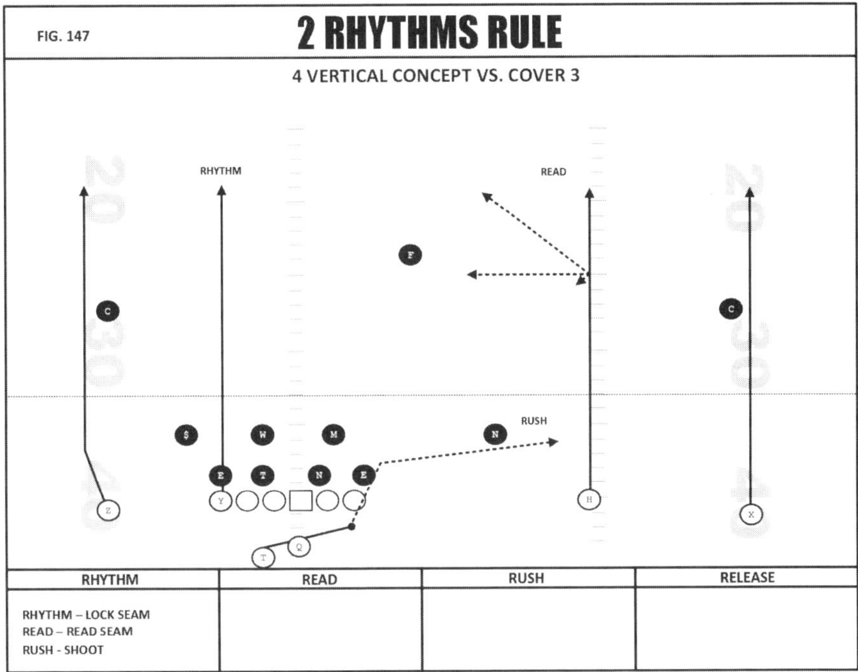

The Rhythm Progression for the 4-Vertical concept is decided based on the design of the 4-Vertical concept. The core design of the 4-Vertical concept is to create a horizontal stretch on a 1-high Safety defense. Therefore, the primary Rhythm progression is to ***Rhythm – Lock Seam, Read – Read Seam, and Rush – Shoot Route.*** The boundary Seam is designated as the Lock Seam because most defenses will rotate and

Blitz from the field. This creates UNCAPPED space in the boundary faster than in the field.

The field Read Seam can snap to UNCAPPED space if the vertical Seam is CAPPED. However, if the field Seam is UNCAPPED the Read Seam will remain a Seam. The Seam will be treated as a Read Route in the progression due to the 2-Rhythms Rule. If the read Seam is CAPPED, then the quarterback will progress to the Rush Shoot Route.

2-RHYTHMS RULE: ***4-Vertical Concept – Read Progression***
The 2-Rhythms rule provides versatility for the 4-Vertical concept by allowing the quarterback to work a boundary progression with a Seam and Fade Route combination. This is an example of a Read progression platform. (FIG. 148)

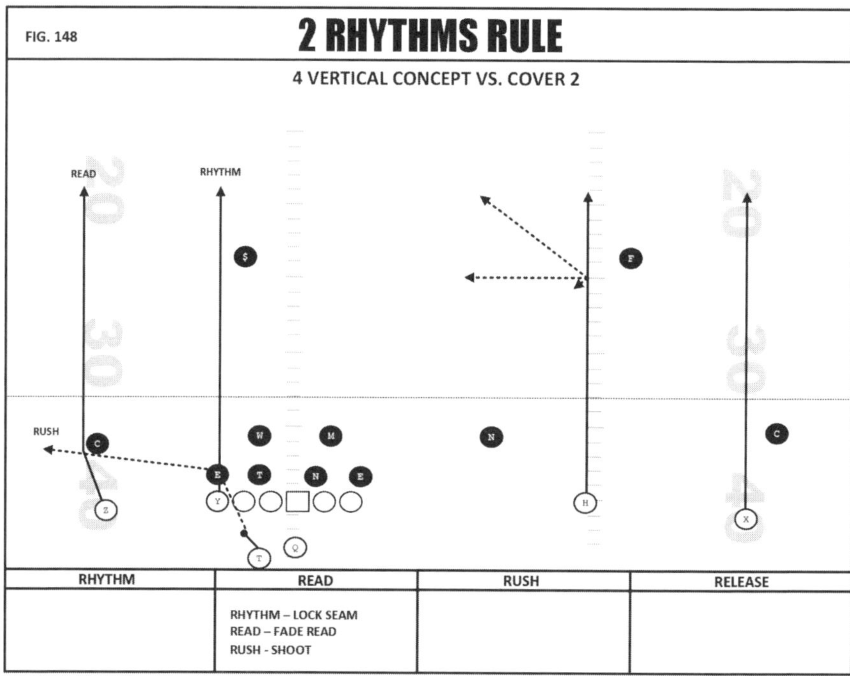

The read progression is favorable against Cover-2 by forcing the boundary deep-half safety in a 2-on-1 stretch. The quarterback would Rhythm the Lock Seam, Read the Fade, and Rush the Shoot route by the tailback.

2-RHYTHMS RULE: ***4-Vertical Concept – Rush Progression***
The 2-Rhythms Rule is also used in a Rush progression of the 4-Vertical

concept. The example of a Rush progression in a 4-Vertical concept can be incorporated by free releasing the back on a Rush Route. (FIG. 149)

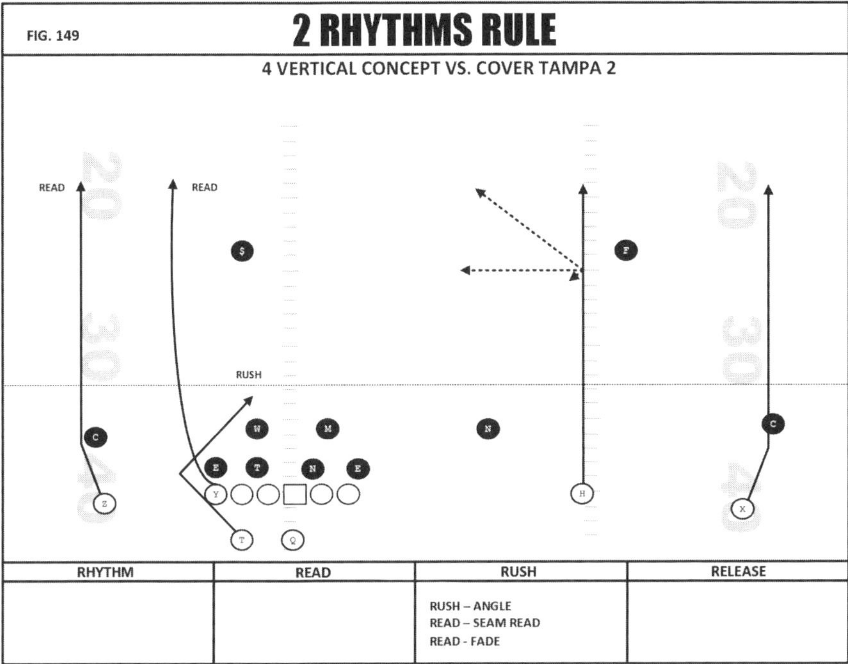

In this play, the running back is running an Angle Route. The Angle Route is a Rush Route. In a Rush progression, the quarterback is going to Rush the Angle Route, Read the Seam Read, and Read the Field Fade. This is an example of a Rush-Read-Read progression. The 2-Rhythms rule allows the Seam and Fade to be treated as Read Routes in the progression. This type of Rush progression platform is used on 3rd downs, when defenses are bringing an attacking 6/7-man Blitzes or Drop 8-man pressure.

2-RHYTHMS RULE: ***4-Vertical Concept – Release Progression***

The final example of applying the 2 Rhythms Rule is seen in the Release progression platform of the 4-Vertical concept. (FIG. 150)

The Release progression will use a Seam Exchange strategy. A Seam Exchange strategy notifies the running back and tagged receiver to exchange routes. The running back will run a Seam for the tagged receiver. The tagged receiver will run a Shallow across the centerline of the formation. This is a game-planned progression. The default progression is to Rhythm running back Seam toward the boundary, Read the Seam Read, and Rush the Shallow Route.

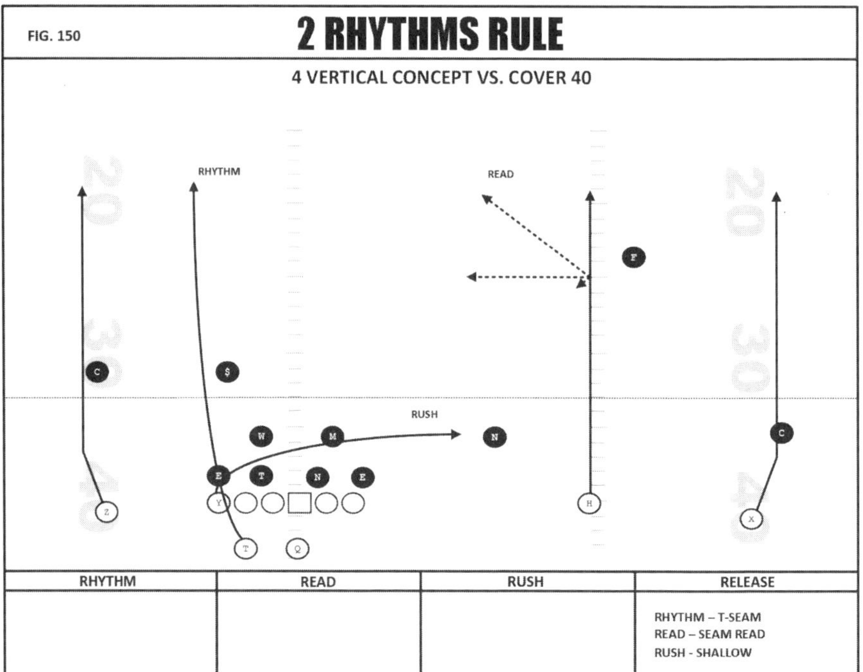

2-RHYTHMS RULE: ***Scissors Concept – Rhythm Progression***

The Scissors concept is another foundational intermediate passing game concept used in most offenses. The Scissors concept derives its name from the crossing of the Post and Corner route. (FIG. 151)

This concept is a Flood concept that is usually run to the field. The Corner Route will break underneath the Post Route. Some coaches may refer to this type of break of the corner under the Post as a Sail Route (15yd Deep Out). Either way, the crossing of two routes requires the use of the 2-Rhythms Rule to increase the progression possibilities.

The Rhythm progression for the Scissors concept is ***Rhythm – Post, Read – Corner, and Rush – Shallow.*** This is the primary progression for the Scissors concept because the Scissors concept is designed to attack soft-zone Coverages like Cover-3 and Cover-4. It is also good against pattern reading Zone Coverages like Cover-8.

2-RHYTHMS RULE: ***Scissors Concept – Read Progression***

Cover-2 and -3 Cloud Zone Coverages are better equipped to delay and disrupt the route timing for the Scissors concept. In these coverages, the field corner can collision the Rhythm Post and then pass it off to a

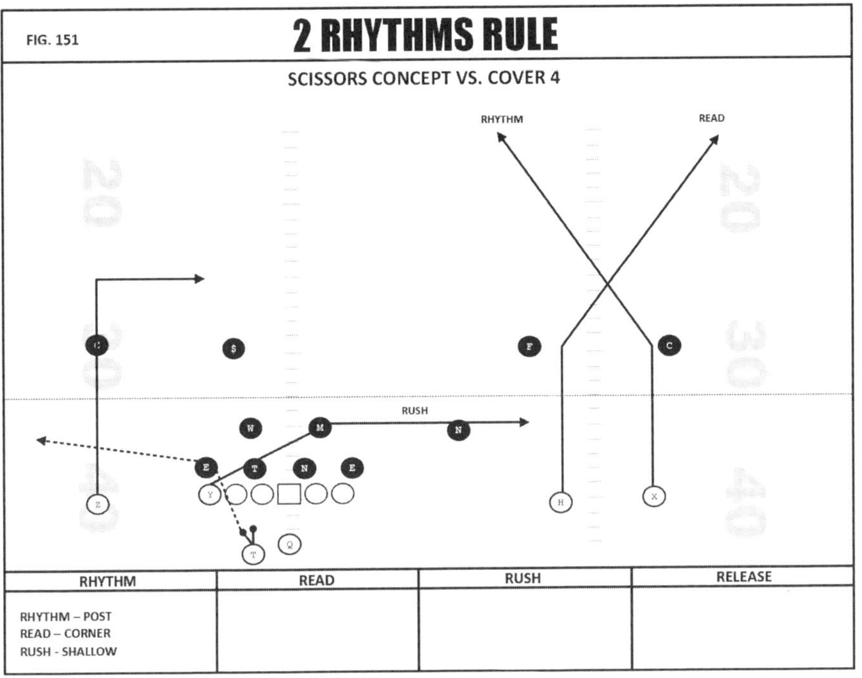
FIG. 151
2 RHYTHMS RULE
SCISSORS CONCEPT VS. COVER 4
RHYTHM
READ
RUSH
RHYTHM
READ
RUSH
RELEASE
RHYTHM – POST
READ – CORNER
RUSH - SHALLOW

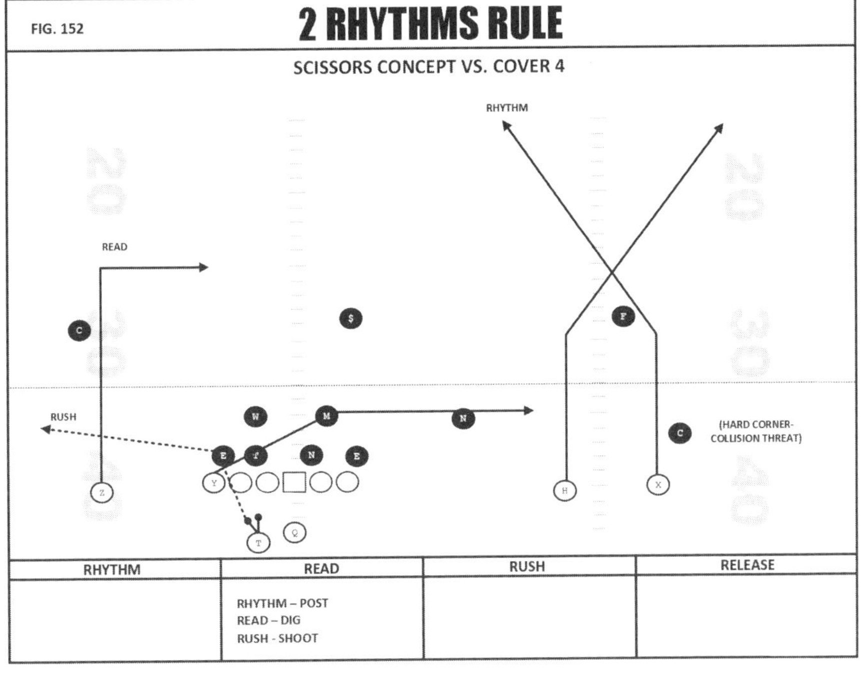
FIG. 152
2 RHYTHMS RULE
SCISSORS CONCEPT VS. COVER 4
RHYTHM
READ
RUSH
(HARD CORNER-
COLLISION THREAT)
RHYTHM
READ
RUSH
RELEASE
RHYTHM – POST
READ – DIG
RUSH - SHOOT

free safety in a CAPPED position. A collision of the Rhythm Post destroys the clear out-route timing for the crossing corner route underneath. The cornerback can fallout after the collision and be in position to undercut the Read Corner route or rally to tackle the Rush Shallow route. (FIG. 152)

We use the term hard-corner to define a cornerback who is under the hard-deck using collision to delay and disrupt a receiver at the line of scrimmage. When running a Scissors concept, we teach the quarterback to adjust into a Read progression against a hard-corner. A Read progression still begins with a ***Rhythm – Post, then resets to the backside Read – Dig, to Rush – Shoot route*** by the running back. This secondary progression better attacks the middle of the field weakness of Cover-2 and weak Seam of 3-Cloud coverages with the Dig route.

2-RHYTHMS RULE: ***Scissors Concept – Rush Progression***

The next defensive weapons used to attack the Scissors concept is to bring Zone Pressure or Man Blitzes. These pressures and Blitzes can inhibit the amount of time needed for the Scissors concept to develop. If a coach is anticipating these types of defensive scheme strategies, then a Rush progression is optimal. (FIG. 153)

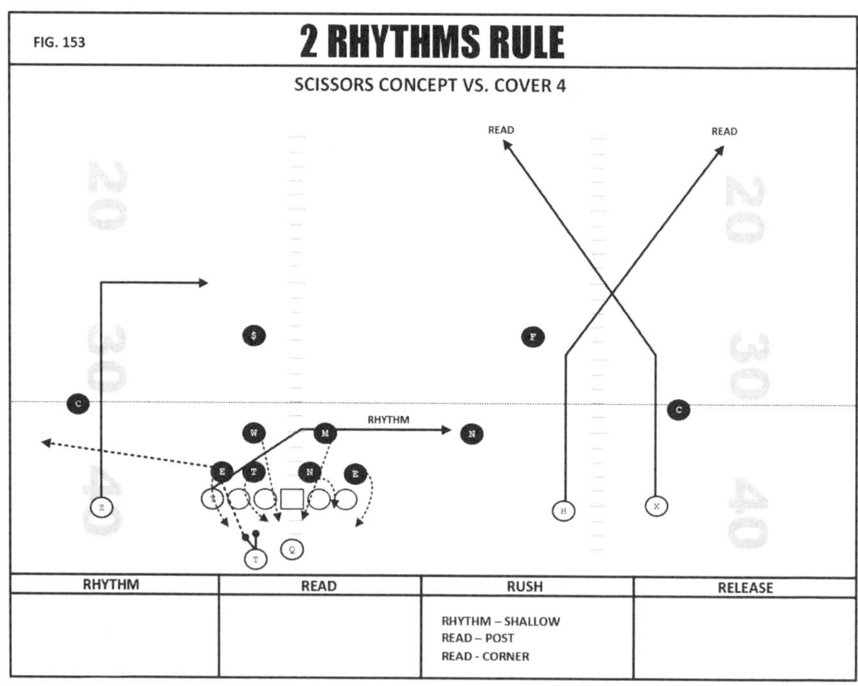

A Rush Progression elevates a Rush Route to replace the Rhythm Route. Therefore, the quarterback's progression begins with the ***Rush – Shallow, to Read – Post, to Read – Corner, then Release.*** Using a Rush Progression allows the quarterback a quick "hot" outlet in the face of pressure, while still allowing him to reset his feet to the Read Post or Read Corner route if pressure is negated.

This is another way the 2-Rhythms rule can be used to treat both Rhythm Routes as a Read Route. Rhythm Routes that intersect take longer to develop. When these routes continue in space without terminating, it allows for them both to be treated as a Read Route.

2-RHYTHMS RULE: ***Scissors Concept – Release Progression***
The Release Progression for the Scissors concept is game-planned at the coach's discretion. The release play is a Shot or Situational Play that is set up by the Core Route structure of the concept and the defender actions used to CAP it. One example would be set up a Dig and go Double-Move Read Route off the Rhythm Progression of the play. (FIG. 154)

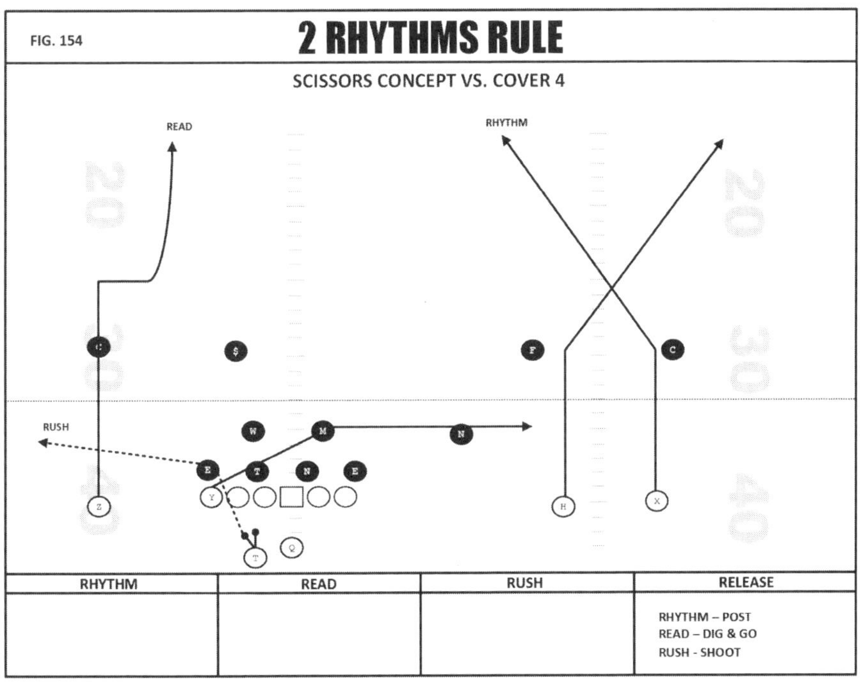

EXAMPLE: You run the Scissors concept a couple of times in a game and the Box Coach see that the backside safety is jumping the Dig Route.

This would be a good time to implement a Release Progression. On the Release Progression, the quarterback will ***Rhythm – Post, Read – Dig & Go, Rush – Shoot, then Release.***

> *The **Rhythm-Side Rule** states that any adjacent routes comprised in a Rhythm-Rush or Rush-Rush combination can be treated as a Rhythm Route combination to that side.*

RHYTHM-SIDE RULE

The next route rule to cover is the Rhythm-Side Rule. The Rhythm-Side Rule states that any adjacent routes comprised in a Rhythm-Rush or Rush-Rush combination can be treated as a Rhythm Route combination to that side. This means that a quarterback can process the Rhythm-Rush or Rush-Rush combinations as a singular Rhythm Route, then reset to a Read Route elsewhere in the progression. (FIG. 155)

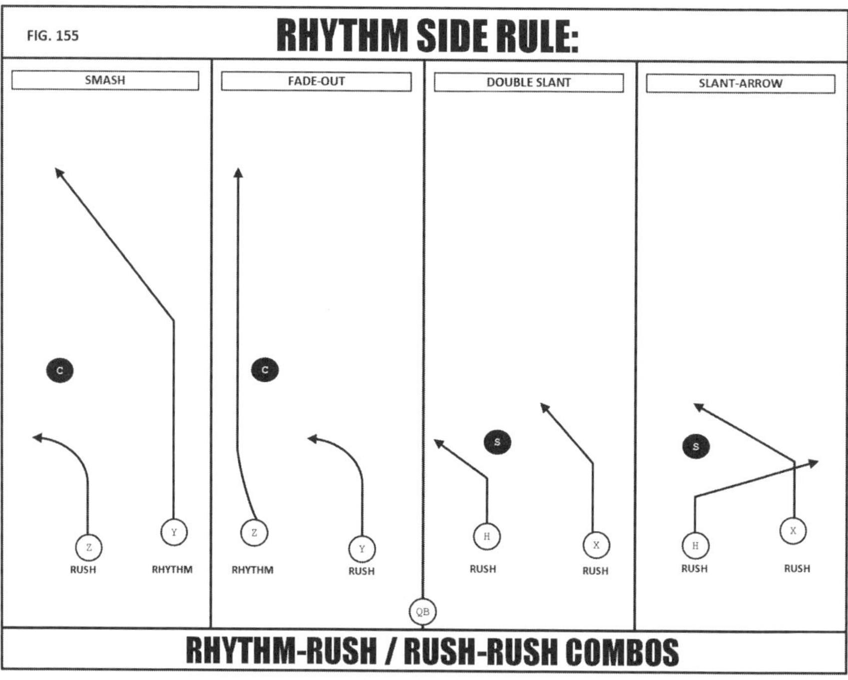

The reason a Rhythm-Rush or Rush-Rush combo can be treated as a Rhythm Route is because both routes in these families break open in 1.8 seconds or less. This is the same timeline with which the Rhythm family operates. Some example of Rhythm-Rush combinations would be a Corner-Quick Out or Fade-Quick Out combo. Some examples of a Rush-Rush combination would be a Double-Slant or Slant-Arrow combo.

The Rhythm-Side Rule allows the coach to break away from using outdated mirrored route concepts. (FIG. 156)

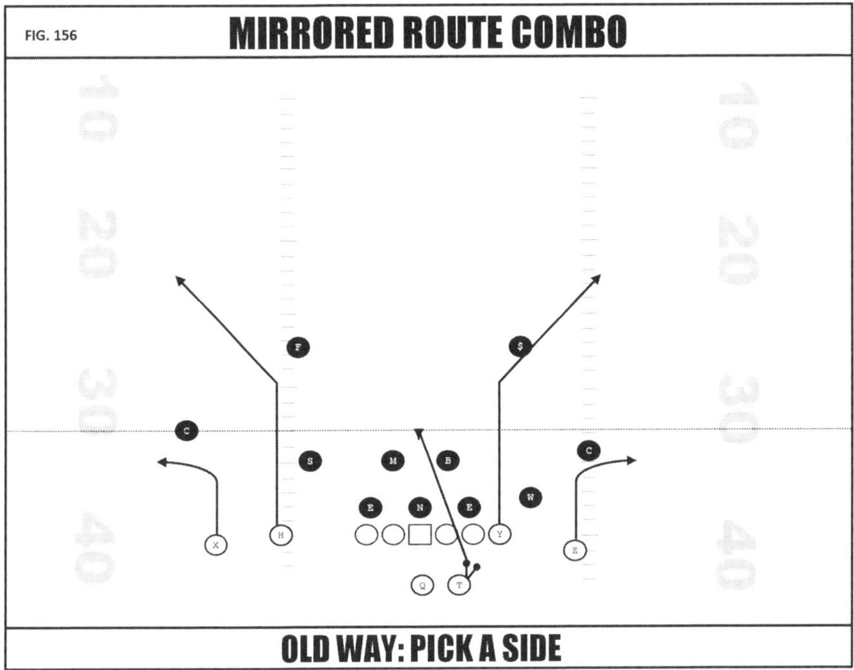

A quarterback who is reading a mirrored route concept must choose which side he likes pre-snap and stay on that side of space. Because the routes are mirrored on each side, the quarterback cannot reset to routes backside and maintain footwork that syncs up with the route breaks. Mirrored route concepts play into the defense's favor by compressing the quarterback's routes to half the field, while usually maintaining a defensive Man advantage to cover that side of space.

The Rhythm-Side Rule enables the blending of concepts. Conceptual blending frees a quarterback who is constrained by pick-a-best side or mirrored route concepts. Versatility and adaptability within concepts are gained using the Rhythm-Side Rule with different route combinations. These combinations are linked together while maintaining the same progression sequence for the quarterback.

RHYTHM-SIDE RULE: ***Smash-Drive Concept – Rhythm Progression***

The benefit of R4 is that it always allows the quarterback to read the full field in Route Break sequence, when necessary. The Rhythm-Side Rule gains the full field back by building a better concept. In this example, we build a Rhythm-side Smash Combo using a Corner and Quick-Out combination. Instead of mirroring the backside, we blend it with a Read and Rush Route combination. The backside combination that is used is determined by the coach, based on the anticipated coverage or adjustments that may occur on the play. (FIG. 157)

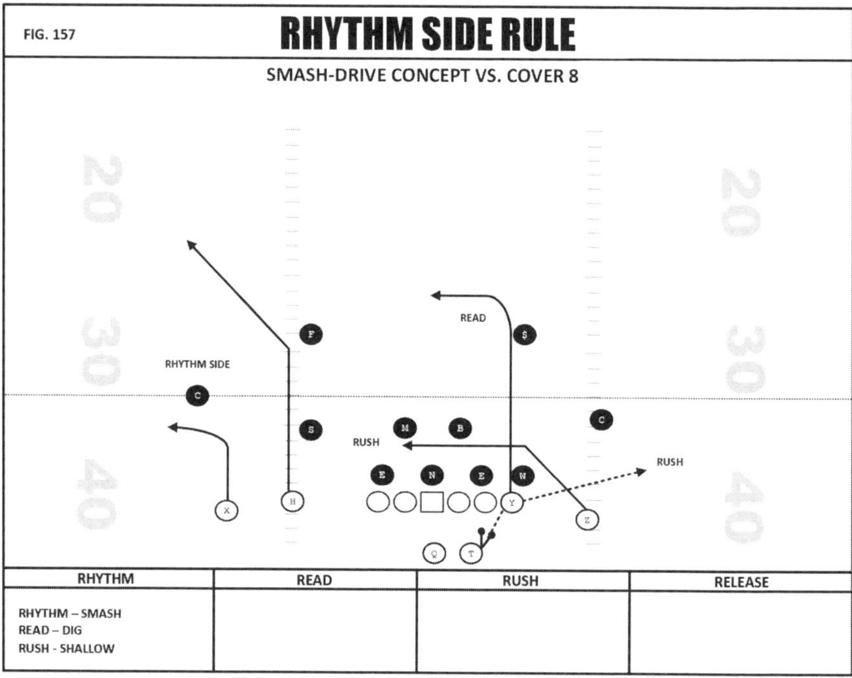

In this example we use a 2-man Drive concept that consists of a Dig Route and Shallow Route. The Drive concept is effective in attacking a variety of coverages and pressures. The base R4 progression used to navigate through the concept would be to ***Rhythm – Smash (Rhythm Side), Read – Dig, Rush – Shallow, then Release.*** The quarterback must maintain a wide-view focus when processing Rhythm-side combinations. The reason is that there are more space and defender movement to CAP than space to process.

RHYTHM-SIDE RULE: ***Smash-Drive Concept – Read Progression***

Concepts that use the Rhythm-Side Rule always work horizontally. Left-to-right or right-to-left in the progression. The benefit of running concepts that are built to operate with the Rhythm-Side Rule is that the base progression always stretches the entire field horizontally. Therefore, a Read progression in the traditional sense is not needed because the quarterback is always working backside in a Rhythm-Read-Rush and Release sequence. (FIG. 158)

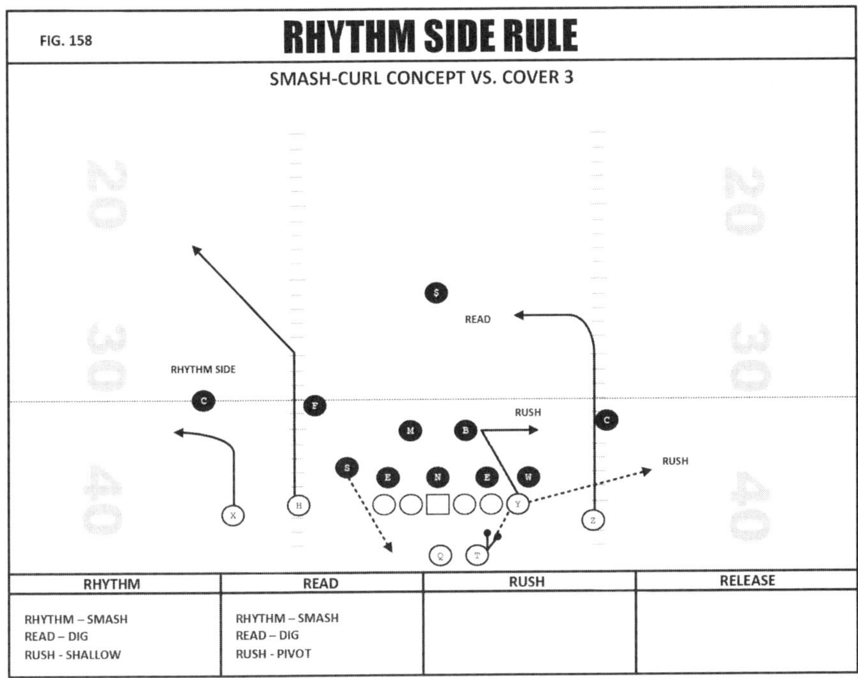

RHYTHM	READ	RUSH	RELEASE
RHYTHM – SMASH READ – DIG RUSH - SHALLOW	RHYTHM – SMASH READ – DIG RUSH - PIVOT		

However, a Read Progression can still be implemented with a Rhythm-side concept to create versatility. A Read Progression in a Rhythm-Side concept would replace the backside Read-Rush Route combo with a different Read-Rush combo that attacks a different anticipated look.

Escape, the 2-Man Drive concept with the Read – Dig and Rush – Shallow is most effective in attacking 2-high safety structures like Cover-2, 4, 8. However, against 1-high safety structures like Cover-1 and 3, they are not as effective. A way to solve this issue would be to attach a 1-high safety Read-Rush Route combination backside, if a 1-high safety coverage is being played. An example would be to use a ***Read – Dig and Rush – Pivot Route combination. The Read progression against a 1-high look would be Rhythm – Smash (Rhythm Side), Read – Dig, Rush – Pivot, then Release.***

It is important to note that the ancillary platform progressions being shown here are to show the versatility and adaptability that is possible with R4. Having multiple progression platforms for every concept is not required.

RHYTHM-SIDE RULE: ***Smash-Drive Concept – Rush Progression***
The Rhythm-Side Rule creates a natural full-field horizontal stretching concept. However, there can be certain Man Coverages, Blitzes or situations that may better be served by using a Rush progression. (Fig 158a)

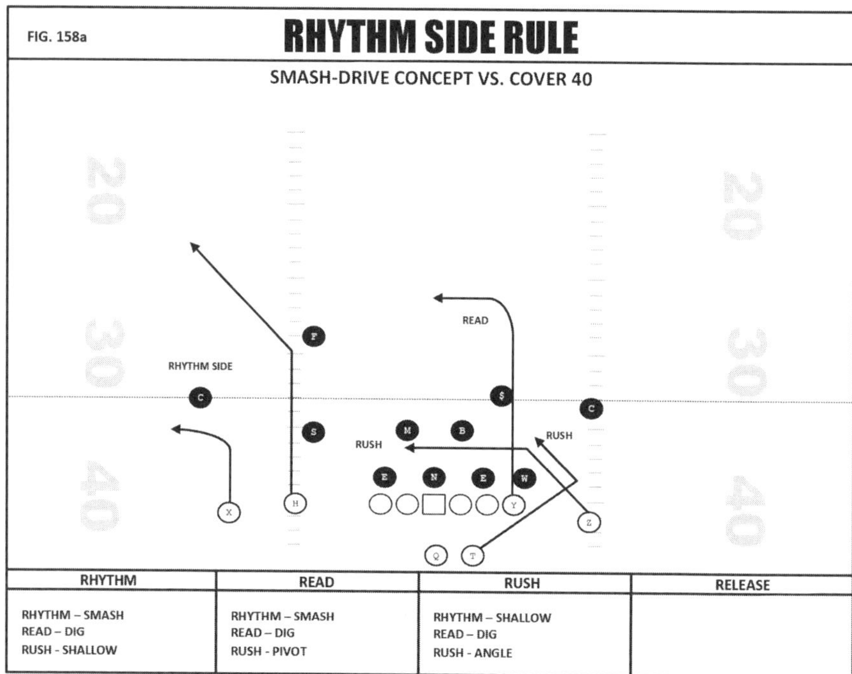

RHYTHM	READ	RUSH	RELEASE
RHYTHM – SMASH READ – DIG RUSH - SHALLOW	RHYTHM – SMASH READ – DIG RUSH - PIVOT	RHYTHM – SHALLOW READ – DIG RUSH - ANGLE	

EXAMPLE: The personnel of the Y and Z on the Drive concept may not be able to UNCAP space against the Man Coverage side of Cover 40. If the pressure of this Man side of coverage is felt, then a good solution is using a Rush progression to involve the running back. The rub of the free release Angle Route with the Shallow route can create space and a mismatch issue for the defense. The Rush progression against this split-field coverage mismatch look would be ***Rhythm – Shallow, Read – Dig, Rush – Angle, then Release.*** The Rush progression informs the quarterback to elevate a Rush route (Shallow) as the Rhythm and then progress to the Read (Dig) and Rush (Angle).

RHYTHM-SIDE RULE: ***Smash-Drive Concept – Release Progression***

A good example of a release progression for the Smash-Drive concept would be to attach a Cross and Corner-Switch concept. The Cross and Corner-Switch combo have initial stems that look identical to the 2-Man Drive (Dig and Shallow) combo. The Rhythm progression of the Smash-Drive concept sets up the Release progression by forcing the defense to pattern-match the Dig and Shallow combo. When the Box Coach sees the defense CAP the backside Drive concept, he will inform the sideline to run the Cross and Corner-Switch combo. (FIG. 159)

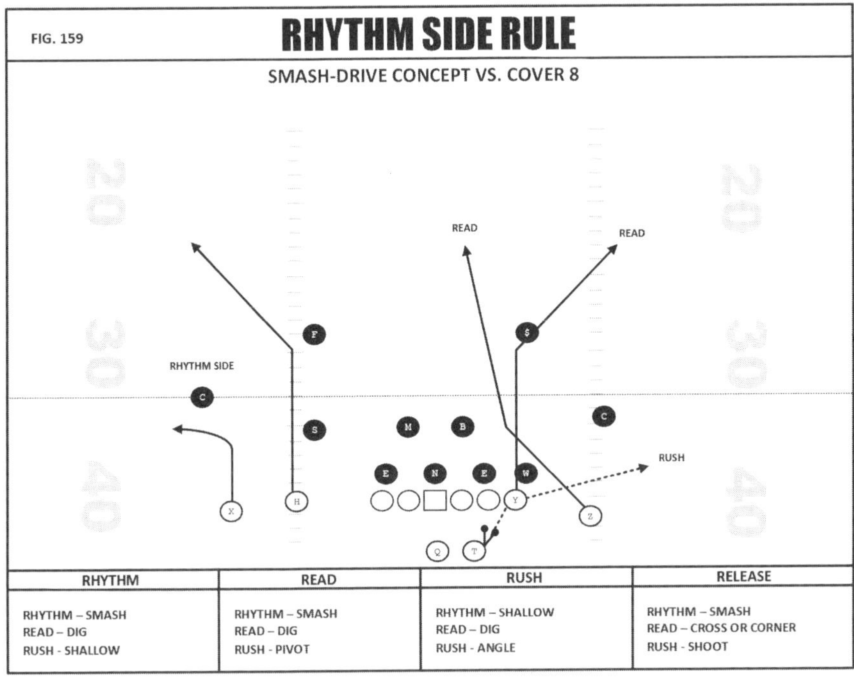

RHYTHM	READ	RUSH	RELEASE
RHYTHM – SMASH READ – DIG RUSH - SHALLOW	RHYTHM – SMASH READ – DIG RUSH - PIVOT	RHYTHM – SHALLOW READ – DIG RUSH - ANGLE	RHYTHM – SMASH READ – CROSS OR CORNER RUSH - SHOOT

The quarterback will Rhythm the Smash (Rhythm Side), then reset to the backside. He will have 2 reset steps to determine the best Read Route. The Cross and the Corner are both treated as Read Routes because they are adjacent and intersect (2-Rhythms Rule). If both routes are CAPPED, then the quarterback will Rush the Shoot and then Release.

RHYTHM-SIDE RULE: ***Double-Slant – Vertical-Switch Concept – Rhythm Progression***

Another example of using the Rhythm-Side Rule can be seen using Rush-Rush combinations. In this example, we use a double-slant combination as the Rhythm Side. The Rhythm-Side Rule provides freedom to blend multiple backside route combinations. This is helpful against defenses who use split filed coverages or disguise coverages well pre-snap.

We are using a Vertical-Switch concept as a dual-read combination backside. This provides a good route combination to attack a post-snap safety rotation to Cover-3 or a split-field coverage, with Cover-0 being played against the Vertical-Switch combination. (FIG. 160)

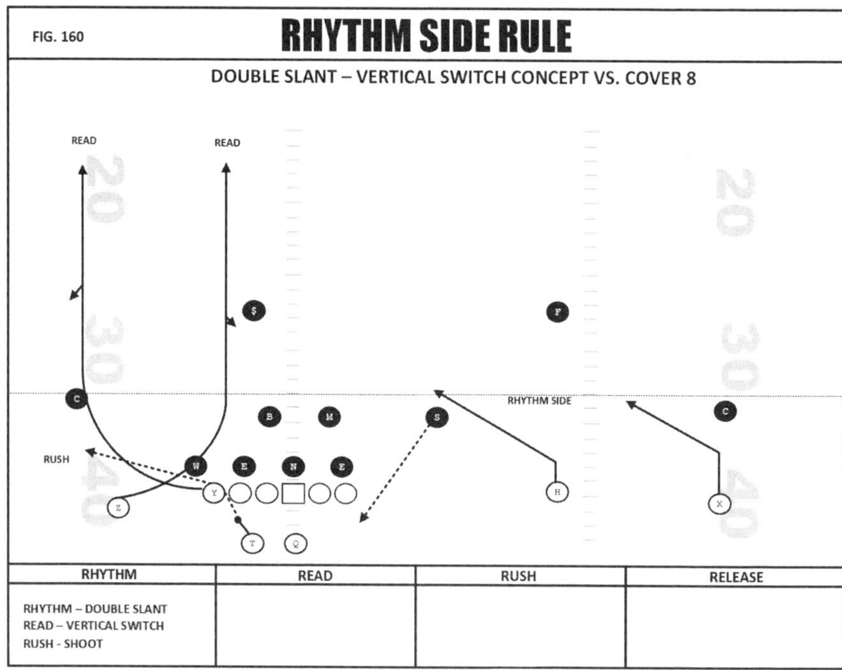

The quarterback will ***Rhythm – Double-Slant (Rhythm Side), Read – Seam or Fade, Rush-Shoot, then Release.*** If the Vertical-Switch concept is a big part of your offense, then we recommend you allow your receivers to convert the Seam into a Curl and Fade into a Comeback if they are CAPPED. We teach them to make this determination pre-snap using the hard deck as a frame of reference.

RHYTHM-SIDE RULE: *Double-Slant – Vertical-Switch Concept – Read Progression*

Read progressions for blended concepts that are using the Rhythm-Side Rule do not always have to be a different backside route combination. They can be a different frontside combination if you determine it is more favorable.

For example, the Double-Slant combination is best to attack 2-High or 0-High safety coverage structures. If a 1-High safety coverage is being played pre-snap, then the Double-Slant concept can be adjusted to a Scat (Slant-Flat) concept. A 2-Man Scat concept is better suited to attack a 1-High coverage structure. (FIG. 161)

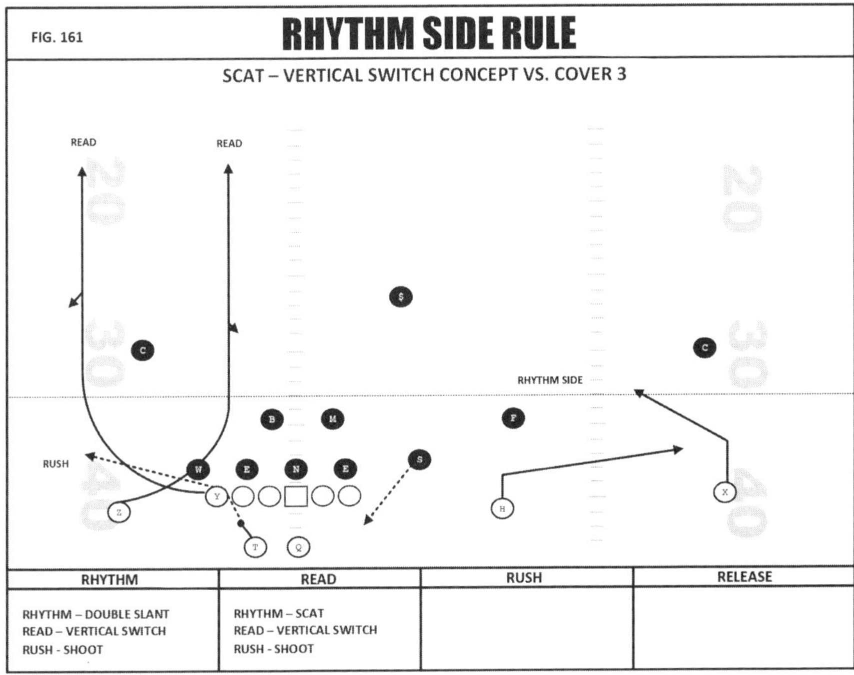

This allows the quarterback to Rhythm – Scat (Rhythm Side), Read – Seam or Fade, Rush – Shoot, then Release. The progression scan remains the same. The benefit to the read progression is that it gets the best quick-game combo to attack the pre-snap coverage shown.

RHYTHM-SIDE RULE: *Double-Slant – Vertical-Switch Concept – Rush Progression*

The Rush progression platform is used to provide a solution for the most anticipated pressure. The Rhythm-side rule naturally elevates Rush Routes into a Rhythm option. The result is a full-field horizontal stretch to the defense that provides "hot" throws to attack rush situations. However, there may be situations or mismatches in games that require a Rush progression platform solution that enhances blended concepts that use the Rhythm-Side Rule.

Screens can be an effective weapon to add onto the Rush progression platform. Attaching a screen with a Rhythm-Side combo can enhance execution against increased pressure shown by the defense. These screen attachments are called P.S.O.s (Pass Screen Options). (FIG 161a)

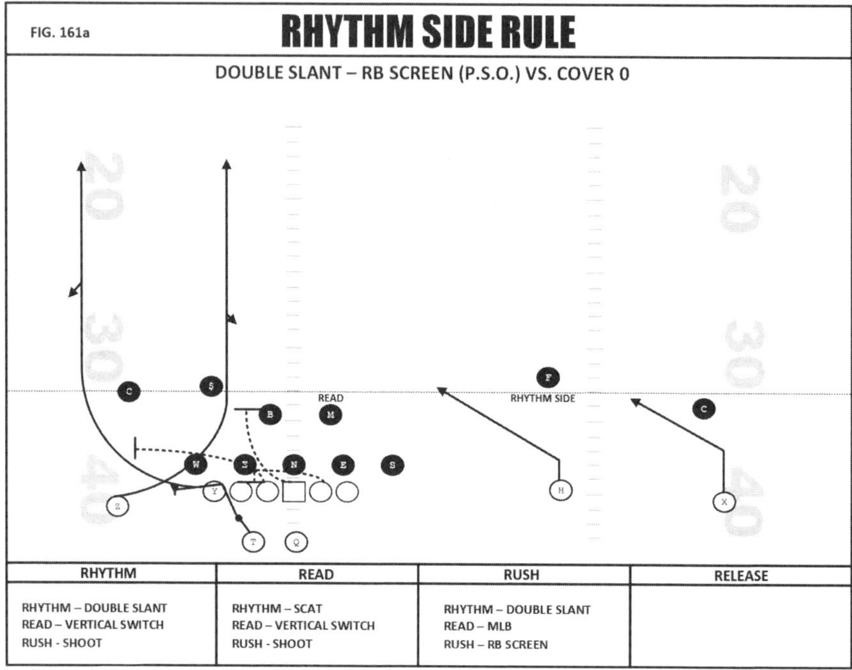

RHYTHM	READ	RUSH	RELEASE
RHYTHM – DOUBLE SLANT READ – VERTICAL SWITCH RUSH - SHOOT	RHYTHM – SCAT READ – VERTICAL SWITCH RUSH - SHOOT	RHYTHM – DOUBLE SLANT READ – MLB RUSH – RB SCREEN	

EXAMPLE: There is only time for one option against a Cover 0 six-man blitz. If you have a clear personnel mismatch, then this situation may not be as threatening. However, if a clear mismatch is not in your favor then P.S.O.s can provide another viable option solution. A P.S.O. is a Rhythm-Side combo attached with a slow screen option. In this scenario, we use the Double Slant combo and attaching a standard running back slow screen to create a P.S.O.

The progression for a P.S.O. is to **Rhythm the Rhythm-Side combo, Read – the conflict defender, and Rush- the Screen.** The specific progression on this play would be to **Rhythm – Double-Slant (Rhythm Side), Read –mlb, Rush-rb screen.**

RHYTHM-SIDE RULE: *Double-Slant – Vertical-Switch Concept – Release Progression*

An example of a release progression for the Double-Slant – Vertical-Switch concept could involve using a Sluggo route. *Sluggo* is a term used for the Slant and Go. When the free safety starts to CAP the Slant route, then a Sluggo is a good counter-route. In this concept, we attach the Sluggo route to the inside Slant and have the outside receiver run a Slant Return. (FIG. 162)

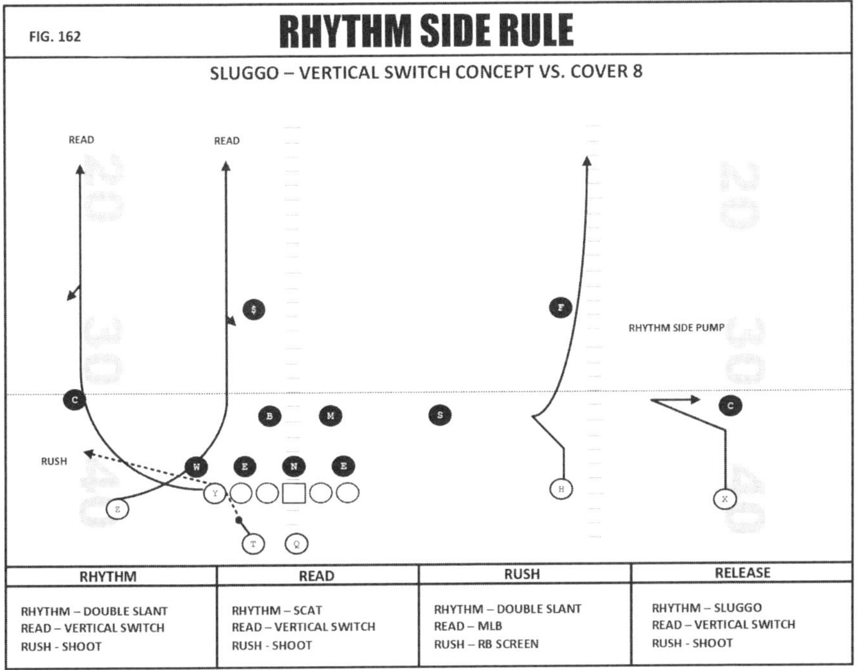

RHYTHM	READ	RUSH	RELEASE
RHYTHM – DOUBLE SLANT READ – VERTICAL SWITCH RUSH - SHOOT	RHYTHM – SCAT READ – VERTICAL SWITCH RUSH - SHOOT	RHYTHM – DOUBLE SLANT READ – MLB RUSH – RB SCREEN	RHYTHM – SLUGGO READ – VERTICAL SWITCH RUSH - SHOOT

A quarterback who has a quick-game double-move route like a Sluggo or Slant Return will use a Rhythm Side Pump. A Rhythm Side Pump is a pump fake that takes place on-Rhythm (last step of the Drop). The quarterback will use a Rhythm-side pump as the decision to reset and throw the double-move route, or to reset and work backside to the dual-Read Route combination.

In this progression, the quarterback will ***Rhythm – Pump*** (if the safety jumps on the pump fake, then QB will reset and throw the Sluggo, if safety does not jump on the pump fake, the quarterback will reset to the ***Dual-Read Route-side, Rush – Shoot, then Release.***

3 Man QUICK RULE

The final route rule is the 3-Man Quick Rule. The 3-Man Quick Rule states that any 3-Man adjacent combination of Rhythm/Rush Routes can be placed in a ***Rhythm-Read-Rush*** progression. In Shotgun, this can only be done by adjusting the footwork of the Drop by the quarterback. For a 3-Man Quick Combination to use a ***Rhythm-Read-Rush*** progression, the quarterback must shorten the timeline of the Drop by taking a 2-step Drop or quick 3-step Drop.

> *The* ***3-Man Quick Rule*** *states that any 3-Man adjacent combination of Rhythm/Rush Routes can be placed in a* ***Rhythm-Read-Rush*** *progression.*

This shortened timeline allows the quarterback to fit 3 quick routes in a progression within their break points. A 2-step or quick 3-step Drop sets up the quarterback to hit the first quick route on-Rhythm, while allowing him to reset to an adjacent Rhythm/Rush Route and hit it with Read Route timing. This also allows him an additional reset step to another adjacent Rhythm/Rush Route and hit it with Rush Route timing.

The goal of the 2-step or quick 3-step Shotgun Drop is to hit the last step of the Drop around 1.4-1.6 seconds. Each reset of the feet is around .40 seconds. A quarterback who hits the last step of the Drop at 1.4 seconds and resets would be at 2.0 seconds on the timeline. This is the Read Route segment of the progression. A quarterback taking an additional reset would be at 2.4 seconds on the timeline. This is the Rush Route segment of the progression.

3 Man QUICK RULE – *SPACING CONCEPT (SPOT – SIT – ARROW)*

Spacing concepts can be created with a variety of routes. In general, a spacing concept consists of 3 adjacent routes that break around or underneath the hard-deck at 7 yards from the line of scrimmage. (FIG. 163)

One of the most common spacing route combinations in football is the Spot-Sit-Arrow. The Spot and Sit Route are Snap Rhythm Routes. A Snap Rhythm is a horizontal breaking route that breaks open around the hard-deck in 1.8 seconds. The Spot and Sit Route terminate in space. Therefore, they require quick-game footwork used in the 3-man quick rule to fit both into a progression.

Using the 3-man quick rule, a quarterback would use a 2-step or quick 3-step Drop and ***Rhythm – Spot, Read – Sit, Rush – Arrow, and then Release.*** The primary Rhythm progression for this spacing concept would be to work the field or strong side of the formation. The secondary read progression would be to work the boundary or weak side of

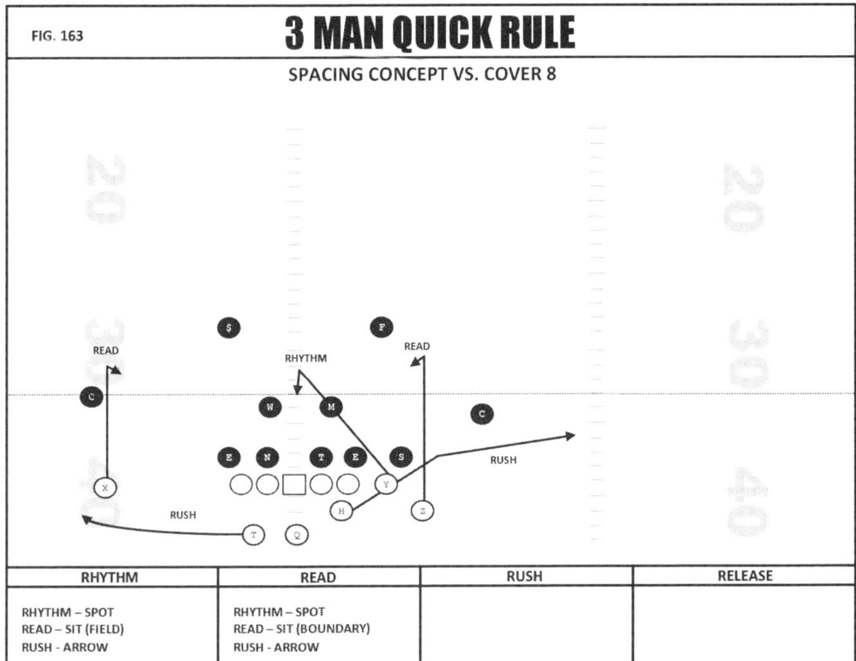

the formation. The read progression is more favorable against safety rotation-strong or pressure-weak.

3-MAN QUICK RULE – ***SPACING CONCEPT (SLANT – SLANT - ARROW)***

Another 3-Man Route combination that creates a spacing concept is a Slant-Slant-Arrow. This variation of spacing is effective against Man Coverages because the Slant routes do not have to terminate in space. A quarterback will use the 3-Man Quick Rule to create a ***Rhythm-Read-Rush*** progression with this spacing concept. The quarterback would accelerate his Drop footwork and ***Rhythm – Inside Slant, Read – Outside Slant, Rush – Arrow.*** (FIG. 164)

The Rhythm progression would be to work the spacing concept to the field or strong side of the formation. The Read progression would be to work the boundary or weak side of the formation.

3-MAN QUICK RULE – ***SPACING CONCEPT (QUICK OUT – STICK – ANGLE)***

The final spacing concept that we will discuss is a 3-man route combination that consists of a Ouick Out-Stick-Angle. This version of spacing is effective against both Man and Zone Coverages. The out-breaks of the Quick Out and stick are good Man beaters with defenders playing

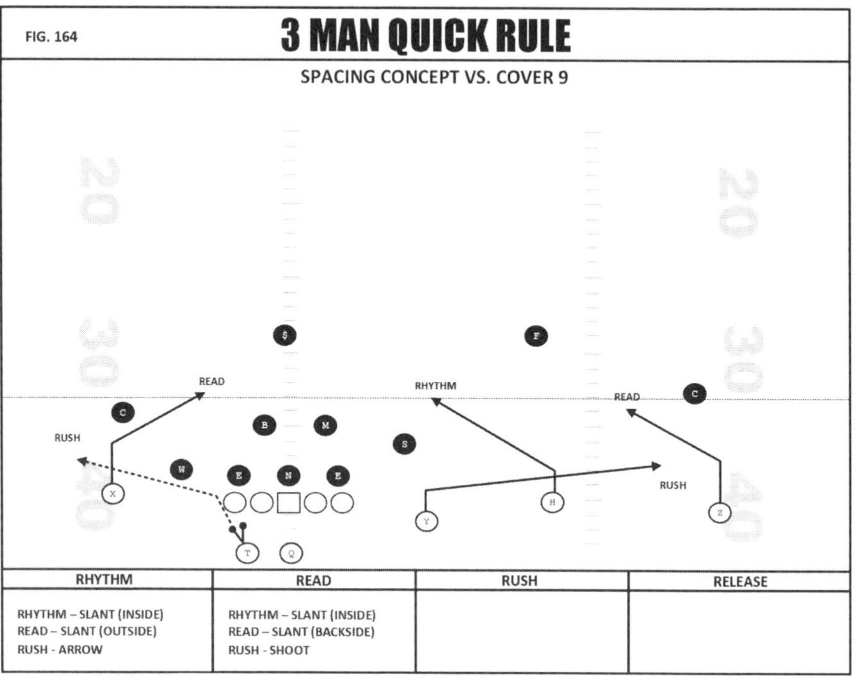

RHYTHM	READ	RUSH	RELEASE
RHYTHM – SLANT (INSIDE) READ – SLANT (OUTSIDE) RUSH - ARROW	RHYTHM – SLANT (INSIDE) READ – SLANT (BACKSIDE) RUSH - SHOOT		

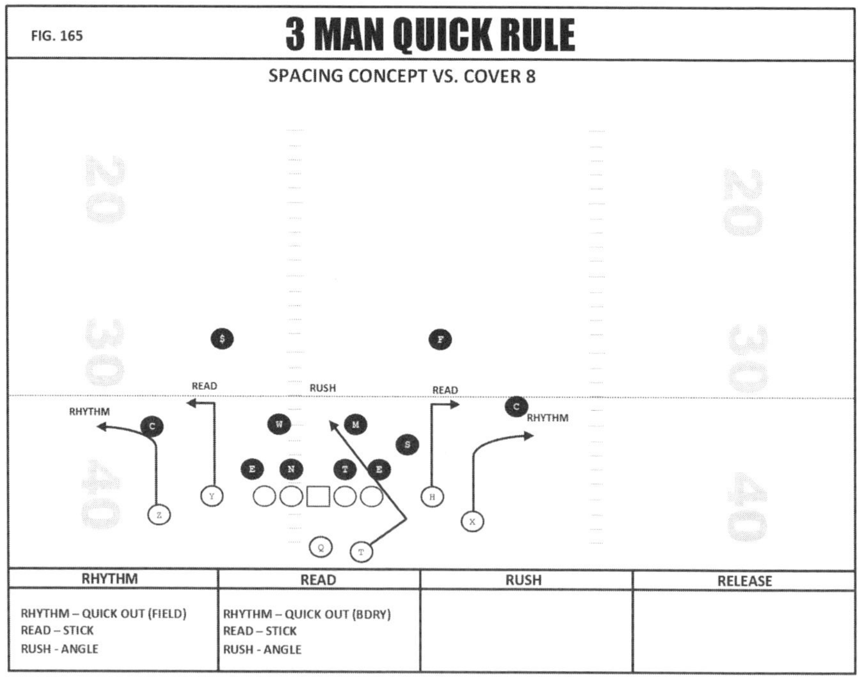

RHYTHM	READ	RUSH	RELEASE
RHYTHM – QUICK OUT (FIELD) READ – STICK RUSH - ANGLE	RHYTHM – QUICK OUT (BDRY) READ – STICK RUSH - ANGLE		

inside leverage on receivers. The spacing of the out-breaking routes places a considerable stretch on Zone flat defenders, along with the angle route attack the middle-void, under-spot, Zone-Dropping linebackers. (FIG. 165)

The quarterback uses the 3-Man Quick Rule to accelerate his footwork Rhythm-Quick Out, Read-Stick, Rush-Angle, and then Release. The Rhythm progression for this concept would be to work the field or strong side of the formation. The read progression would be to work the boundary or weak side of the formation.

CREATING CONCEPTS THAT USE MULTIPLE RULES

The individual R4 route rules create a context to increase adaptability within concepts. The R4 route rules can also be stacked together within a concept to further accelerate versatility and adaptability. A prime example of this is seen in using the Stick concept. (Fig. 166)

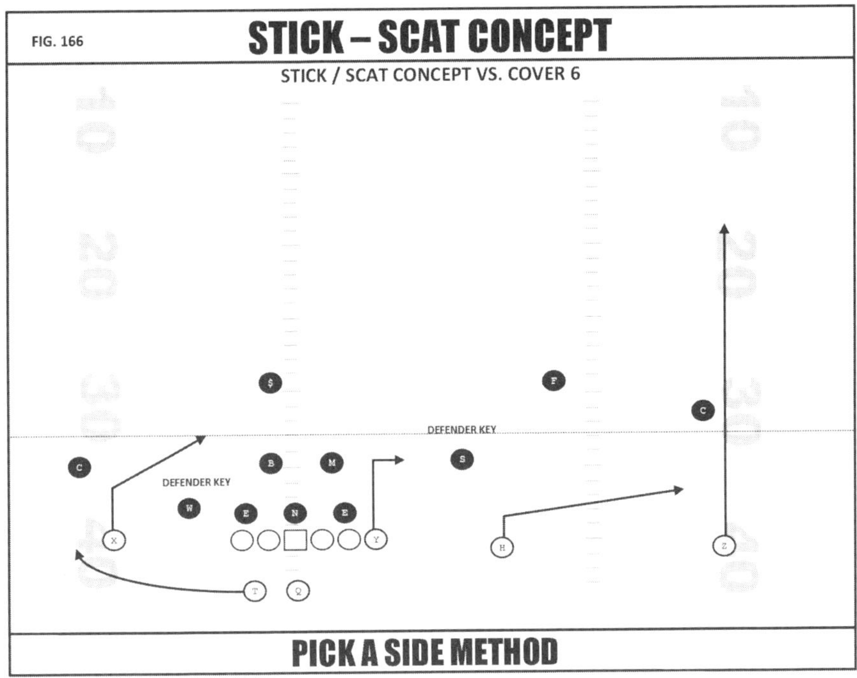

EXAMPLE: In this diagram, there is a Stick (Fade-Stick-Flat) concept on the right and a Scat (Slant-Flat) concept on the left. Generally, the quarterback is taught to pick the side he likes best, based on mismatch, Blitz, or space, and throw opposite of a single defender-key post-snap to only routes on that side post-snap. While this method can work, there is a lot of opportunity missed and information that is left for loose interpretation by the quarterback.

RHYTHM-SIDE RULE + 3 Man QUICK RULE:
Stick – Scat Concept – Rhythm Progression
The advantage of using the R4 route combination rules is that it streamlines that decision-making process for the quarterback. The route rules provide different full-field platform progressions that can be used based on the intent of the defensive actions. Opening the quarterback's opportunities to read the full field keeps his field of view wide so he can process more than a single defender move. It also applies more stress on the defense when a consistent full-field attack is available. (FIG. 167)

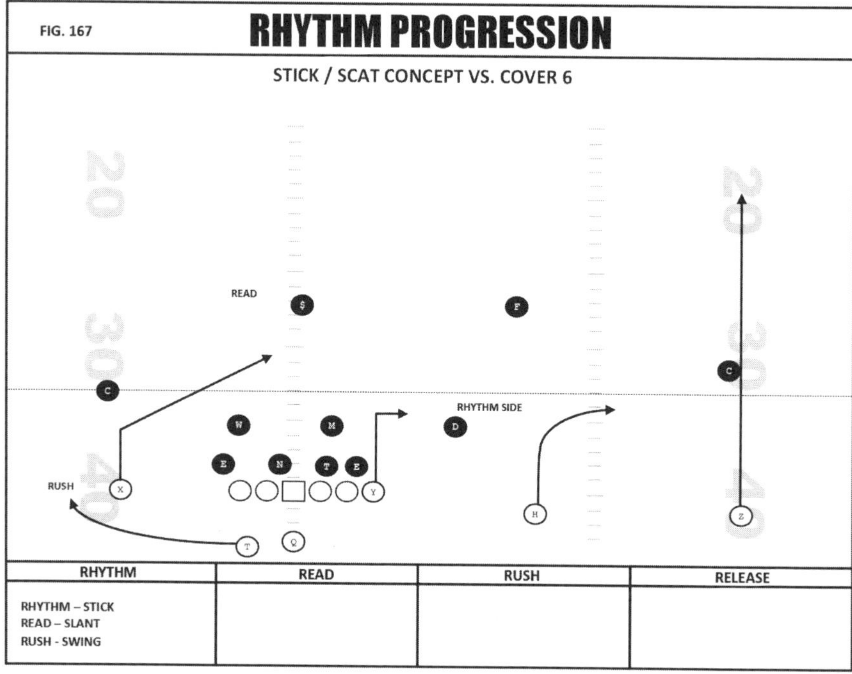

The Rhythm-Side Rule allows the quarterback to Rhythm the Stick concept with Rhythm timing. The quarterback will determine pre-snap and post-snap on the Drop which route of the Stick concept is UNCAPPED. Combining the Rhythm-Side Rule with the 3-Man Quick Rule allows the quarterback to bring the backside Scat concept online. This creates a ***3-Man Quick Rhythm – Stick, Read – Slant, Rush – Swing*** progression.

Now the quarterback can accelerate his footwork on the Drop to Rhythm the Stick concept, reset his feet to the ***Read – Slant, reset again to Rush – Swing, and then Release.*** The footwork and resets of the quarterback must be accelerated as stated in the 3-Man Quick Rule. This is the primary Rhythm progression for the Stick – Scat concept.

RHYTHM-SIDE RULE:

Stick – Read Route Concept – Read Progression

One of the adjustments that the defense will use to CAP the Stick-Scat concept is to push the under-coverage to the field, to CAP the stick and use inside Man or Zone leverage by the boundary cornerback to CAP the backside Slant space. To counter this defensive adjustment, use a Read Progression. The Read Progression for the Stick-Scat concept is to transplant the Slant route with a Read Route that attacks the UNCAPPED space of the backside coverage. (FIG. 168)

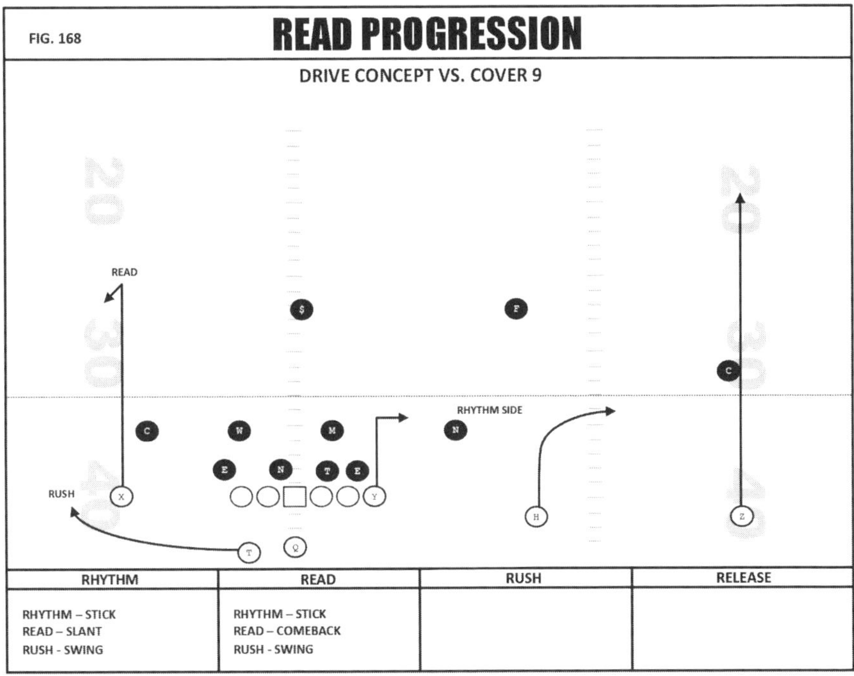

RHYTHM	READ	RUSH	RELEASE
RHYTHM – STICK READ – SLANT RUSH - SWING	RHYTHM – STICK READ – COMEBACK RUSH - SWING		

EXAMPLE: If the defense is playing a Man technique on the backside Slant and the receiver cannot own inside route-space, then replace the slant with a Read Route that attacks outside space. A comeback route is used here. The quarterback would ***Rhythm -Stick (Rhythm side), Read – Comeback, Rush – Swing, and then Release.***

The route that is used can be signaled or tagged onto the play. The signal, or tag, alerts the quarterback to use the read progression for the concept.

RHYTHM-SIDE RULE: ***Stick – Read Route Concept – Rush Progression***
Another adjustment the defense would use to CAP the Stick-Scat concept is to play Man Coverage and bring Blitz pressure. The quarterback would use a Rush Progression in this situation. (FIG. 169)

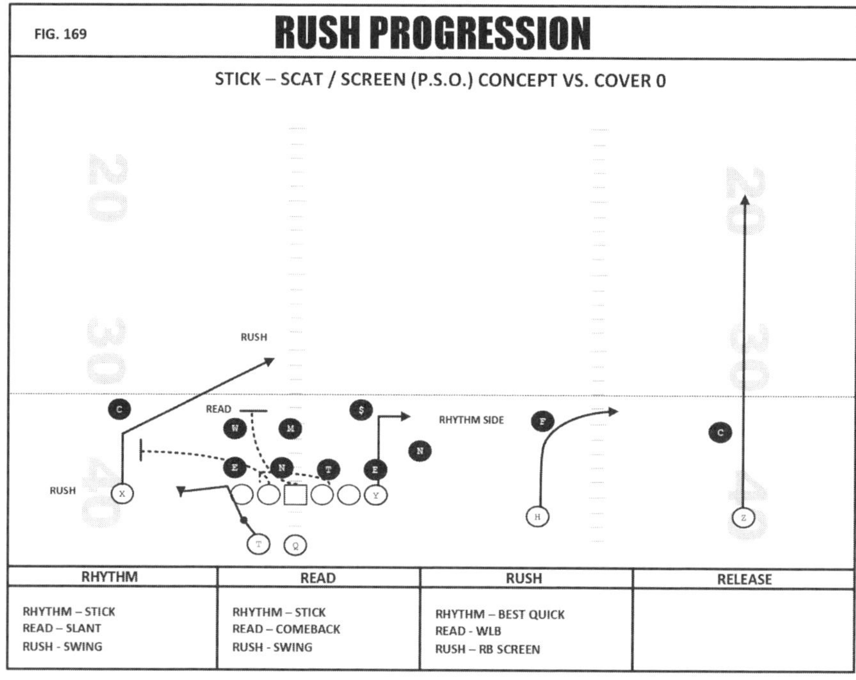

RHYTHM	READ	RUSH	RELEASE
RHYTHM – STICK READ – SLANT RUSH - SWING	RHYTHM – STICK READ – COMEBACK RUSH - SWING	RHYTHM – BEST QUICK READ - WLB RUSH – RB SCREEN	

A good Rush Progression strategy to use with Rhythm Side Rule + 3 Quick Rule concepts is to use a P.S.O. adjustment. Pass Screen Option concepts provide an additional weapon into the progression if the quick route is CAPPED on rhythm. The Rush progression for this P.S.O. is ***Rhythm – Best quick, Read – wlb and Rush – rb screen.***

We teach the quarterback to use the mental coaching phrase, “If you feel the Rush, throw the Rush.” Meaning that whenever the Rush pressure is felt to a side, then you will throw the best Rush Route into the pressure to that side.

RHYTHM-SIDE RULE: ***Stick – Read Route Concept – Release Progression***
The Release Progression for the Stick-Read Route concept is a game-planned progression based on the post-snap defensive reactions to a specific progression. (FIG. 170)

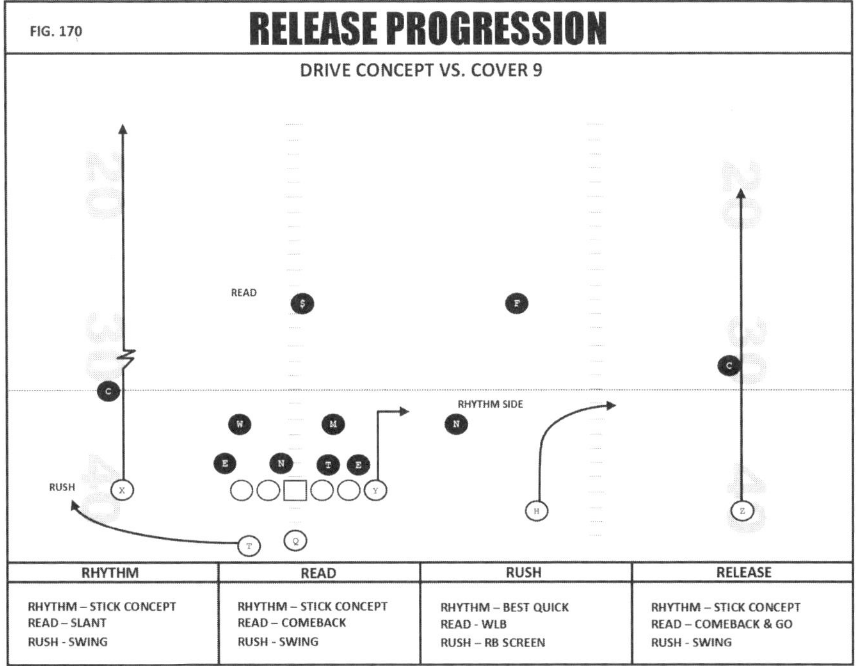

RHYTHM	READ	RUSH	RELEASE
RHYTHM – STICK CONCEPT READ – SLANT RUSH - SWING	RHYTHM – STICK CONCEPT READ – COMEBACK RUSH - SWING	RHYTHM – BEST QUICK READ - WLB RUSH – RB SCREEN	RHYTHM – STICK CONCEPT READ – COMEBACK & GO RUSH - SWING

EXAMPLE: Say you have been using a Read Progression with a ***Rhythm – Stick, Read – Comeback and Rush – Swing.*** You anticipate that a Man defender covering the Comeback may quickly close and therefore make a play on the Comeback throw. To protect the Comeback Route, go to a Release progression and replace the Comeback with a Comeback-and-Go-Double-Move Route.

On the Release progression, the quarterback would ***Rhythm – Stick, Read – Comeback & Go, Rush – Swing, and then Release.***

CHAPTER 12

RPO – Rush Attachments and R4 Progression Platforms

RHYTHM READ
R4
RUSH RELEASE

RPO – RUSH ATTACHMENTS AND R4 PROGRESSION PLATFORMS

If you have ever fired a tactical rifle, chances are there are parts of the rifle you liked and parts of the rifle you would like to modify. The preferences between shooters gave rise to customizable rifles like the AR-15. There are virtually endless ways an AR-15 can be upgraded with certain components that are tailored to best suit the shooter and the intent of the use of the weapon.

RPOs (Run Pass Option) concepts have similar characteristics to these customized weapons. RPOs provide extreme customization by the coach and his players. Mixtures of runs with perimeter screens or quick passes can be assorted in many ways to provide maximum stress on a defense. This can enhance versatility within an offense. However, it can also create an environment for confusion.

With so many options, it is easy for a coach to get lost in the fun of drawing up new schemes that can attack a defense. If the coach gets lost, then the players will soon follow. R4 progression platforms can provide the guardrails needed for coaches and players to network their RPO concepts without losing their way in the mist of battle.

Before we go through how to network different RPO attachments on progression platforms, we need to show how to use an R4 progression to navigate a quarterback through a concept. RPOs begin with a Run concept. The Run concept used replaces the Rhythm Route of a passing progression. Therefore, each RPO will always begin and be built upon the Rhythm Run of the play. The Read Route will be replaced by the defender who is not being blocked in the RPO concept. This could be a 1st, 2nd or 3rd level defender. Whoever the coach determines is the unblocked defender will become the quarterback's Read on the play. The Rush Route is replaced by a perimeter screen or Quick-Game Rush Route/Concept that creates a stretch on a defender. (FIG. 171)

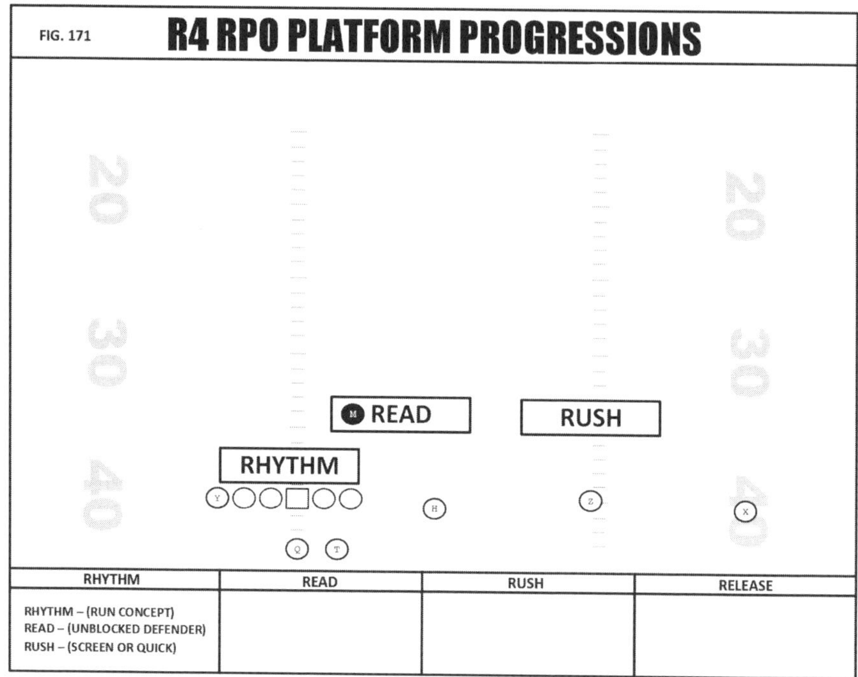

RHYTHM	READ	RUSH	RELEASE
RHYTHM – (RUN CONCEPT) READ – (UNBLOCKED DEFENDER) RUSH – (SCREEN OR QUICK)			

A quarterback using a R4 progression to navigate a RPO would ***Rhythm – Run, Read – Unblocked Defender, Rush – Perimeter Screen/Quick, and then Release – Escape.***

Rush attachments are singular routes, perimeter-Key Screens or Quick-Game Route combinations that provide the pass option to the Run concept of an RPO. Like the upgrade components that can be added onto an AR-15 tactical rifle, so are the Rush attachments to the RPOs.

It is important to understand the cost-benefit that comes in using different Rush attachments with a Rhythm Run concept. Some run schemes may not fit well with the timing needed to let the routes develop. For example, pairing a One-Back Power Run concept with a Slant-and-Go Rush attachment may not sync well. Pulling a guard on a One-Back Power Run could place the puller too far downfield by the time the throw of the Slant is made. These are factors to consider when building your RPO concepts.

Coaches must also consider which Rush attachment best attacks the defensive-intent on a given play. Rush attachments in RPOs are best used to attack Zone Coverage. There are many variations of Zone Coverage that can be used to attack RPOs. There are also many different post-snap defender reactions within a coverage that can take away a Rush attachment.

3 key factors must be considered when building and selecting the best RPOs for a situation:

> *1. Does the Rush attachment have time to develop before the Rhythm Run scheme gets linemen downfield?*
>
> *2. Does the Rush attachment attack the anticipated coverage of the defense?*
>
> *3. Does the Rush attachment have a counter scheme or move that attacks the post-snap defensive personnel reactions to the concept?*

These questions can be answered faster by grouping Rush attachments into families.

RUSH ATTACHMENTS – KEY SCREENS FAMILY

The Key Screen Rush attachment family consists of any 2- or 3-man combination of routes that has at least one route that breaks on or behind the line of scrimmage. Key Screen concepts develop in 1-1.4 seconds and attach better with run schemes that have linemen who may quickly get downfield. There are 5 families of 3-Man Key Screen Rush attachments. We have chosen to use the 3-Man Key Screens to teach the relationships. The 2-man Key Screen Rush attachments would carry the same route properties.

ARROW SCREEN

The first Rush attachment in the Key Screen family is the Arrow screen. The Arrow screen is a 3-man route concept that contains only one route option for the quarterback. The #3 receiver pushes off his inside foot and runs flat down the line of scrimmage toward the sideline. (FIG. 172)

The Arrow Route in this concept is not to be run at full-speed. It is important that the Arrow runner throttle his route down to allow time for the quarterback to mesh and read the Rhythm Run progression of the RPO.

The #2 receiver will block the first defender outside the apex line. The #1 receiver will block the cornerback. This Rush attachment is best used to attack Zone Coverages with a cornerback who is above the hard-deck. Coverage examples the Arrow Screen would attack are Cover-3, 4, 6, 8, and 9.

Some coaches run the Bubble Route by the #3 receiver instead of the Arrow Route. The Bubble attacks the same space and maintains the same conceptual integrity. If this is desired, then the Bubble Screen replaces the Arrow Screen.

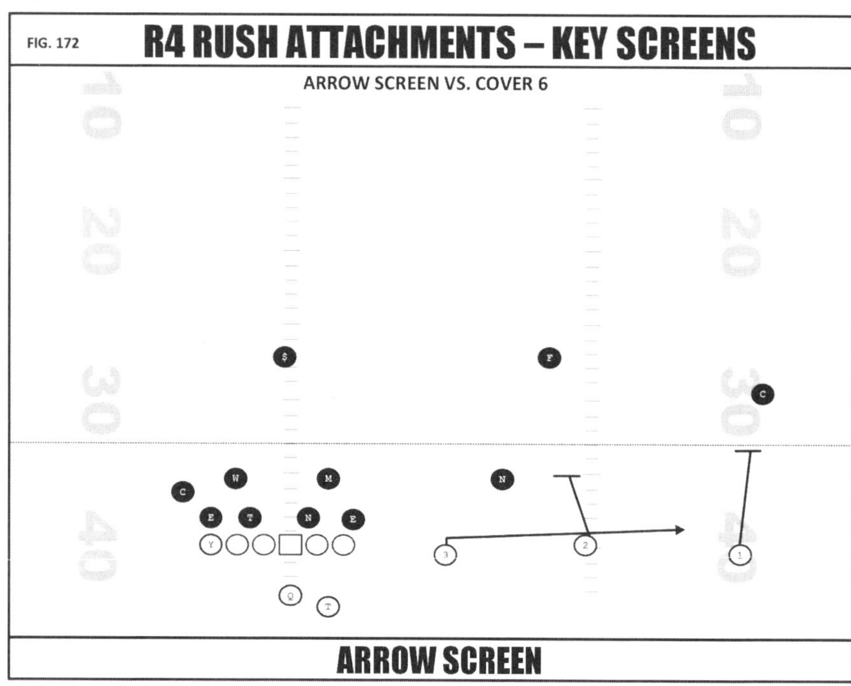

FIG. 172

STICK SCREEN

The next Rush attachment in the Key Screen family is the Stick Screen. The Stick Screen is a 3-man route concept that creates two route options for the quarterback. The #3 receiver drives for 5 yards and turns inside on a Stick Route. If the #3 receiver is attached to the formation like a tight end, then he would turn outside at 5 yards on the Stick Route. The #2 receiver will run a no-step Arrow Route down the line of scrimmage as instructed in the Arrow Screen. The #1 receiver blocks the most dangerous defender. (FIG. 173)

The Stick Screen Rush attachment is best to attack Zone Coverages with the cornerback above the hard-deck. Coverage examples the Stick Screen would attack are Cover-3, 4, 6, 8, and 9. The Stick Route provides

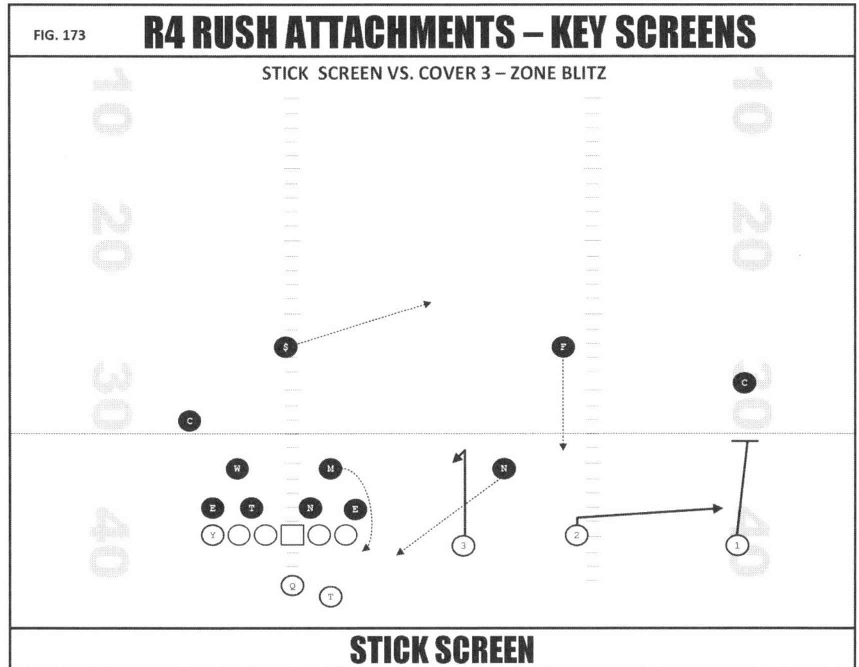

a "hot" route option against Zone Dog (single linebacker pressure) or Zone Blitzes (double linebacker pressures). This is an important counter to have available against a defense who shows intent to use these types of pressures.

NOW SCREEN

The next Rush attachment in the Key Screen family is the Now Screen. The Now Screen is a 3-Man Route concept with two route options for the quarterback. The #3 receiver blocks the most dangerous flat defender head-up to outside his pre-snap alignment. The #2 receiver jabs one step forward and throttles down the line of scrimmage toward the quarterback. The #1 receiver runs a Fade Route. (FIG. 174)

The Now Screen attachment is best used to attack Zone Coverages with a cornerback who is below the hard-deck. Coverage examples that the Now Screen would attack are Cover-2, 3-Cloud, and 7. Running the Now by the #2 receiver and blocking out with the #3 receiver attacks the leverage positions of the flat and hook/curl defenders in these coverages. The Fade by the #1 receiver is a pure match-up throw. This is used mostly as a run-off block in this concept.

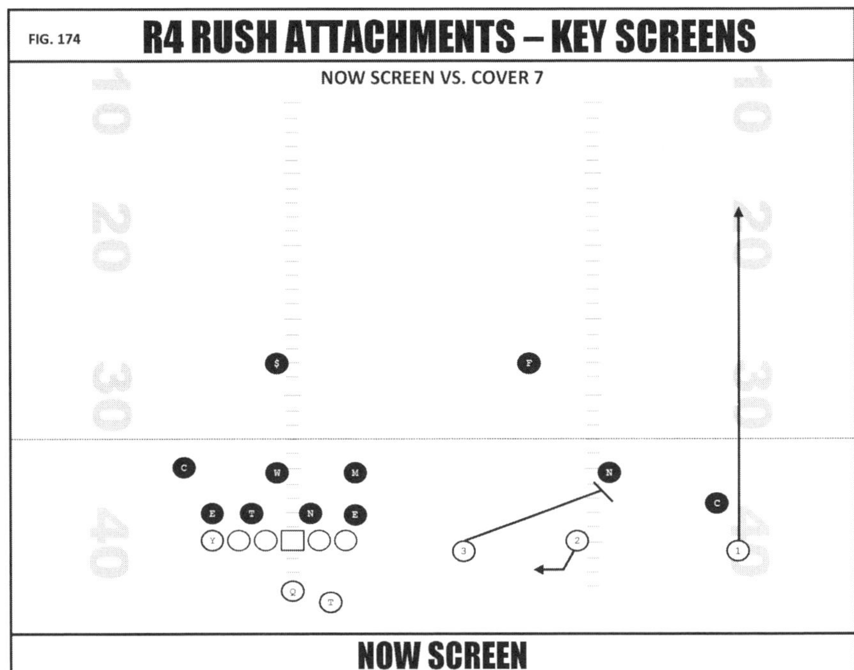

SMOKE SCREEN

The next Rush attachment in the Key Screen family is the Smoke Screen. The Smoke Screen is another 3-man route concept with two route options for the quarterback. The #3 receiver runs a Stick Route. The #2 receiver blocks the most dangerous Man who is head-up to outside-leverage of his pre-snap alignment. The #1 receiver runs a 1-step Now Route that throttles down and attacks the quarterback down the line of scrimmage. (FIG. 175)

The Smoke Screen attachment is best used to attack Man and Zone Coverages that play a cornerback below the hard-deck. Coverage examples would be Cover-0, 1, 2, and 3-Cloud. The Stick Route provides the "hot" route benefit against Zone pressures. The Now Route by the #1 receiver and out block by the #2 receiver provides an improved leverage block against a Hard-Zone or Man cornerback. It also creates a natural Pick Route against Man Coverages like Cover-0 or 1.

SHOT SCREENS -TORCH

Shot Screens are designed double-move route combos that mirror the initial stems of the Key Screen Rush attachments. Shot Screens attack the post-snap personnel accelerator actions that are CAPPING a Key

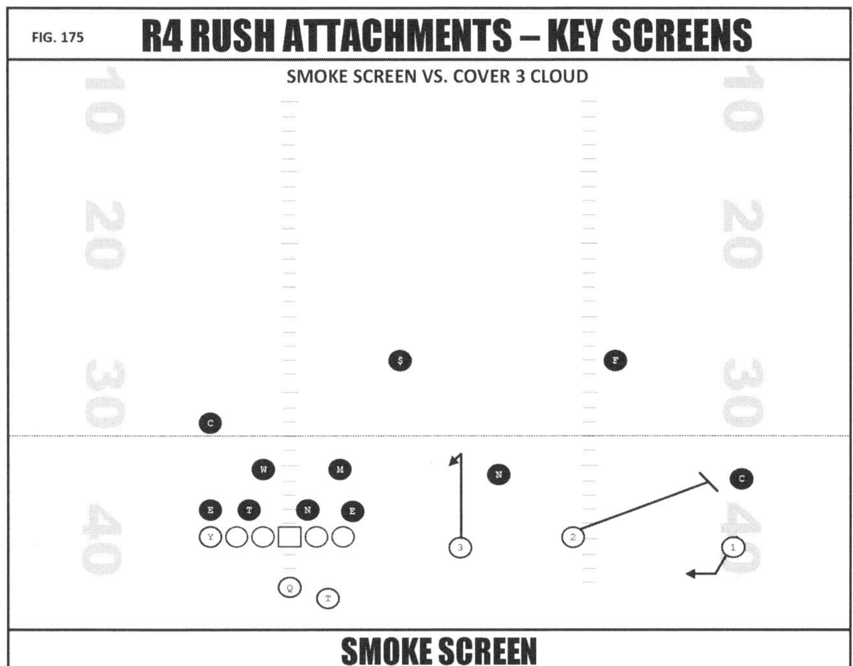

Screen concept. Shot Screens can be used in a RPO or with play-action pass-protection, depending on how long it takes for them to develop. (FIG. 176)

EXAMPLE: You have been running an RPO with a Smoke Screen Rush attachment. The Torch Screen is a Shot Screen concept that counters post-snap defensive personal actions that attempt to CAP it. The initial stem of the Torch Screen looks exactly like the Smoke Screen causing the defenders to trigger and CAP the flat route-space. This UNCAPs the vertical space that the Torch Screen attacks. The Torch Screen takes longer to develop due to the buzz of the feet to sell the Stick Route and block on the Now Route. Play-action pass-protection would be used on the Torch Shot Screen to allow enough time to set up.

Ideally, you should have Shot Screens built to use from your most commonly used Rush attachments. However, some Key Screen concepts can be protected by Quick-Game combinations.

RUSH ATTACHMENTS – QUICK-GAME FAMILY

The Quick-Game Rush attachment family consists of any 2 or 3-man combination of routes that has at least one route that breaks on or behind the line of scrimmage. Quick-Game concepts are different the Key Screen concepts in that they push vertical beyond the line of scrimmage before the break. This forces the routes to develop in 1.4-1.8 seconds. The benefit of Quick-Game Rush attachments is that they attack vertically, delaying the defender's post-snap CAPPING ability for a moment in time. This can give the quarterback more time to process the best route-space to attack in an RPO.

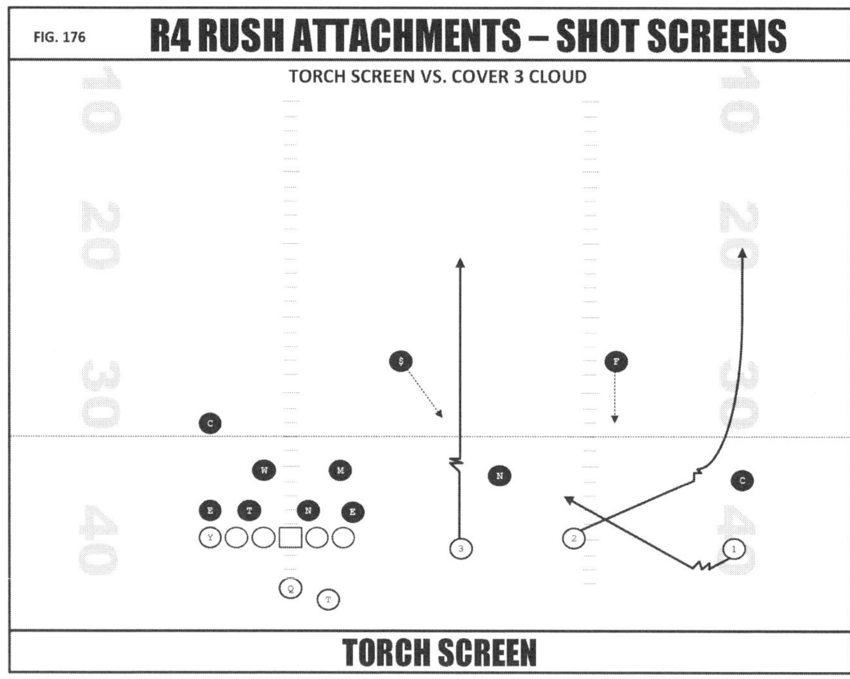

RPO concepts that use Quick-Game Rush attachments may require Rhythm Run Schemes that do not get linemen immediately downfield. Examples would be inside-zone and outside-zone Run concepts. There are 5 families of 3-man Quick-Game Rush attachments.

3-SCAT QUICK

The first Rush attachment in the quick family is 3-Scat. 3-Scat consists of a double-slant and flat route. The 3 in 3-Scat signifies that the #3 receiver runs the flat. The #2 receiver runs a 3-step Slant. The #3 receiver runs a 5-step Slant. This Quick-Game Rush attachment is an all-weather concept in that it can attack both Man and Zone Coverage well. (FIG. 177)

The 3-Scat Rush attachment has an initial stem that mirrors the Arrow Screen Rush attachment. This is another benefit of the 3-Scat Rush attach-

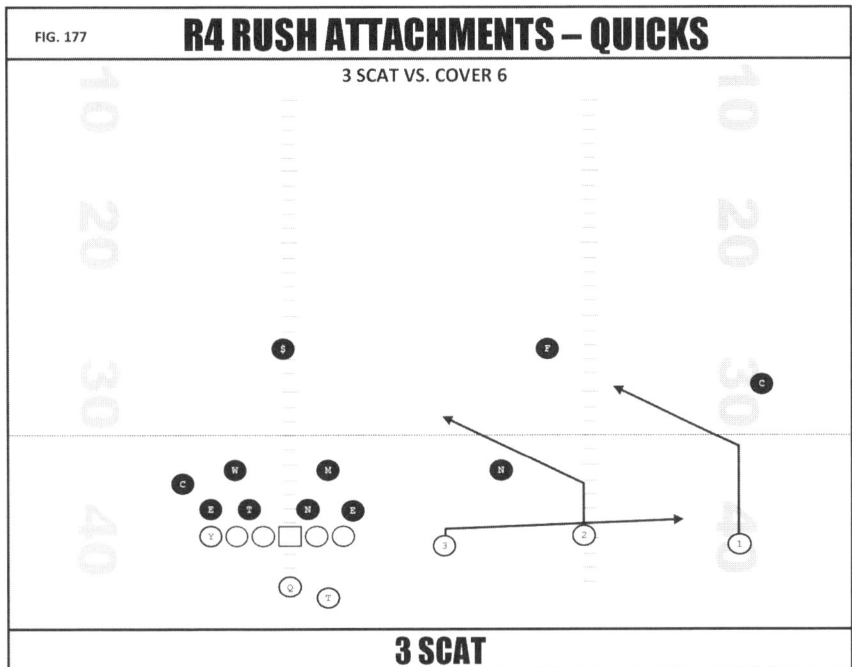

ment. It protects the Arrow Screen concept from defenders who are aggressive in CAPPING the Arrow Route, post- snap.

SCAT QUICK

The next Rush attachment in the Quick family is Scat. Scat consists of two Slants and a Flat Route. The difference between Scat and 3-Scat is that the #3 receiver runs a 3-step Slant instead of a Flat. The #2 receiver runs the Flat Route. The #1 receiver runs a 5-Step Slant. (FIG. 178)

Scat is designed to provide a "hot" throw with the #3 receiver running a Slant. This attacks the interior pressure of a Blitzing linebacker quicker. Scat is another all-weather concept that attacks both Man and Zone Coverage well. The priority of using Scat over 3-Scat depends on the anticipation of a Blitz or how the flat defender reacts to the Flat Route, post-snap.

DITCH QUICK

The next Rush attachment in the Quick family is Ditch. Ditch consists of double-hitches and a Fade Route. The #1 receiver runs a Fade. The #2 and #3 receivers run Hitches. The Ditch Rush attachment is designed to attack Zone Coverages that have a corner below the hard-deck. The Ditch concept best attacks Cover-2, 3 Cloud, and 7. (FIG. 179)

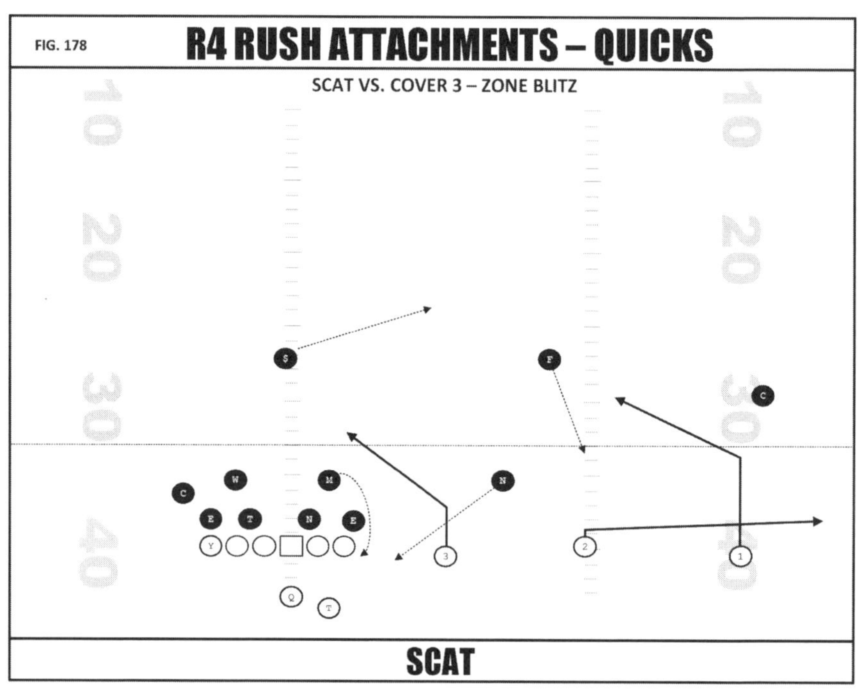
FIG. 178
R4 RUSH ATTACHMENTS – QUICKS
SCAT VS. COVER 3 – ZONE BLITZ
SCAT

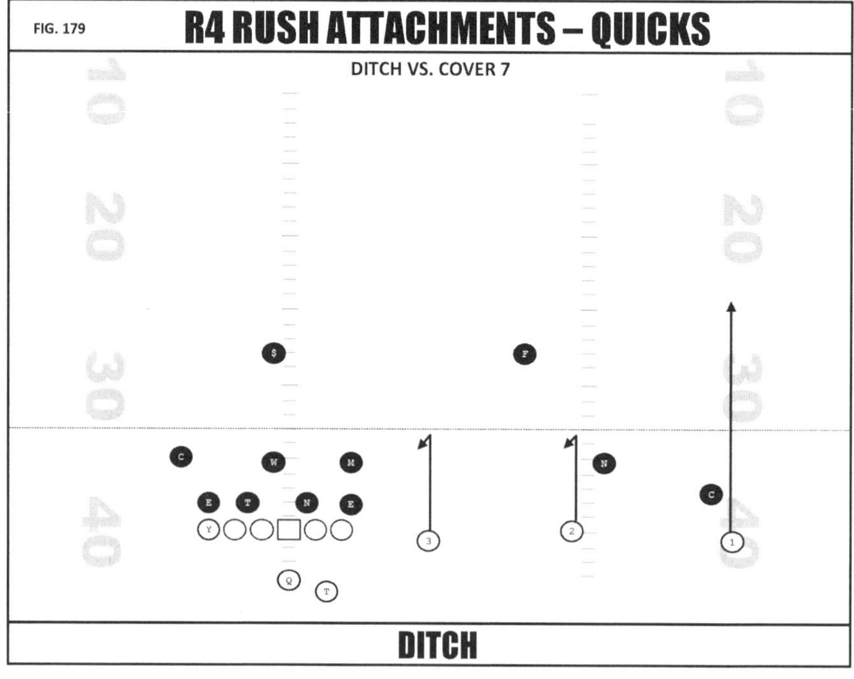
FIG. 179
R4 RUSH ATTACHMENTS – QUICKS
DITCH VS. COVER 7
DITCH

STICK QUICK

The next Rush attachment in the Quick family is the Stick concept. The Stick concept consist of a Fade by the #1 receiver, Quick-Out by the #2 receiver, and a Stick Route by the #3 receiver. The vertical value of the Fade, Out, and Stick allows more time for the quarterback to read the flat defender post-snap to determine the best UNCAPPED route. The Stick concept best attacks Zone Coverages with cornerbacks above the hard-deck. Cover-3, 4, 6, 8, and 9 are examples. (FIG. 180)

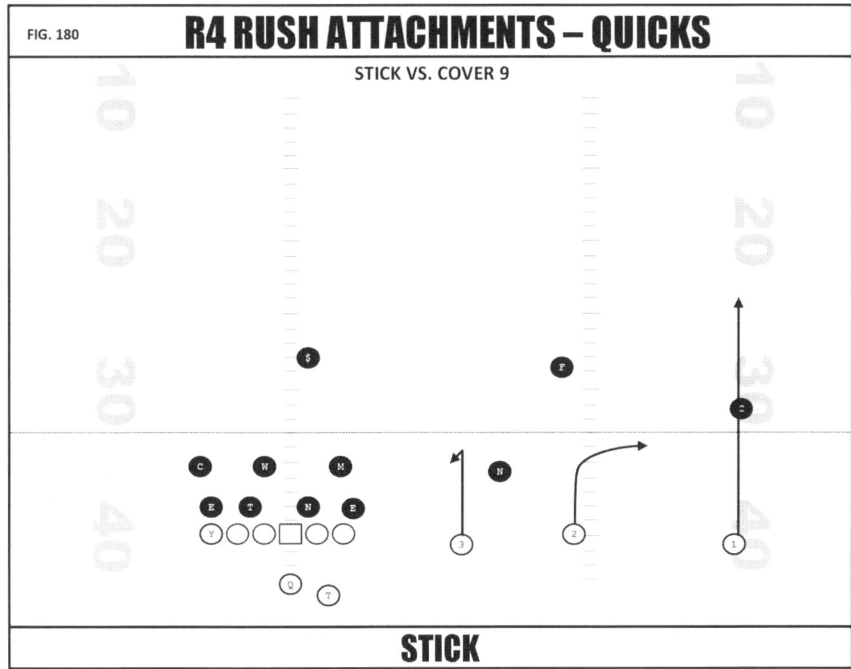

QUICK PUMPS - SHAKE

The final Rush attachment in the Quick family is Quick Pumps. Quick Pumps are concepts that are designed to have at least one Double-Move Route that counters the breaks of a Base-Quick concept.

EXAMPLE: We use the Stick Quick Rush attachment in a RPO concept. The defensive personnel have started to CAP the Stick concept post-snap, or we are anticipated a coverage adjustment to take the Stick concept away. This is the time to use a Quick-Pump concept.

The Shake concept is an example of a Quick-Pump Rush attachment that counters the breaks of the Stick concept. The #1 receiver still runs a Fade. The #2 receiver runs a Whip Route. The #3 receiver runs a Shake Route (Stick-and-Go). Quick-Pumps are like Shot Screens in that they can be used in an RPO or with play-action pass protection. (FIG. 181)

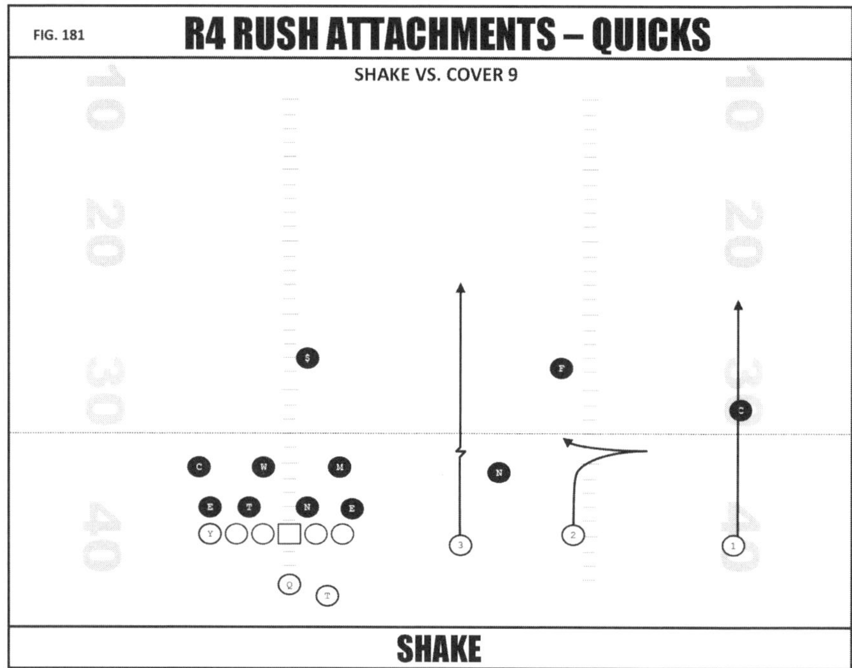

The Shake concept should be used with play-action pass-protection because of the time it takes for the concept to develop. The quarterback Play-Fakes with the running back and Pump-Fakes like he is throwing the Stick Route. If the defenders trigger to CAP the Stick Route, then the quarterback resets to throw the Shake. If they defenders do not trigger, then the quarterback resets to the Whip Route.

We recommend that you have Quick-Pumps built to counter your most commonly used Quick Rush attachments. Quick-Pumps provide explosive play opportunities that every offense needs in the game plan.

RPO – R4 PROGRESSION PLATFORMS

The Key Screen and Quick-Game Rush attachments families reveal the relationships between concept and provide context to what attachment is best used against a specific coverage. They also helped determine what attachments work best with the Rhythm Run scheme of an RPO. Lastly, it shows how to protect and set up a Base Rush attachment for an explosive play by using a Shot Screen or Quick-Pump concept.

Rush attachment families provide the coach and players the ability to customize the best RPOs to attack a defense. That is only the first step in the process. The real magic is being able to build a network of RPOs together that provide answers to the reactions of the defense. R4 progression platforms provide the foundation necessary to sequence concepts in this manner.

PIN-PULL RPO: ***R4 Progression Platforms -Rhythm Progression***
The Rhythm progression platform for RPOs is determined based on the most anticipated front and coverage that the defense will play to an offensive formation.

EXAMPLE: We plan a TE closed-trips formation and the defense is expected to play an Over-Front with Cover-9 against it. First determine your Rhythm run scheme that best attacks the Over-Front. In this example, we decided to use a Pin-Pull Scheme as our Rhythm Run. (FIG. 182)

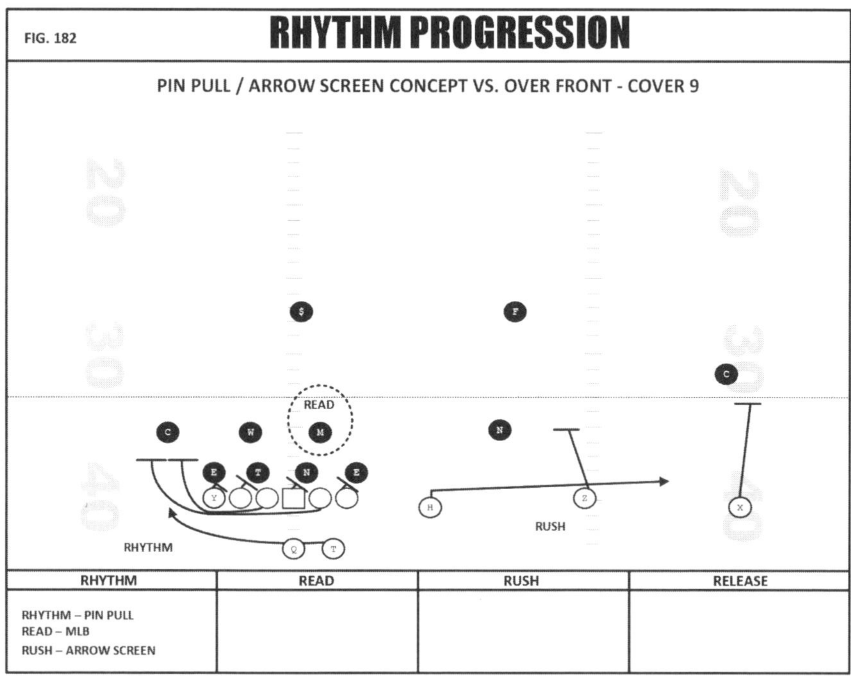

RHYTHM	READ	RUSH	RELEASE
RHYTHM – PIN PULL READ – MLB RUSH – ARROW SCREEN			

The read for the RPO is the unblocked defender who we are trying to place in conflict. In the Pin-Pull concept, the read is the backside inside linebacker. The goal is to delay the pursuit of this defender with the Key Screen and quarterback run-threat on the backside of the run play.

The Rush attachment for this RPO concept was the Arrow Key Screen. The Arrow Key Screen attacks soft cornerback coverages like Cover-9.

The quarterback's progression on this RPO concept would be to ***Rhythm – Pin-pull scheme, Read – the middle linebacker on the mesh, Rush – Arrow Screen, Release – Scramble Drill.***

PIN-PULL RPO: ***R4 PROGRESSION PLATFORMS - READ PROGRESSION***
The Read progression platform for RPOs is determined based on the most anticipated front or coverage adjustment that the defense will make to CAP the Rhythm progression. The Read progression for an RPO would be accomplished by changing the Run Scheme or Rush attachment within the RPO to best attack the anticipated defense adjustment. (FIG. 183)

FIG. 183 **READ PROGRESSION**

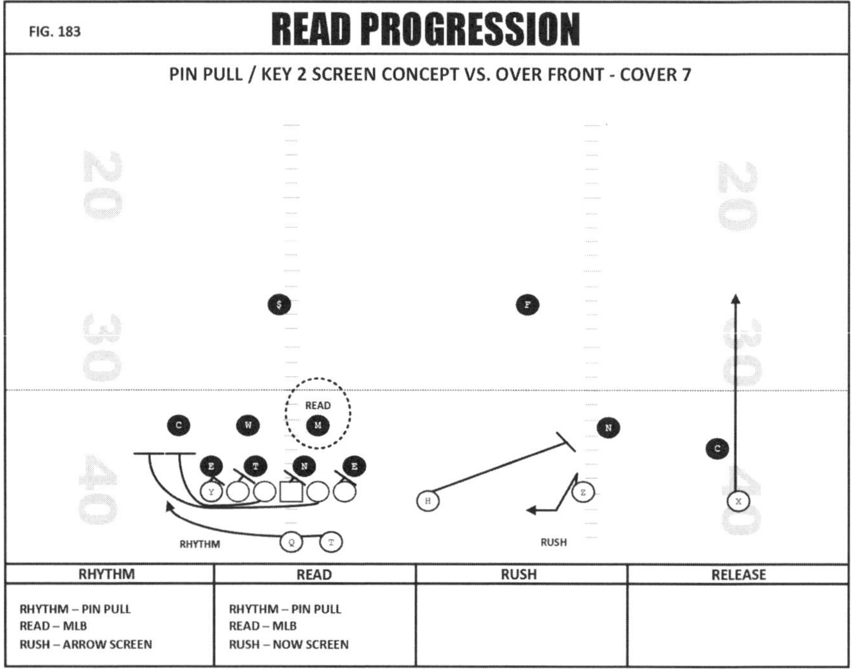

RHYTHM	READ	RUSH	RELEASE
RHYTHM – PIN PULL READ – MLB RUSH – ARROW SCREEN	RHYTHM – PIN PULL READ – MLB RUSH – NOW SCREEN		

EXAMPLE: The most anticipated adjustment that the defense could make to take away the Arrow Screen concept would be by playing Cover-7. Cover-7 places the nickel-backer in an outside-leveraged position to better CAP the Arrow Route of the Key Screen concept. Therefore, the Now Screen concept would be a better Key Screen Rush attachment to use to attack the inside UNCAPPED space of the Cover-7 adjustment.

The quarterback's progression on this RPO concept would be to ***Rhythm – Pin pull scheme, Read – the middle linebacker, Rush – Now Screen concept, Release – Scramble Drill.***

PIN-PULL RPO: ***R4 Progression Platforms -Rush Progression***
The Rush progression platform for RPOs is used to determine the best concept to attack the most anticipated defensive pressure. Pressure in the form of Man or Zone Blitzes is inevitable for offenses that incorporate RPOs. It is important to have a plan of attack against these actions. We recommend adjusting the RPO into a pure pass progression against Man pressure. This can be done by checking to a pass protection that will provide time against a Man Blitz. (FIG. 184)

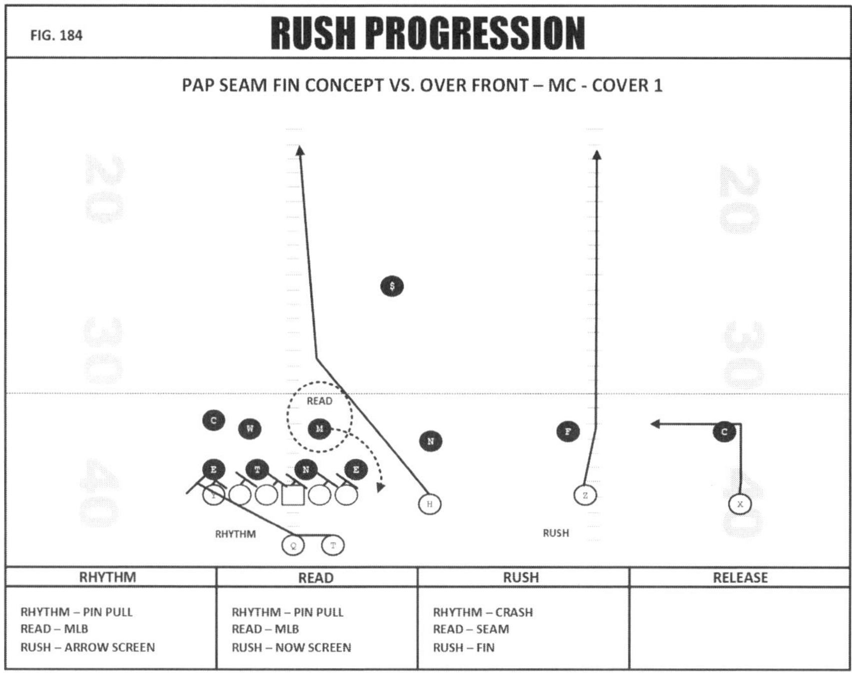

In this Rush progression, a full Slide Protection is called, and the pass routes would be checked into a Seam-Fin concept. The Seam-Fin concept provides a vertical threat that attacks the weakness of Cover-1. The quarterback would ***Rhythm – Crash, Read – Seam, Rush – Fin, and then Release – Scramble Drill.***

PIN-PULL RPO: ***R4 PROGRESSION PLATFORMS -RELEASE PROGRESSION***
The release progression platform for RPOs is used to protect the Rhythm progression and set up the defense for an explosive play. The release progression should contain a Shot Screen, Quick-Pump, or route concept that attacks post-snap CAPPING reactions of defenders to the Rhythm progression RPO. (FIG. 185)

The 3-Scat Concept Rush attachment is used to build an RPO release progression here. The 3-Scat concept has initial stems that look identical to the Arrow Key Screen used in the Rhythm RPO progression. This makes it a favorable match-and-release RPO progression. The quarterback would ***Rhythm – Pin Pull scheme, Read – middle linebacker, Rush – 3 Scat Concept, Release – Scramble Drill.***

INSIDE ZONE RPO: ***R4 Progression Platforms -Rhythm Progression***
There are 3 key questions that a coach should ask himself when building or game-planning RPOs to attack an opponent.

1. *What is the best Run Scheme that attacks the most anticipated front?*
2. *Can my personnel execute this Run Scheme against the opponents' personnel?*
3. *What Rush attachments best fit the timing of this run scheme?*

EXAMPLE: You are facing an odd front. Inside-zone is a favorable concept to use to attack an Odd Front defense. In a TE formation it provides 2 double-teams along with extra time to throw Quick-Game concepts as Rush attachments. We will use the same TE closed trips formation to provide another example of how to build R4 progression platforms to network concepts together to protect the Rhythm progression RPO. (FIG. 186)

EXAMPLE: The most anticipated coverage used here is Cover-9. Cover-9 can be effectively attacked with a Quick-Game Stick Concept Rush attachment. Paring the Inside-zone with the Stick concept makes for a sound RPO against Zone Coverage. The quarterback would ***Rhythm – Inside Zone, Read – middle linebacker, Rush – Stick Concept, Release – Scramble Drill.***

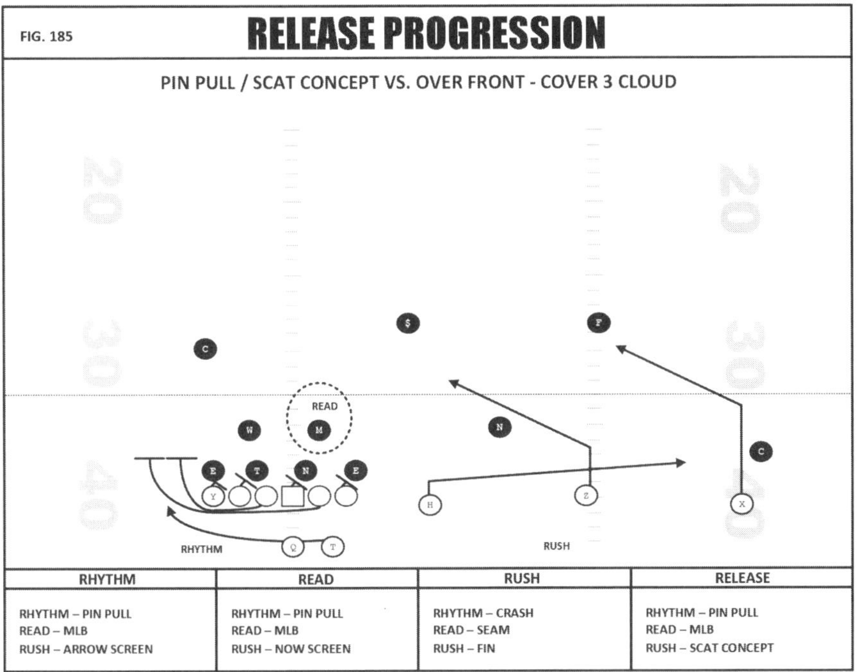

RHYTHM	READ	RUSH	RELEASE
RHYTHM – PIN PULL READ – MLB RUSH – ARROW SCREEN	RHYTHM – PIN PULL READ – MLB RUSH – NOW SCREEN	RHYTHM – CRASH READ – SEAM RUSH – FIN	RHYTHM – PIN PULL READ – MLB RUSH – SCAT CONCEPT

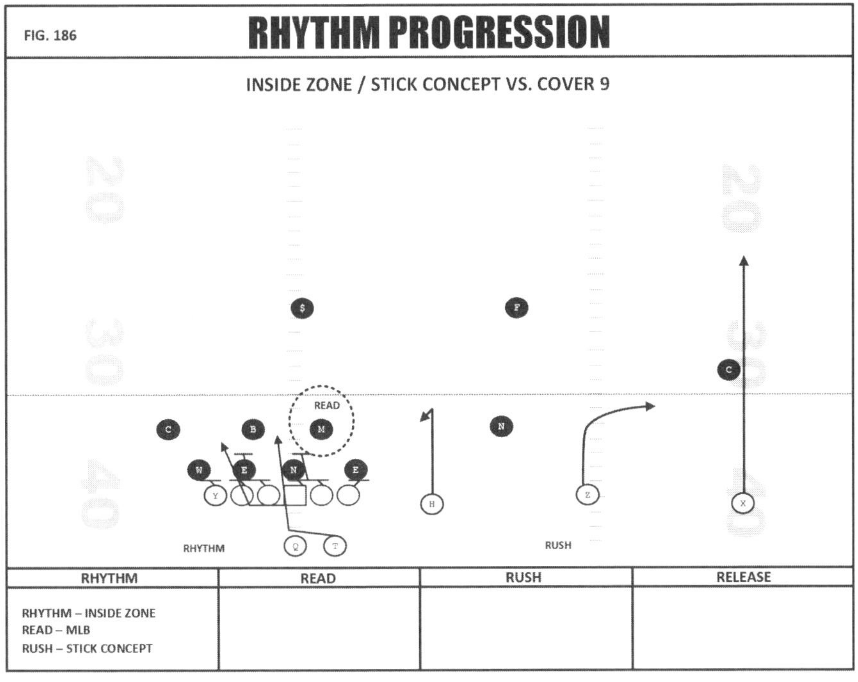

RHYTHM	READ	RUSH	RELEASE
RHYTHM – INSIDE ZONE READ – MLB RUSH – STICK CONCEPT			

INSIDE ZONE RPO: ***R4 Progression Platforms -Read Progression***
The Read progression for RPOs is based on the most anticipated adjustment to CAP the Rhythm progression RPO. (FIG. 187)

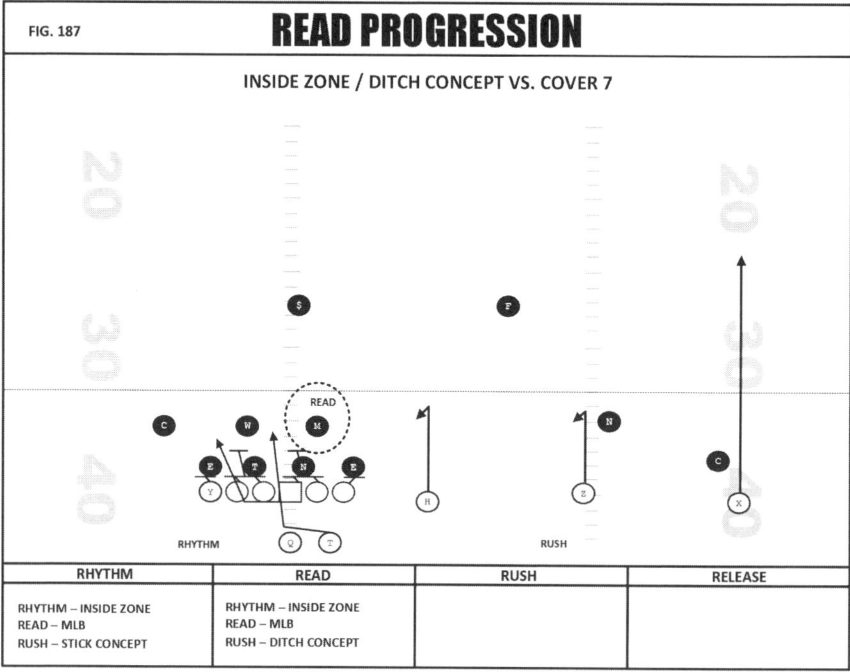

EXAMPLE: The most anticipated adjustment that the defense could make to take away the Stick concept would be playing Cover-7. Cover-7 places the nickel-backer in an outside-leveraged position to CAP the Quick-Out of the Stick concept. Therefore, the Ditch concept would be a better Quick-Game Rush attachment to attack the inside UNCAPPED space of the Cover-7 adjustment.

The quarterback's progression on this RPO concept would be to ***Rhythm – Inside Zone scheme, Read – the middle linebacker, Rush – Ditch concept, Release – Scramble Drill.***

INSIDE ZONE RPO: ***R4 Progression Platforms -Rush Progression***
The Rush progression for RPOs is based on the most anticipated pressure adjustment. Man pressure poses the biggest threat to RPO concepts. Therefore, it is often best to have a max-protection and man-beater concept planned to use for a Rush progression. (FIG. 188)

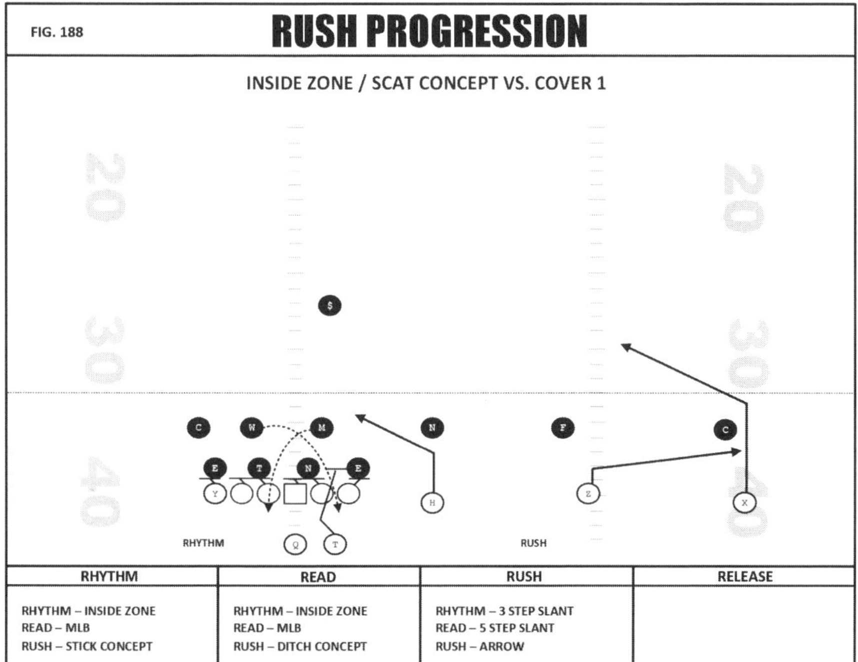

RHYTHM	READ	RUSH	RELEASE
RHYTHM – INSIDE ZONE READ – MLB RUSH – STICK CONCEPT	RHYTHM – INSIDE ZONE READ – MLB RUSH – DITCH CONCEPT	RHYTHM – 3 STEP SLANT READ – 5 STEP SLANT RUSH – ARROW	

EXAMPLE: A Cover-1 Cross Pop Blitz is anticipated to CAP the inside zone/Stick concept. A protection call to alert the linemen from getting downfield and running-back to insert and block the first inside linebacker to his side could be used here. A Rush attachment that could be used to attack Cover-1 would be the Scat Quick-Game concept.

The quarterback would ***Rhythm – 3 step Slant, Read, 5-Step Slant, Rush – Arrow, Release – Scramble Drill.***

INSIDE ZONE RPO: ***R4 Progression Platforms - Release Progression***
The release progression for the Inside Zone RPO would be the best Run or Route concept adjustment to attack aggressive post-snap CAPPING defenders to the Rhythm progression. (FIG. 189)

The Shake concept is an effective Quick-Pump Rush attachment to use to protect the Stick Rush attachment. The quarterback would ***Rhythm – Pump the Stick, Read – Shake, Rush – Whip, and then Release – Scramble Drill.***

Defenses are becoming more versatile in the ways that they are disguising and removing the conflicted defender that RPO concept are built to attack. The 5-family structure of RPO attachments can help define and determine the best run or pass concept to adjust to within these defensive strategies. The R4 progression platforms provide the foundation to network the best attachments together in and easy progression-based decision-making tree. The result is accelerated adaptability with simplicity.

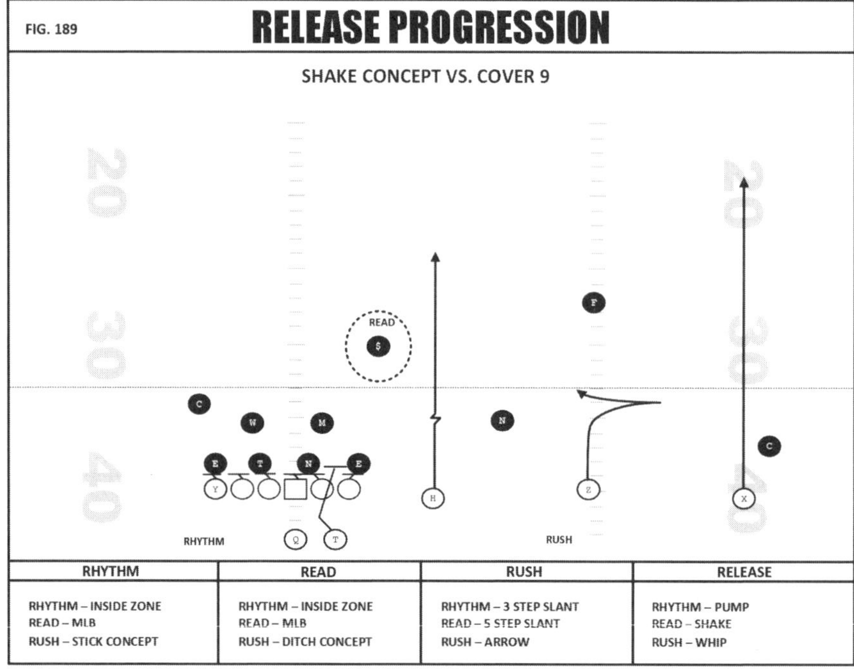

CONCLUSION

Many books have been written since the battles in Fallujah, Iraq in 2004. Most of them have been about the lessons-learned that sparked an evolution of modern warfare. The U.S. Military had to adapt or die. These same lessons are learned every year in the game of football. This book was born out of those lessons. The goal of this book was to give you a field manual that can be used with your players to accelerate the R4 passing system. It was also to give you a peek inside to the advancements of R4 that has accelerated the modern passing game. However, we can't stop there.

We had to find a way to take the R4 process that accelerated decision-making for the quarterback and his coach and infuse it into every coach and player on the team. We discovered that the R4 process for the intermediate passing game provides the roadmap of how to accelerate decision-making for quick game, screen game, RPOs, run game, game-planning and play-calling. Accelerated decision-making in every conceptual phase of the game provides the adaptability that we missed in this modern era of football.

The next evolution in the modern game of football is a shared consciousness among all 11 players on the field, along with their coaches on the sideline. The result is accelerated adaptability and decision-making of any run or pass concept through a common language and simple process of R4.

R4 isn't a new offensive scheme, it's a total offensive solution. It's an ever-present consultant to your game preparation, practice planning, and play-calling approach. It's quite possibly the last four words you will ever need to seamlessly integrate your existing schemes to do more with less – less time, less players, and less coaches. R4 isn't just about drawing up new plays, it's about drilling down your process deeper than ever before, while maintaining clear and achievable objectives.

Bottom line, you will know more than ever, WHY you do what you do, and HOW best to do it.

It doesn't change what you do best, it confirms, constrains, and connects it all together seamlessly. We aren't here to reinvent your wheel...We're just going to make it turn faster and more smoothly than ever before.

We have built on online R4 modular sequential teaching platform that fills in the knowledge gaps in each staff, affirms the best practices already in place, and gives a simple process that provides a:

- Common language that defines defensive space, intent, and technique during film breakdown,
- Template that guides and influences playbook design, practice-scripting, and play-calling,
- Platform that maintains scheme simplicity, flexibility and adaptability that isn't personnel dependent,
- Source code for tagging and enhancing existing schemes without having to replace them, and
- Sequential set of procedures that increase staff/player productivity and efficiency

It's a streamlined learning engine for sustainable improvement in all phases of the offense...Pass Game, Run Game, Film Review, Game-Planning, and Play-Calling

This isn't just a library of content, plays, drills and schemes... it's a language of connection with your players and staff like never before. If you are interested in diving into a better way to accelerate everything you do in the game of football, go to **www.r4footballsystem.com** and become an online member today.

Adapt or die...